Financial Analysis with Lotus 1-2-3 for Windows

Timothy R. Mayes
Metropolitan State College of Denver

Todd M. Shank
University of Portland

THE DRYDEN PRESS
Harcourt Brace College Publishers

Fort Worth   Philadelphia   San Diego   New York   Orlando   Austin   San Antonio
Toronto   Montreal   London   Sydney   Tokyo

Executive Editor: Mike Reynolds
Development Editor: Shana Lum
Project Editor: Andrea Wright
Art Director: Brian Salisbury
Production Manager: Darryl King

Address for orders:
Harcourt Brace & Company
6277 Sea Harbor Drive, Orlando, FL 32887-6777
1-800-782-4479

Address for editorial correspondence:
Harcourt Brace College Publishers
301 Commerce Street, Suite 3700, Fort Worth, TX 76102

Printed in the United States of America

ISBN: 0-03-016014-6

6 7 8 9 0 1 2 3 4 5 066 9 8 7 6 5 4 3 2 1

The Dryden Press

Contents

Preface **xi**

Purpose of the Book   **xi**
Organization of the Book   **xii**
Outstanding Features   **xiii**
  Pedagogical Features   **xiii**
  Supplements   **xiv**
Intended Audience   **xiv**
  A Note to Students   **xv**
Typography Conventions   **xv**
Acknowledgments   **xvi**

CHAPTER 1

Spreadsheet Basics   **1**

  Spreadsheet Uses   **2**
Starting Lotus 1-2-3   **2**
Using the Mouse   **3**
The 1-2-3 Screen   **4**

Contents

The Title Bar **4**
The Menu Bar **5**
The SmartIcons **6**
The Edit Line **6**
The Worksheet Area **6**
Worksheet Tabs **7**
Status Bar **7**

Navigating the Worksheet **8**
Selecting a Range of Cells **9**
Entering Text and Numbers **9**
Formatting and Alignment Options **10**
Number Formats **12**
Entering Formulas **13**
Copying and Moving Formulas **15**
Mathematical Operators **17**
Parentheses and the Order of Operation **17**

Using 1-2-3's Built-in Functions **18**
Using the @Function List **20**

Creating Graphs **21**
Creating Embedded Charts **22**
Formatting Charts **22**

Printing **24**

Saving and Opening Files **26**

Quitting 1-2-3 **27**

Summary **27**

CHAPTER 2

The Basic Financial Statements **29**

The Income Statement **30**
Building an Income Statement in 1-2-3 **30**
Common-Size Income Statements **35**

The Balance Sheet **36**
Building a Balance Sheet in 1-2-3 **37**
Creating a Common-Size Balance Sheet **39**

Building a Statement of Cash Flows **39**

Summary **44**

CHAPTER 3

The Cash Budget **45**

The Worksheet Area **47**
   Collections 47
   Purchases and Payments 48

Collections And Disbursements **50**

Calculating The Ending Cash Balance **51**
   Using the Cash Budget for Timing Large Expenditures 54

Adding Interest and Investment of Excess Cash **56**
   Calculating Current Borrowing 58
   Calculating Current Investing 59
   Working Through the Example 59

Summary **62**

CHAPTER 4

Evaluating Performance with Financial Ratios **63**

Liquidity Ratios **64**
   The Current Ratio 65
   The Quick Ratio 66

Efficiency Ratios **67**
   Inventory Turnover Ratio 67
   Accounts Receivable Turnover Ratio 68
   Average Collection Period 68
   Fixed Asset Turnover Ratio 69
   Total Asset Turnover Ratio 70

Leverage Ratios **70**
   The Total Debt Ratio 71
   The Long-term Debt Ratio 72
   The Long-term Debt to Total Capitalization Ratio 72
   The Debt to Equity Ratio 73
   The Long-term Debt to Equity Ratio 73

Coverage Ratios **74**
   The Times Interest Earned Ratio 75
   The Cash Coverage Ratio 75

Profitability Ratios **76**
   The Gross Profit Margin 76
   The Operating Profit Margin 77
   The Net Profit Margin 77

Return on Total Assets 78
Return on Equity 78
Return on Common Equity 79
Analysis of EPI's Profitability Ratios 79

Using Financial Ratios 81
Trend Analysis 81
Comparing to Industry Averages 81
Company Goals and Debt Covenants 82
Automating Ratio Analysis 83

Summary 85

CHAPTER 5

Financial Forecasting 89

The Percent of Sales Method 90
Forecasting the Income Statement 90
Forecasting Assets on the Balance Sheet 92
Forecasting Liabilities on the Balance Sheet 94
Discretionary Financing Needed 96

Other Forecasting Methods 97
Linear Trend Extrapolation 97
Regression Analysis 101

Summary 106

CHAPTER 6

Break-even and Leverage Analysis 109

Break-even Points 110
Calculating Break-even Points in 1-2-3 112
Other Break-even Points 113

Leverage Analysis 114
The Degree of Operating Leverage 115
The Degree of Financial Leverage 117
The Degree of Combined Leverage 119
Extending the Example 120

Summary 122

CHAPTER 7   *The Time Value of Money   125*

Future Value   **126**
   Using 1-2-3 to Find Future Values   127
Present Value   **129**
Annuities   **130**
   Present Value of an Annuity   131
   Future Value of an Annuity   133
   Solving for the Annuity Payment   135
   Solving for the Number of Periods in an Annuity   136
   Solving for the Interest Rate in an Annuity   137
   Deferred Annuities   139
Uneven Cash Flow Streams   **141**
   Solving for the Yield in an Uneven Cash Flow Stream   143
Non-annual Compounding Periods   **145**
   Continuous Compounding   148
Summary   **149**

CHAPTER 8   *Valuation and Rates of Return   153*

What is Value?   **154**
Fundamentals of Valuation   **155**
Determining the Required Rate of Return   **156**
   A Simple Risk Premium Model   157
   CAPM: A More Scientific Model   158
Valuing Common Stocks   **161**
   The Constant-Growth Dividend Discount Model   162
   Other Common Stock Valuation Models   166
Bond Valuation   **167**
Bond Return Measures   **171**
   Current Yield   172
   Yield to Maturity   172
   Yield to Call   173
Preferred Stock Valuation   **174**
Summary   **177**

Contents

CHAPTER 9   *The Cost of Capital*   **179**

The Appropriate 'Hurdle' Rate   **180**
   The Weighted Average Cost of Capital   *181*
   Determining the Weights   *182*
WACC Calculations in 1-2-3   **183**
Calculating the Component Costs   **184**
   The Cost of Common Equity   *185*
   The Cost of Preferred Equity   *187*
   The Cost of Debt   *187*
Using 1-2-3 to Calculate the Component Costs   **189**
   The After-tax Cost of Debt   *189*
   The Cost of Preferred Stock   *190*
   The Cost of Common Stock   *190*
The Role of Flotation Costs   **191**
   Adding Flotation Costs to our Worksheet   *193*
   The Cost of Retained Earnings   *193*
The Marginal WACC Curve   **195**
   Finding the Break-points   *195*
Summary   **199**

CHAPTER 10   *Capital Budgeting*   **203**

Estimating the Cash Flows   **204**
   The Initial Outlay   *205*
   The Annual After-tax Cash Flows   *206*
   The Terminal Cash Flow   *207*
   Estimating the Cash Flows: an Example   *208*
Making the Decision   **212**
   The Payback Method   *213*
   The Discounted Payback Period   *214*
   Net Present Value   *216*
   The Profitability Index   *219*
   The Internal Rate of Return   *220*
   Problems with the IRR   *221*
   The Modified Internal Rate of Return   *223*
Sensitivity Analysis   **225**
   NPV Profile Charts   *226*

Scenario Analysis   **227**

The Optimal Capital Budget   **231**

Optimal Capital Budget Without Capital Rationing   232
Optimal Capital Budget Under Capital Rationing   234
Other Techniques   239

Summary   **239**

CHAPTER 11   *Risk, Capital Budgeting, and Diversification   241*

Review of Some Useful Statistical Concepts   **242**
The Expected Value   242
Measures of Dispersion   244
The Variance and Standard Deviation   244
The Coefficient of Variation   246

Using 1-2-3 to Measure Risk   **247**
A Short Example   247
Finding Expected Values in 1-2-3   248

Calculating the Measures of Dispersion with 1-2-3   **249**
The Variance   249
The Standard Deviation   250
The Coefficient of Variation   251
Charting the Probability Distribution   251

Incorporating Risk into Capital Budgeting Decisions   **252**
The Risk-Adjusted Discount Rate   253

Alternatives to the RADR   **257**
The Certainty Equivalent Approach   257
The Decision Tree Approach   259
Monte-Carlo Simulation   261

Portfolio Diversification Effects   **261**

Determining Portfolio Risk and Return   **264**
Expected Portfolio Return   264
Portfolio Standard Deviation   264
Portfolios with More Than Two Securities   268

Summary   **269**

APPENDIX A   *Menu Descriptions*   **273**

The *F*ile Menu   **273**

The *E*dit Menu   **274**

The *V*iew Menu   **275**

The *S*tyle Menu   **276**

The *T*ools Menu   **276**

The *R*ange Menu   **277**

The *W*indow Menu   **277**

The *H*elp Menu   **278**

APPENDIX B   *Using COMPUSTAT*® *Data with 1-2-3*   **279**

Using Pre-defined Reports   **280**

Using the Universal Report Builder   **281**

Building Reports Manually   **287**

     The SPWS Add-in Functions   **288**

     Creating a Monthly Stock Price Report   **289**

Summary   **291**

Preface

Electronic spreadsheets have been available for microcomputers since the introduction of VisiCalc® for the Apple I in the late 1970's. The first version of Lotus 1-2-3® in 1982 convinced businesses that the IBM PC was a truly useful, productivity-enhancing tool. Today, any student who leaves business school without at least basic spreadsheet skills is truly at a disadvantage. Much as earlier generations had to be adept at using a slide rule or calculator, today's manager needs to be proficient in the use of a spreadsheet. International competition means that U.S. companies must be as efficient as possible. No longer can the manager count on having a large staff of "number crunchers" at her disposal.

As of this writing, the most recent version of 1-2-3 is Release 5.0 for Windows. We use this version throughout the book, but we are running it under Windows 95. The difference is that 1-2-3 has the "look and feel" of Windows 95. This should not cause any confusion, since the interface differences are very minor, and most users will eventually upgrade to Windows 95.

Purpose of the Book

We feel strongly that the trend in textbooks of providing pre-built spreadsheet templates for students to use should be reversed. We believe that students can gain valuable insights and a deeper understanding of financial analysis by actually building their own templates. Programming requires the student to actually confront many issues that might otherwise be swept under the carpet. It also allows us to tightly integrate the finance material and the spreadsheet techniques so that students learn both simultaneously. It continually amazes us how thankful students are when they are actually forced to think rather than just to "plug and go". For this reason the book concentrates on spreadsheet building skills (though all of the templates are included for instructors) so that students will be encouraged to think and understand.

Anyone who has been exposed to Microsoft Excel®, Quattro® Pro, or any of the multitude of other available spreadsheets, will find it easy to adapt to 1-2-3 for Windows. The differences between 1-2-3 and the other spreadsheets are great enough however, that we feel it is necessary to have a book dedicated solely to the art of financial analysis with 1-2-3. Furthermore, the Microsoft Windows environment is so different from that of DOS that users of any DOS-based spreadsheet will need some amount of retraining to effectively use 1-2-3.

Students with no prior experience with spreadsheets will find that using 1-2-3 is very intuitive, especially if they have used other Windows applications. For these students, *Financial Analysis with Lotus 1-2-3 for Windows* (FALW) will provide a thorough introduction to the use of spreadsheets from basic screen navigation skills to building fairly complex financial models.

Organization of the Book

Financial Analysis with Lotus 1-2-3 for Windows is organized along the lines of an introductory financial management textbook. The book is intended as an adjunct to a regular text, but it is not "just a spreadsheet book." In most cases topics are covered at the same depth as in the usual textbooks; in many cases the topics are covered in greater depth. For this reason we believe that FALW is complete enough that it may also be used as a primary text. The book is organized as follows:

- CHAPTER 1: Spreadsheet Basics
- CHAPTER 2: The Basic Financial Statements
- CHAPTER 3: The Cash Budget
- CHAPTER 4: Evaluating Performance with Financial Ratios
- CHAPTER 5: Financial Forecasting
- CHAPTER 6: Break-even and Leverage Analysis

- CHAPTER 7: The Time Value of Money
- CHAPTER 8: Valuation and Rates of Return
- CHAPTER 9: The Cost of Capital
- CHAPTER 10: Capital Budgeting
- CHAPTER 11: Risk, Capital Budgeting, and Diversification

Outstanding Features

FALW's outstanding feature is its use of 1-2-3 as a learning tool rather than just a fancy calculator. Students using FALW will be able to demonstrate to themselves how and why things are the way they are. Once a student creates a worksheet, they understand how it works and the assumptions behind the calculations. Thus, unlike the more usual "template" approach, the student gains a deeper understanding of the material. In addition, FALW greatly facilitates the professor's use of spreadsheets in their courses.

This text takes a self-teaching approach used by many other "how-to" spreadsheet books, but it provides opportunities for much more in-depth experimentation than the competition. For example, sensitivity analysis is an often recommended technique but is rarely demonstrated in any depth. FALW uses the tools that are built into 1-2-3 to greatly simplify such computation-extensive techniques, eliminating the boredom of tedious calculation. Other examples include regression analysis and linear programming. FALW encourages the use of such techniques by concentrating on the interpretation of results. Thus, FALW encourages students to use tools that they have learned in their statistics and management science classes.

Pedagogical Features

FALW begins by teaching the basics of using 1-2-3, including the features that differentiate it from other spreadsheet programs. Then, the text uses 1-2-3 to build the basic financial statements that students encounter in all levels of financial management courses. This coverage then acts as a "springboard" into more advanced material such as performance evaluation, forecasting, valuation, and capital budgeting. Each chapter builds upon the techniques learned in prior chapters so that the student becomes familiar with 1-2-3 and finance at the same time. This type of approach facilitates the professor's incorporation of 1-2-3 into a financial management courses since it reduces, or eliminates, the necessity of teaching spreadsheets. It also helps students to see how this vital "tool" is used to solve the financial problems faced by practitioners.

The chapters are set up so that a problem is introduced, solved by traditional methods, and then solved using 1-2-3. We believe that this approach relieves much of the quantitative complexity, while enhancing student understanding through repetition and experimentation. This approach also generates interest in the subject matter that a traditional lecture cannot (especially for non-finance business majors that are required to take a finance course). Once they are familiar with spreadsheets, our students typically enjoy using them, and spend more time with the subject than they otherwise would. In addition, since graphics are used extensively (and they are created by the student), the material may be better retained.

A list of learning objectives precedes each chapter, and a summary of the major 1-2-3 functions discussed in the chapter is included at the end.

Supplements

An instructor's manual and disk is available that contain the following:

1. Templates with solutions to all problems covered in the text. Having this material on disk allows the instructor to easily create transparencies or give live demonstrations via computer projection panel in class.

2. A set of three 1-2-3 spreadsheet problems for each chapter that relate directly to the concepts covered in that chapter. Each problem requires the student to build a worksheet to solve a common financial management problem. Often, the problems require solutions in a graphical format.

3. Complete solutions to these student projects and instructions for accessing data on the Standard & Poor's Compustat database that can be used to develop additional, "real world," projects. (See Appendix B, page 279)

4. In addition, since FALW may be used with any standard financial management text, the instructor's manual contains a cross-reference of corresponding chapters. This allows the instructor to easily determine the appropriate FALW chapters to assign.

Intended Audience

Financial Analysis with Lotus 1-2-3 for Windows is aimed at a wide variety of students and practitioners of finance. The topics covered generally follow those in an introductory financial management course for undergraduates or first-year MBA students. Because of the emphasis on spreadsheet building skills, the book is also appropriate for case-oriented courses in which the spreadsheet is used extensively.

We have tried to make the book complete enough that it may also be used for self-paced learning. We assume however, that the reader has some familiarity with the basic concepts of accounting and statistics. Instructors will find that their students can use this book on their own time to learn 1-2-3 thereby minimizing the amount of class time required for teaching the rudiments of spreadsheets. Practitioners will find that the book will help them to transfer skills from other spreadsheets to 1-2-3, and at the same time update their knowledge of corporate finance.

A Note to Students

As we have noted, this book is designed to help you to learn finance and to understand spreadsheets at the same time. Learning finance alone can be a daunting task, but we hope that learning to use 1-2-3 at the same time will make your job easier and more fun. However, you will likely find that learning is more difficult if you do not work the examples presented in each chapter. We encourage you to work along with the book as each example is discussed.

Typography Conventions

The main text of this book is set in the 10 point Times New Roman True Type font. Text or numbers that the student is expected to enter are set in the 10 point `Courier New` True Type font.

The names of built-in functions are set in small-caps and bolded. Function inputs can be either required or optional. Required inputs are set in small-caps and are italicized and bolded. Optional inputs are set in small-caps and are italicized. As an example, consider the **@PVAL** function (introduced in Chapter 7):

@PVAL(*PAYMENTS; INTEREST; TERM; TYPE; FUTURE-VALUE*)

In this function, **@PVAL** is the name, ***PAYMENTS, INTEREST***, and ***TERM*** are the required variables and *TYPE* and *FUTURE-VALUE* are optional. In equations and the text, equation variables (which are distinct from function input variables) are italicized. As an example, consider the *PV* equation:

$$PV = \frac{FV_N}{(1 + i)^N}$$

We hope that these conventions will help to avoid confusion due to similar terms being used in different contexts.

Acknowledgments

All books are collaborative projects with input from more than just the listed authors. That is true in this case as well. We wish to thank those colleagues and students who have reviewed and tested the book to this point. In particular, we would like to thank Stuart Michelson of Eastern Illinois University for his editing and ideas, and Nancy Jay of Mercer University (who wrote the Instructor's Manual). Gary McClure of Skidmore College, John Settle of Portland State University, and David Suk of Rider College through their contributions to a previous book for helped to improve this one. Mitch Abeyta, Beth Bonczek, and the support staff at Standard & Poor's Compustat in Denver provided invaluable support while we were writing Appendix B. Without them, the appendix wouldn't exist.

Students at several schools tolerated early drafts of the book and they have our gratitude for helpful comments and suggestions. In particular, we would like to thank Pete Ormsbee, Marjo Turkki, Kevin Hatch, and Ron LeClere at Metropolitan State College of Denver. Thanks also to Worachai Chongpipatanasook for reading early drafts of the manuscript.

Finally, we wish to express our thanks to Shana Lum, Craig Johnson, and Mike Reynolds of the Dryden Press. Without their help, confidence, tolerance and support this book never would have been written. To anybody we have forgotten, we heartily apologize.

We encourage you to send your comments and suggestions, however minor they may seem to you, to one of our e-mail addresses. Thanks in advance.

Timothy R. Mayes (MayesT@clem.mscd.edu)
Todd M. Shank (Shank@uofport.edu)

September, 1996

CHAPTER 1

Spreadsheet Basics

After studying this chapter, you should be able to:

1. *Explain the basic purpose of a spreadsheet program and the use of the mouse in a Windows program.*

2. *Identify the various components of the Lotus 1-2-3 screen.*

3. *Navigate the 1-2-3 worksheet (entering, correcting, and moving data within the worksheet).*

4. *Explain the purpose and usage of 1-2-3's built-in functions.*

5. *Create graphics and show how to print and save files in 1-2-3.*

The term "spreadsheet" covers a wide variety of elements useful for quantitative analysis of all kinds. Essentially a spreadsheet is a simple tool consisting of a matrix of cells which can store numbers, text, or formulas. The spreadsheet's power comes from its ability to recalculate results as you change the contents of other cells. No longer does the user need to do these calculations by hand or on a calculator. Instead, with a properly constructed spreadsheet, changing a single number (say, a sales forecast) can result in literally thousands of automatic changes in the model. The freedom and productivity enhancement provided by modern spreadsheets presents an unparalleled opportunity for learning financial analysis.

Spreadsheet Uses

Spreadsheets today contain built-in analytical capabilities previously unavailable in a single package. Users often had to learn a variety of specialized software packages to do any relatively complex analysis. With the newest versions of Lotus 1-2-3, users can perform tasks ranging from the routine maintenance of financial statements to multivariate regression analysis to Monte Carlo simulations of various hedging strategies.

It is literally impossible to enumerate all of the possible applications for spreadsheets. You should keep in mind that spreadsheets are useful not only for financial analysis, but for any type of quantitative analysis whether your specialty is in marketing, management, engineering, statistics, or economics. For that matter, a spreadsheet can also prove valuable for personal uses. With 1-2-3 it is a fairly simple matter to build a spreadsheet to monitor your investment portfolio, do retirement planning, experiment with various mortgage options when buying a house, keep a mailing list, etc. The possibilities are literally endless. The more comfortable you become with the spreadsheet, the more valuable uses you will find. Above all, feel free to experiment! Try new things. Using a spreadsheet can help you find solutions that you never would have imagined on your own.

1-2-3 v. 5 Icon

Starting Lotus 1-2-3

Before you can do any work in 1-2-3, you have to run the program. In Windows, programs are generally started by double-clicking on the program's icon. The location of the 1-2-3 icon will depend on the organization of your system. In Windows 3.x, if you are using Program Manager as the main shell, there may be a program group titled "Lotus Applications." If so, open this group by double-clicking the icon and then double-click the 1-2-3 icon, pictured at left, to start the program. If you are not using Program Manager, or if your system is organized differently, locate the 1-2-3 icon and double-click on it. In Windows 95 click on the Start button and choose Programs, "Lotus Applications", and then "Lotus 1-2-3 Release 5," or find the 1-2-3 icon and double-click on it.

Using the Mouse

A mouse is a soap-bar sized piece of equipment that enables you to move a pointer on the screen. Most of the actions that you might want to take in 1-2-3 can be accomplished with either the mouse or keyboard. Normally, using the mouse greatly simplifies these actions. In fact, sometimes there is no way to accomplish an action without using the mouse.

For the most part, we will describe both keyboard and mouse movements to accomplish any necessary actions. In order for you to understand the mouse, you should be familiar with some terms as used in this book.

- **Left button** - The button used for common tasks such as menu selection. Usually, this button is on the left-side of the mouse, but it is possible in Windows to reverse the functionality of the buttons. This is normally done for left-handed users who prefer to use the mouse on the left-side of the PC.

- **Mouse pointer** - You will usually see the mouse pointer as either an arrow-shape or in the shape of a fat cross. The mouse pointer indicates where on the screen an action will take place. The shape of the pointer will change depending on its location and actions that are taking place.

- **Click** - To press and release a mouse button quickly at the specified screen location. Usually, unless a particular button is specified, we'll use the term to refer to the left mouse button.

- **Double-click** - To press and release a mouse button quickly *twice* at the specified screen location. Ordinarily, double-clicking is done with the left mouse button.

- **Drag** - To press and hold a mouse button while moving the mouse. This action is usually used to move a graphical object such as a chart or line.

The 1-2-3 Screen

FIGURE 1-1
LOTUS 1-2-3 RELEASE 5.0

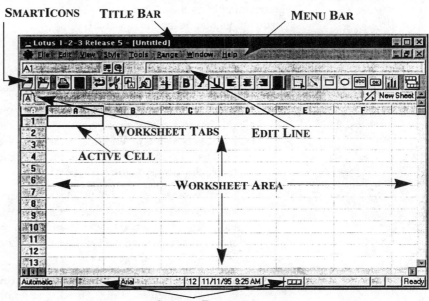

SMARTICONS   TITLE BAR   MENU BAR

WORKSHEET TABS   EDIT LINE

ACTIVE CELL

WORKSHEET AREA

STATUS BAR

The Title Bar

The title bar is the area at the very top of the 1-2-3 screen. It serves a number of functions:

- Identifies the program as Lotus 1-2-3 and displays the name of the currently active worksheet.

- Will be brightly colored when 1-2-3 has the input focus.

- Can be "grabbed" with the mouse to move the window around within the Windows environment.

- Contains the system menu and the minimize and maximize buttons. The system menu, in the upper left corner, provides choices for moving the window or changing its size as well as the ability to switch to or run other programs. The minimize button will collapse the window down to an icon at the bottom of the Windows screen where it is still active, but out of the way. The maximize button causes the program to occupy the entire screen.

- When it is double-clicked, duplicates the functioning of the maximize button.

- As you scroll through the menus with the arrow keys, 1-2-3 will display a short message on the title bar describing the selected menu command.

The Menu Bar

FIGURE 1-2
THE LOTUS 1-2-3 RELEASE 5.0 MAIN MENUS

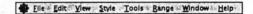

The main menu bar in 1-2-3 provides access to eight menus, each of these leading to further choices. There are two ways to select a menu: click on the menu of choice with the mouse, or use the Alt key in combination with the underlined letter in the menu name. For example, to choose the File menu, we could either click on the word "File" or press Alt-F on the keyboard. Either method will lead to the File menu dropping down, allowing you to make another choice.

In Windows, menus are persistent, meaning that they stay visible on the screen until you either make a selection or cancel the menu by pressing the Esc key. While the menu is visible, using the arrow keys to highlight the individual menu choices will cause a short help message to be displayed on the title bar of the 1-2-3 screen. This help message describes what action the highlighted menu selection performs. Scrolling through the menus in this manner is especially useful when learning to use 1-2-3. Once you locate the option that you want to select, simply press Enter.

At times, some menu selections are displayed in a light gray color. These options are not available for selection at the time that the menu is selected. For example, if you have not cut or copied a cell, the Paste option from the Edit menu has nothing to paste, so it is grayed. Only the menu options displayed in black may be selected.

Refer to Appendix A for a short description of each menu selection.

The SmartIcons

FIGURE 1-3
THE LOTUS 1-2-3 SMARTICONS

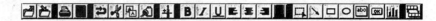

Immediately below the menu bar, 1-2-3 displays a series of short-cut buttons. The exact buttons, and their order, may be different on different machines. The buttons provide a quick way to carry out certain commands without wading through menus and dialog boxes. To add, delete, or rearrange buttons choose **T**ools Smart**i**cons from the menus. You can learn what function each button performs by simply moving the mouse pointer over the button. After a few seconds, a message will appear near the cursor that informs you of the button's function.

The Edit Line

FIGURE 1-4
THE LOTUS 1-2-3 EDIT LINE

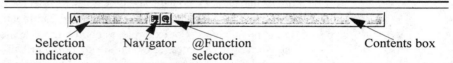

Selection   Navigator   @Function   Contents box
indicator   selector

The edit line displays information about the currently selected cell. The left part of the edit line indicates the name of the selected cell. The right part of the edit line displays the contents of the selected cell. If the cell contains a formula, the edit line displays the formula, and the cell displays the result of the formula. The Navigator button is equivalent to selecting **E**dit **G**o To from the menus, and the @Function selector makes it easy to insert functions into the selected cell. While you are entering data into a cell, the edit line also shows buttons to accept or reject changes.

The Worksheet Area

The worksheet area is where the real work of the spreadsheet is done. The worksheet is a matrix (256 columns and 8,192 rows) of cells, each of which can contain text, numbers, formulas, or graphics. Each cell is referred to by a column letter and a row number. Column letters (A,B,C,...,IV) are listed at the top of each column, and row numbers (1,2,3,...,8,192) are listed to the left of each row. The cell in the upper left corner of the worksheet is therefore referred to as cell A1, the cell immediately below A1 is referred to as cell A2, the cell to the right of A1 is cell B1, and so on. This naming convention is common to all spreadsheet programs and will become comfortable once you have practiced a bit.

The active cell (the one into which any input will be placed) can be identified by a solid black border around the cell. Note that the active cell is not always visible on the screen, but it is always named in the leftmost portion of edit line.

Worksheet Tabs

FIGURE 1-5
THE 1-2-3 RELEASE 5.0 WORKSHEET TABS

A B C D
New Sheet

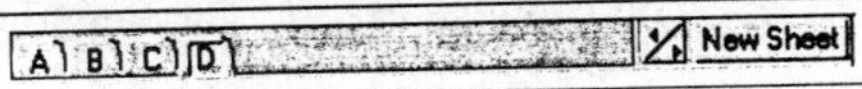

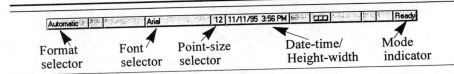

Beginning with version 4.0, 1-2-3 worksheets are stored in a new format (*.wk4) which combines multiple worksheets into one file known as a workbook. This new format saves several related worksheets in one file. The sheet tabs, near the top of the screen, allow you to switch between sheets in a workbook. You may rename, copy, or delete any existing sheet or insert a new sheet by double-clicking a tab. The VCR-style buttons to the right of the sheet tabs are the sheet tab control buttons, and allow you to scroll the list of sheet tabs. The New Sheet button allows you to insert a new worksheet into the workbook.

Status Bar

FIGURE 1-6
THE STATUS BAR

Automatic
Arial
12
11/11/95 3:56 PM
Ready
Format selector
Font selector
Point-size selector
Date-time/ Height-width
Mode indicator

The status bar contains information regarding the current state of 1-2-3, as well as certain messages. For example, most of the time the only message is “Ready” indicating that 1-2-3 is waiting for input. At other times, 1-2-3 may add “Calc” to the status bar to indicate that it needs to recalculate the worksheet because of changes.

Navigating the Worksheet

There are two principle methods for moving around within the worksheet area: the arrow keys and the mouse. Generally speaking, for small distances the arrow keys provide an easy method of changing the active cell, but moving to more distant cells is usually easier with the mouse.

Most keyboards have a separate keypad containing arrows pointing up, down, left and right. If your keyboard does not, then the numeric keypad can be used if the NumLock function is off. To use the arrow keys, simply press the appropriate key once for each cell that you wish to move across. For example, assuming that the current cell is A1 and you wish to move to cell D1, simply press the Right arrow key three times. To move from D1 to D5 press the Down arrow key four times. You can also use the Tab key to move one cell to the right.

A Scroll Bar

The mouse is even easier to use once you have developed the hand-eye coordination skills required for its use. When the mouse pointer is over the worksheet area it will be in the shape of an arrow. To change the active cell move the mouse pointer over the destination cell and click the left button. To move to a cell which is not currently displayed on the screen, click on the scroll bars until the cell is visible and then click on it. For example, if the active cell is A1 and you wish to make A100 the active cell, merely click on the arrow at the bottom of the scroll bar on the right-hand part of the screen until A100 is visible. Move the mouse pointer over cell A100 and click with the left button. Each click on the scroll bar moves the worksheet up or down one page. The thumb is the small button that moves up and down the scroll bar to indicate your position in the worksheet. If you wish to move up, click above the thumb. If down, click beneath the thumb. To move more quickly, you can drag the thumb to the desired position, and 1-2-3 will let you know your location with a message on the left side of the edit line.

If you know the address of the cell to which you wish to move (for large models this is not always the case) use the Goto command. The Goto command will change the active cell to whatever cell you indicate. The Goto command can be used by choosing the **E**dit menu and then the **G**o To command, or by pressing the F5 function key. To move to cell A50, simply press F5, type: A50 in the edit box, and then press Enter. You will notice that cell A50 is now highlighted and visible on the screen. Notice that you can also use this command to go to a chart, drawn object (lines, circles, etc.), or a database query table in any open file.

Selecting a Range of Cells

Many times you will need to select more than one cell at a time. For example, you may wish to apply a particular number format to a whole range of cells, or you might wish to clear a whole range. Since it would be cumbersome to do this one cell at a time, especially for a large range, 1-2-3 allows you to simultaneously select a whole range and perform various functions on all of the cells at once. The easiest way to select a contiguous range of cells is to use the mouse. Simply point to the cell in the upper left corner of the range, click and hold down the left button, and drag the mouse until the entire range is highlighted.

You can also use the keyboard to select a range. First change the active cell to the upper left corner of the range to be selected, press and hold down the Shift key, and use the arrow keys to highlight the entire range. Note that if you release the Shift key while pressing an arrow key you will lose the highlight.

Sometimes it is also useful to select a discontiguous range (i.e., two or more unconnected ranges) of cells. To do this, simply select the first range as usual, and then hold down the Ctrl key as you select the other ranges.

The ability to select cells is crucial because 1-2-3, like most other Windows applications, works in the "select, then act" mode. (Users of DOS programs are probably more familiar with the "act, then select" method of operation.) In 1-2-3, you first select the cells that you wish to act on, then choose the operation (e.g., Edit Copy) that you want to perform. This would seem to be a minor point, but it is actually quite important. In the "select, then act" method, the cells stay selected after the operation has been performed, thereby allowing another operation on those cells without reselecting them.

Entering Text and Numbers

Each cell in 1-2-3's worksheet can be thought of as a miniature word processor. Text can be entered directly into the cell and then formatted in a variety of ways. To enter a text string, first select the cell where you want the text to appear and then begin typing. It is that simple.

1-2-3 is smart enough to know the difference between numbers and text, so there are no extra steps for entering numbers. Let's try the following example of entering numbers and text into the worksheet.

Move the cell pointer to cell A1 (using the arrow keys, mouse, or the Edit Go To command) and type: Microsoft Corporation Sales. In cell A2 enter: (Millions of Dollars). Select cell A3 and type: 1989 to 1995. Note that the entry in cell A3 will be treated as text by 1-2-3 because of the spaces and letters included. In cells A4 to G4 we now want to enter the years. In A4 type: 1995, in B4 type: 1994, and so on until you reach G4 and type: 1989. As an alternative, you could use the Drag and Fill feature. Enter the first two years in A4 and B4, select the cells, and then position the mouse pointer over the lower-right corner of the selection (the cursor will change so that it looks like the one at left). Click and drag the selection to the right to fill in the rest of the series. You should now have the numbers 1989 through 1995 entered into the cells. Notice that the most recent data is typically entered at the left, and the most distant data at the right. This convention allows us to easily recognize and concentrate on the most recent and usually the most important data.

We have now set up the headings for our first worksheet. Now let's add Microsoft's sales (in millions of dollars) for the years 1989 to 1995 into cells A5 to G5. Exhibit 1-1 shows how your worksheet should appear.

EXHIBIT 1-1
THE FIRST WORKSHEET

	A	B	C	D	E	F	G
1	Microsoft Corporation Sales						
2	(Millions of Dollars)						
3	1989 to 1995						
4	1995	1994	1993	1992	1991	1990	1989
5	5937.000	4649.000	3753.000	2758.725	1843.432	1183.446	803.530

Formatting and Alignment Options

The worksheet in Exhibit 1-1 isn't very attractive. Notice that the text is displayed at the left side of the cells, while the numbers are at the right. By default this is the way that 1-2-3 aligns text and numbers. However, we can easily change the way that these entries are displayed through the use of the formatting and alignment options.

Before continuing, we should define a few typographical terms. A "typeface" is a particular style of drawing letters and numbers. For example, the main text of this book was set in the Times New Roman typeface. However, the text that you are expected to enter into a worksheet is displayed in the `Courier New` typeface. Typeface also refers to whether the text is drawn in **bold**, *italics*, or perhaps ***bold italics***.

The term "type size" refers to the size of the typeface. When typewriters were commonly used, type size was defined in characters per inch (CPI). This convention was somewhat confusing because the larger the CPI number, the smaller was the text. Today, with computers we normally refer to the type size in "points." Each point represents an increment of 1/72nd of an inch, so there are 72 points to the inch. A typeface printed at a 12 point size is larger than the same typeface printed at a size of 10 points.

Generally, we refer to the typeface and type size combination as a font. So when we say "change the font to 12 point bold Times New Roman," it is understood that we are referring to a particular typeface (Times New Roman, bolded) and type size (12 point).

For text entries, the term "format" refers to the typeface and type size and cell alignment used to display the text. Let's change the font of the text that was entered to Times New Roman, 12 point, bold. First, select the range from A1 to A3 by clicking on A1 and dragging to A3. Now select the Style menu and choose Fonts & Attributes. A dialog box allows you to change the various attributes of the cells. We want to select Times New Roman from the Face list, bold from the Attributes list, and 12 from the size list. Notice that there is a sample of this font displayed at the bottom of the dialog box, so you can see how the chosen font will look on the worksheet. Since none of these changes actually take effect until you validate them by choosing the OK button, you can experiment until the text in the sample window looks right. Click on the OK button or press the Enter key to make the change take effect. You can also make all of these changes on the status bar.

We can just as easily change the font for numbers. Suppose that we want to change the years in cells A4..G4 to 12 point Times New Roman Italic. First select the range A4..G4 by clicking on A4 and dragging the mouse until the highlight extends to G4. Choose Style Fonts & Attributes and select the attributes. Press the OK button and the change will be made.

Our worksheet is now beginning to take on a better look, but it still isn't quite right. We are used to seeing the titles of tables nicely centered over the table, but our title is way over at the left. We can remedy this by using 1-2-3's alignment options. 1-2-3 provides for three different horizontal alignments within a cell. We can have the text (or numbers) aligned with the left or right sides of the cell or centered within the cell boundaries. 1-2-3 also allows centering text across a range of cells.

Let's change the alignment of our numbers first. Highlight cells A4..G5 and select Style Alignment from the menu. Horizontal alignment refers to the left and right alignment, vertical refers to the up and down alignment, and orientation refers to the way that the font is rotated. For now, we simply want to change the horizontal alignment to centered. Choose "Center" from the horizontal choices and press the OK button. Notice that the numbers are all centered within their respective cells.

Next, we want to center our table title across the whole range of numbers that we have entered. To do this, we must select the entire range across which we want to center our titles. Highlight cells A1..G3 and select Style Alignment from the menu. You will again be presented with the alignment dialog box from which you should select "Center" and "Across columns." Press the OK button and notice that the titles are indeed centered across the columns A to G.

Number Formats

Aside from changing the typeface and type size, when dealing with numbers we can also change their appearance by adding commas and dollar signs, and by altering the number of decimal places displayed. Furthermore, we can make the numbers appear different depending on whether they are positive or negative. For example, we might want negative numbers to be displayed in parentheses rather than using the negative sign.

Microsoft is a large company, and their sales have ranged from the hundreds of millions to billions of dollars over the 1989 to 1995 time period. Numbers this large, even when expressed in millions of dollars, become difficult to read unless they are written with commas separating every third digit. Let's format our sales numbers so that they are easier to read.

Select the range of sales numbers (A5..G5) and choose Style Number Format from the menus. You are presented with the number format dialog box which has a list of available formats. We want to display the sales numbers with commas separating every third digit and two decimal places, so select ", Comma" from the list and set the number of decimal places to 2. Press the OK button and notice that the numbers are now displayed in this more readable format.

At this point, we have made several formatting changes to the Microsoft Sales worksheet. Your worksheet should look like the one in Exhibit 1-2. All of this formatting may seem tedious at the moment, but it will quickly become easy as you become more familiar with the menus. Furthermore, the payoff in readability will be worth far more than the few seconds spent in formatting the worksheet.

EXHIBIT 1-2
ORIGINAL WORKSHEET REFORMATTED

	A	B	C	D	E	F	G
1	Microsoft Corporation Sales						
2	(Millions of Dollars)						
3	1989 to 1995						
4	*1995*	*1994*	*1993*	*1992*	*1991*	*1990*	*1989*
5	5,937.00	4,649.00	3,753.00	2,758.73	1,843.43	1,183.45	803.53

Entering Formulas

So far, we haven't done anything that couldn't just as easily be done in any word-processing application. The real power of spreadsheets becomes obvious when formulas are used. Formulas will enable us to convert the data that we have entered into useful information.

At the moment, our sample worksheet contains only sales data for Microsoft. Suppose, however, that we are interested in performing a simple analysis of the profitability of Microsoft over the 1989 to 1995 time period. In this case we would also need to see the net income for each of the years under study. Let's make some modifications to the worksheet to make it more useful.

Add the data from Table 1-1 to the sample worksheet in cells A6..G6, immediately below the sales data. Now, we have a couple of problems. The title of our worksheet, in cell A1, is no longer accurate. We are now putting together a profitability analysis, so we should change the title to reflect this change of focus. Select cell A1 (even though the title is centered across A1..G1, 1-2-3 still keeps the data in A1) by clicking on it. Notice that the text appears in the right-hand side of the formula bar. To edit the title, click on the edit line just to the right of the word "Sales." Backspace over the word "Sales" and then type: `Profitability Analysis`, and press Enter to make the change take effect.

TABLE 1-1
MICROSOFT NET INCOME

Year	Net Income
1995	1,453.000
1994	1,146.000
1993	953.000
1992	708.060
1991	462.743
1990	279.186
1989	170.538

Our only remaining problem is that the data in the table are not clearly identified. Ideally, we would like to have the data labeled in the column just to the left of the first data point. But, there is no column to the left of the data! There are several ways to overcome this problem. The easiest is to simply tell 1-2-3 to insert a column to the left of column A. To accomplish this feat, select the whole of column A by clicking on the column header where it has an "A." Notice that the whole column is highlighted (we can do this with rows as well). Now, from the menus, choose Edit Insert. The new column is magically inserted, and all of our data have been moved one column to the right. In cell A5 type: Sales, and in A6 type: Net Income.

If you are following the examples exactly, the words Net Income probably do not fit exactly into A6. Instead, part of the text is cut off so as not to overflow onto the data in B6. We can easily remedy this by changing the width of column A. Again select column A, and then choose Style Column Width which will cause a dialog box to be displayed. In the edit box type: 20 and press the Enter key. Column A should now be wide enough to hold the text that we have added and will add later.

We can now proceed with our profitability analysis. Because of the dramatic growth in sales, it isn't immediately clear from the data whether Microsoft's profitability has improved over the years or not, even though net income has increased steadily over this time. In this type of situation, it is generally preferable to look at net income as a percentage of sales (net profit margin) instead of dollar net income. Thankfully, we do not have to type in more data to do this. Instead, we can let 1-2-3 calculate these percentages for us. All we need to do is to enter the formulas.

Formulas in 1-2-3 are based upon cell addresses. To add two cells together, we simply tell 1-2-3 to take the contents of the first cell and add it to the contents of the second. The result of the formula will be placed in the cell in which the formula is entered. In our problem, we need to find net income as a percentage of sales. We will do this first for 1995.

Before entering our first formula, we should insert a label identifying the data. In cell **A7** type: Net Profit Margin. Change the active cell to **B7** where we want to place the result of the calculation. The problem that we want to solve is to take the number in cell B6 and divide it by the number in B5. In 1-2-3, division is represented by the forward slash (/), so in **B7** type: +B6/B5. *The plus sign must precede all formulas in 1-2-3*, otherwise it will treat the formula as text and will not calculate the result. Press the Enter key to make 1-2-3 calculate the formula (you should get 0.244736 as the result).

In this example, we typed the formula directly into the cell because the small size of our worksheet made it easy to know what cells we wanted to use in the formula. In many instances, this is not the case. In more complicated worksheets it is usually easier to use the "pointer mode" to enter formulas. In pointer mode, we merely use the mouse to point to the cells that we want included, and 1-2-3 inserts them into the formula. Move to C7 and we will enter the formula using the pointer mode. First, type + which places 1-2-3 in edit mode. Now, instead of typing C6, click on C6 with the mouse. Notice that C6 appears in the formula bar to the right of the equals sign. Press the forward slash key to indicate division and then point to C5. In the formula bar you should see the formula "+C6/C5". Press the Enter key calculate the result of the formula (you should get 0.246505 as the result).

Let's change the format of these cells so that they are easier to read. In this case, it would be nice to see them in percentage format with two decimal places. First, highlight cells B7..C7. Choose **S**tyle **N**umber Format. From the **F**ormat list click on **P**ercentage and then set the number of decimal places to 2. Press the Enter key or click the OK button.

Copying and Moving Formulas

We have now calculated the net profit margin for 1995 and 1994, but that still leaves five years for which we need to enter formulas. Repeatedly typing essentially the same formula can get tedious. Fortunately, we can simply copy the formula, and 1-2-3 will update the cell addresses to maintain the same relative relationships. For example, we know that for 1993, the formula should read "+D6/D5". If we copy the formula from C7 to D7, 1-2-3 will change the formula from

"+C6/C5" to "+D6/D5" automatically. This works because 1-2-3 treats all cell references as relative. When you typed the formula in cell B7 (+B6/B5) 1-2-3 read that as "take the contents of the cell that is one row above the current cell and divide that by the contents of the cell that is two rows above the current cell." When copying formulas, 1-2-3 maintains the same relative cell relationships so that the formulas are updated.

Rather than retyping the formula for our other cells, let's simply copy from C7. First, select C7 and then choose Edit Copy from the menus. Now highlight cells D7..H7 and choose Edit Paste from the menus. At this point, your worksheet should closely resemble the one in Exhibit 1-3.

EXHIBIT 1-3
A PROFITABILITY ANALYSIS FOR MICROSOFT

	A	B	C	D	E	F	G	H
1		Microsoft Corporation Profitability Analysis						
2		(Millions of Dollars)						
3		1989 to 1995						
4		1995	1994	1993	1992	1991	1990	1989
5	Sales	5,937.00	4,649.00	3,753.00	2,758.73	1,843.43	1,183.45	803.53
6	Net Income	1,453.00	1,146.00	953.00	708.06	462.74	279.19	170.54
7	Net Profit Margin	24.47%	24.65%	23.59%	21.22%	25.10%	23.59%	21.22%

We can see from Exhibit 1-3 that Microsoft's net profit margin has been mostly increasing in since 1989. The increase in profitability since 1990 is probably the result of the phenomenal success of the Microsoft Windows environment after the May 1990 release of version 3.0 and the follow-on release of Windows 3.1.

In addition to copying formulas (which maintains the relative cell references) they can also be moved. Moving a formula to a different cell has no effect on the cell references. For example, we could move the formula in B7 (+B6/B5) to B8. To do this, select B7 and then choose Edit Cut from the menus. Next, select B8 and choose Edit Paste from the menus. Notice that the result in B8 is exactly the same as before. Furthermore, the formula is unchanged.

Formulas (or anything else) may also be moved with the mouse. Simply select the cells containing the data that you want to move, position the mouse pointer at the edge of the cell so that it changes to a hand, and then click the left mouse button and drag the cell to its new location. Now move the formula back to B7. Highlight B8 and drag it back to B7. Or, select B8 and choose Edit Cut, select B7 and choose Edit Paste. The worksheet should again resemble the one pictured in Exhibit 1-3.

Mathematical Operators

Aside from division, which we have already seen, there are four additional primary mathematical operations: addition, subtraction, multiplication, and exponentiation. All of these operations are available in 1-2-3 and can be used as easily as division. Table 1-2 summarizes the five basic operations and the result that you should get from entering the example formula in cell B8.

TABLE 1-2
MATHEMATICAL OPERATIONS

Operation	Key	Example	Result in B8
Exponentiation	^	+15^2	225.00
Multiplication	*	+B5*B7	1,453.00
Division	/	+B6/B7	5,937.00
Addition	+	+B5+B6	7,390.00
Subtraction	-	+B5-B6	4,484.00

Parentheses and the Order of Operation

Using the mathematical operators provided by 1-2-3 is straightforward in most instances. However, there are times when it gets a bit complicated. For example, let's calculate the rates of growth of Microsoft's sales and net income. To calculate the growth rates we will usually want the compound annual growth rate (geometric mean growth rate) rather than the arithmetic average growth rate. The general equation for the geometric mean growth rate is:

$$\overline{G} = {}^{(N-1)}\!\sqrt{\frac{X_N}{X_1}} - 1 = \left(\frac{X_N}{X_1}\right)^{\frac{1}{(N-1)}} - 1 \qquad (1\text{-}1)$$

where $\overline{G}$ is the geometric mean, N is the count of the numbers in the series, X_1 is the first number in the series (1989 sales in our example), and X_N is the last number in the series (1995 sales).

Translating this equation into 1-2-3 is not as simple as it may at first appear. To do this correctly requires knowledge of operator precedence. In other words, 1-2-3 doesn't necessarily evaluate equations from left to right. Instead, some operations are performed before others. Exponentiation is usually performed first. Multiplication and division are usually performed next, but they are considered equal in precedence so any multiplication and division are evaluated from left to right. Finally, addition and subtraction are evaluated, and they are also considered equal in precedence to each other.

We can modify the order of precedence by using parentheses. Operations enclosed in parentheses are always evaluated first. As a simple example, how would you evaluate the following expression?

$$X = 2 + 4/3$$

Is X equal to 2 or 3.33? Algebraically, X is equal to 3.33 because the division should be performed before the addition (as 1-2-3 would do). If the answer we were seeking was 2, we could rewrite the expression using parentheses to clarify:

$$X = (2 + 4)/3$$

The parentheses clearly indicate that the addition should be performed first, so the answer is 2.

To calculate the compound annual growth rate of sales, move to cell **A8** and type: `Sales Growth`. Now, enter the following into **B8**: `+(B5/H5)^(1/6)-1`. Pressing the Enter key will reveal that the growth rate of sales for the seven year period was 39.56% per year (you may have to reformat the cell to display as a percentage). To determine the average growth rate of net income, type: `Net Income Growth` into **A9**, and then copy the formula from **B8** to **B9**. You should find that the compound annual rate of growth of net income has been 42.91% per year. And, that the formula in **B9** is: `+(B6/H6)^(1/6)-1`.

Using 1-2-3's Built-in Functions

We could build some pretty impressive worksheets with the techniques that we have examined so far. But why should we have to build all of our formulas from scratch, especially when some of them can be quite complex, and therefore error-prone? 1-2-3 comes with hundreds of built-in functions; about 27 of them are financial functions. These functions are ready-to-go, all they need is for you to supply cell references as inputs. We will be demonstrating the use of many of these functions throughout the book, but for now let's redo our growth rate calculations using the built-in functions.

Since we want to know the compound annual rate of growth, we can use 1-2-3's built-in **@GEOMEAN** function. To use this function the syntax is:

@GEOMEAN(*LIST*)

where *LIST* is any number of inputs separated by commas. As is usual in 1-2-3, we can also supply a range of cells rather than specifying the cells individually. Remember, we want to find the geometric mean *rate of growth of sales*, not the geometric mean of sales. Since the **@GEOMEAN** function simply finds the N*th* root of the product of the inputs, we need to redefine our inputs (we used sales in our custom-built formula.) Let's add a row of percentage changes in sales to our worksheet.

Move to A10 and enter the label: `% Change in Sales`, then move to B10 and enter the formula: `+B5/C5-1`. The result in B10 should be 0.2770, indicating that sales grew by 27.70% from 1994 to 1995. Now copy the formula from B10 to each cell in the C10..G10 range. Note that we don't copy the formula into H10 because that would cause an error since I10 doesn't contain any data (try it, and you will see ERR in H10 because your formula tried to divide by zero).

Now, to calculate the compound annual rate of sales growth we need to enter the **@GEOMEAN** function into B11: `@geomean(B10..G10)`. Since our data points are in one contiguous range, we chose to specify the range rather than each individual cell. Let's also supply a label so that when we come back later we can recall what this cell represents. Move to A11 and enter: `Sales Growth`.

Have you noticed any problems with the result of the **@GEOMEAN** function? The result was 0.3823, rather than the 0.3956 we got when using our custom formula. Either our custom formula is incorrect, or we have misused the **@GEOMEAN** function. Actually, this type of error is common, and easily overlooked. What has happened is that when using the **@GEOMEAN** function, we didn't fully understand what went on behind the scenes. Remember that **@GEOMEAN** simply takes the Nth root of the product of the numbers. When multiplying numbers that are less than one, the result is even smaller, not larger as is the case with numbers greater than one. What we should have done is taken the geometric mean of the relative changes (i.e., one plus the percentage change).

To correct the error, replace the formula in B10 with: `+B5/C5` and copy it to the other cells. Now replace the formula in B11 with: `@geomean(B10..G10)-1`. The result is 0.3956, exactly the same as our previous result. To avoid errors like this one, you absolutely must understand what the built-in formula is doing. Never blindly accept results just because 1-2-3 has calculated them for you. There is an old saying in computer science, "garbage in, garbage out."

At this point, your worksheet should closely resemble the one pictured in Exhibit 1-4.

EXHIBIT 1-4
ANALYSIS OF MICROSOFT'S GROWTH RATES

	A	B	C	D	E	F	G	H
1		Microsoft Corporation Profitability Analysis						
2		(Millions of Dollars)						
3		1989 to 1995						
4		1995	1994	1993	1992	1991	1990	1989
5	Sales	5,937.00	4,649.00	3,753.00	2,758.73	1,843.43	1,183.45	803.53
6	Net Income	1,453.00	1,146.00	953.00	708.06	462.74	279.19	170.54
7	Net Profit Margin	24.47%	24.65%	23.59%	21.22%	25.10%	23.59%	21.22%
8	Sales Growth	39.56%						
9	Net Income Growth	42.91%						
10	% Change in Sales	1.2770	1.2387	1.3604	1.4965	1.5577	1.4728	
11	Sales Growth	39.56%						

Using the @Function List

 With the hundreds of built-in functions that are available in 1-2-3, it can be difficult to remember the name of the one you want to use, or the order of the parameters, etc. To help you with this problem, 1-2-3 provides the @Function List, a series of dialog boxes that guide you through the process of selecting and entering a built-in formula.

Let's use the @Function list to insert the **@GEOMEAN** function into B11. First, select cell B11 and then clear the current formula by choosing **E**dit Clear **B**oth from the menus. Now, insert a + into the cell. Notice that there is a button just to the left of the + sign (pictured at left) on the edit line. Click this button on the edit line to bring up the @Function list.

Click on List All and then choose Statistical in the **C**ategory list. The @Function list, Exhibit 1-5, will now show the built-in statistical functions. Scroll down this

EXHIBIT 1-5
THE 1-2-3 V. 5.0 @FUNCTION LIST

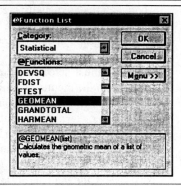

list and click on **@GEOMEAN**. Notice that there is a definition of the function at the bottom of the dialog box. Click the OK button to insert the function into B11.

Now, highlight cells B10..G10 so that they replace *LIST* in the function. Before pressing the Enter key, we need to subtract 1 from the result of the function, so type −1 after the **@GEOMEAN** function and then press Enter. The formula in B11 should be: @Geomean(B10..G10)-1.

The @Function list is an easy way to discover new functions and to use familiar ones. Using it will make 1-2-3 much easier for you to learn.

Creating Graphs

In our simple profitability analysis it is obvious that Microsoft's profitability has been growing at a faster rate in the last three years. Many times, you will build much more complicated worksheets where the key trends are not so easy to spot; especially for others who didn't build the worksheet. You may also find that you need to give a presentation, to a group of investors perhaps, to convince them to invest in your firm. In cases such as these, tables full of numbers may actually obscure your point. People (and students too!) tend to get a glazed look in their eyes when examining tables of numbers. The solution to this problem is to present a chart of the numbers to illustrate your point. Fortunately, high-quality graphics are a snap with 1-2-3.

Creating Embedded Charts

Until a few years ago, worksheets and graphics were separate entities. The original Lotus 1-2-3 actually used a separate program to create charts of worksheet data. Today, charts are usually created within the main program. In 1-2-3, we can create a chart simply by selecting the data and then choosing **T**ools **C**hart. Let's try creating a graph of sales versus net income for Microsoft.

First you must select the data. Select the A5..H6 range and then choose **T**ools **C**hart from the menus. At this point, you need to tell 1-2-3 where to place the chart in your worksheet. Click on the upper-left corner of A12, and a bar chart of the data will appear. Note that the chart can be resized by dragging the selection handles (little squares around the border). Make your chart larger by dragging the upper-right corner of the chart to H12.

Next, we'll add the chart title and label the X- and Y-axes. Double-click the title at the top of the chart and enter: `Microsoft Sales vs. Net Income` for Line **1** in the dialog box. Note that, instead of entering the title text, you can also specify a cell reference which contains the text for the title. Repeat this procedure for each axis title. For the X-axis enter the title: `Years`. For the Y-axis enter: `Dollars`.

By default, the Y-axis labels are scaled by a factor of 1,000. We can change this by choosing **C**hart **A**xis **Y**-Axis from the menus. Now, press the **O**ptions button and set the Axis units to M**a**nual and the **E**xponent to 0. You can change the scaling of the Y-axis by changing the **E**xponent to any amount desired. Note that an indication of the scale (e.g., thousands, millions, etc.) will automatically be entered on the Y-axis.

Finally, we need to add labels to the X-axis. Click on the axis and choose **C**hart **R**anges. From the **S**eries list, choose X-Axis Labels and highlight B4..H4 on the worksheet. Press the OK button, and the labels will appear. Your worksheet should now resemble that in Exhibit 1-6.

Formatting Charts

We have now created a basic chart of sales versus net income, but it may not be exactly what you wanted. The colors may be wrong, you may want a different type of chart, etc. Before we can perform any editing on the embedded chart, select the chart by clicking anywhere on the chart. This will highlight the chart and some of the menus will change to those specific to editing charts.

EXHIBIT 1-6
A WORKSHEET WITH AN EMBEDDED CHART

	A	B	C	D	E	F	G	H
1		Microsoft Corporation Profitability Analysis						
2		(Millions of Dollars)						
3		1989 to 1995						
4		1995	1994	1993	1992	1991	1990	1989
5	Sales	5937.00	4649.00	3753.00	2758.73	1843.43	1183.45	803.53
6	Net Income	1453.00	1146.00	953.00	708.06	462.74	279.19	170.54
7	Net Profit Margin	24.47%	24.65%	23.59%	21.22%	25.10%	23.59%	21.22%
8	Sales Growth	39.56%						
9	Net Income Growth	42.91%						
10	% Change in Sales	1.2770	1.2387	1.3604	1.4965	1.5577	1.4728	
11	Sales Growth	39.56%						

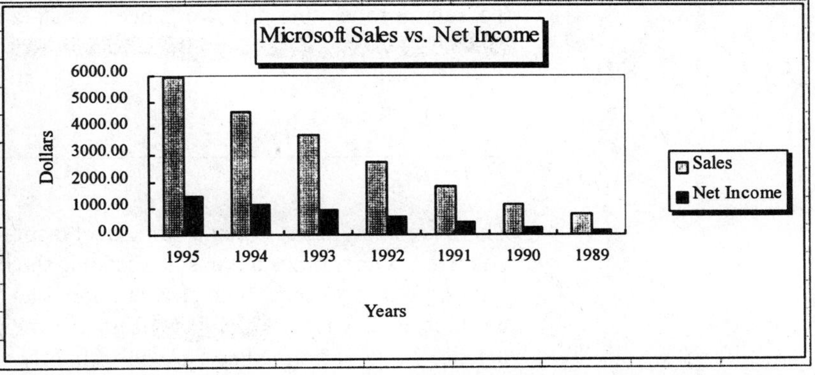

Microsoft Sales vs. Net Income

In 1-2-3, every element of a chart is treated as a separate "object." This means that each element can be selected and edited separately from the other elements. In addition, these chart objects are somewhat intelligent. They "know" what actions can be performed on them, and will present a menu of these actions if you click on them with the right mouse button. The major objects in any chart include each data series, the axes, the axes titles, the chart title, and any other text strings entered into the chart. To select an object, all you need to do is to click on it with the left button. Once the object is selected, it will be redisplayed with small squares (selection boxes) surrounding it. With this knowledge let's edit our chart.

Suppose that rather than the default bar chart, we wanted the data presented as lines. To make the change, simply right-click one of the bars and choose Chart Type from the shortcut menu. You will now be presented with 12 different chart types to choose from. Select Line and then click the OK button to make the change. It's that simple! To change the line color or symbols, simply right-click one of the lines and choose Lines & Color from the shortcut menu.

We can also reformat the text on the chart. For example, to make the chart title appear in a smaller font, right-click the title and choose Fonts & Attributes from the shortcut menu. Select the appropriate font size, press the OK button, and the change will be made. Any other text object on the chart can be reformatted similarly.

Next, let's move the legend to the bottom of the chart so that the chart doesn't have to be so wide. Click on the legend with the right button and choose Legend from the shortcut menu. Now, choose Below Plot from among the choices. Press the Enter key to return to the chart.

To return to editing the worksheet, click anywhere in the worksheet. Your worksheet should now resemble the one in Exhibit 1-7.

Printing

There are many times when a worksheet displayed on screen accomplishes all that you need. Other times there is no escaping the need for hard copy. 1-2-3 makes the printing of a worksheet both easy and flexible. For small worksheets, all that need be done is to choose File Print from the menus, and let 1-2-3 worry about the details. Larger printing tasks are only slightly more complex.

Suppose that our profitability analysis of Microsoft needs to be printed so that it can be distributed at a conference. As a first step, we need to decide if we want to print the entire worksheet or only a portion of it. In this case, let's assume that we wish to print the whole worksheet, except that we want to print the graph on a separate page so that it can more easily be converted to an overhead transparency.

EXHIBIT 1-7
WORKSHEET WITH REFORMATTED CHART

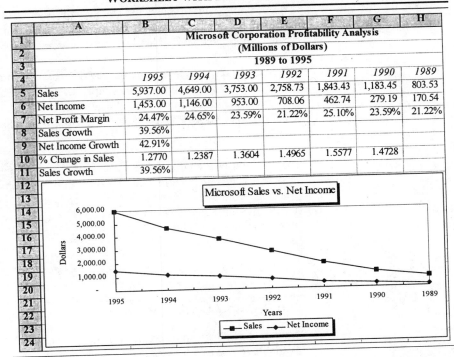

	A	B	C	D	E	F	G	H
1			Microsoft Corporation Profitability Analysis					
2			(Millions of Dollars)					
3			1989 to 1995					
4		1995	1994	1993	1992	1991	1990	1989
5	Sales	5,937.00	4,649.00	3,753.00	2,758.73	1,843.43	1,183.45	803.53
6	Net Income	1,453.00	1,146.00	953.00	708.06	462.74	279.19	170.54
7	Net Profit Margin	24.47%	24.65%	23.59%	21.22%	25.10%	23.59%	21.22%
8	Sales Growth	39.56%						
9	Net Income Growth	42.91%						
10	% Change in Sales	1.2770	1.2387	1.3604	1.4965	1.5577	1.4728	
11	Sales Growth	39.56%						
12								
13								
14								
15								
16								
17								
18								
19								
20								
21								
22								
23								
24								

Because we wish to print the numbers and chart separately, we need to tell 1-2-3 the range of cells that we want printed. Select the range A1..H11 and then choose File Print from the menus. In the dialog box you will see that 1-2-3 has already decided that you want to print the selected range (you can change the range if necessary). Because our worksheet is relatively wide, we want to make sure that it prints on only one page. Click on the Page Setup button to see the printing options that are available. On this dialog box you can enter headers and footers (text which prints at the top or bottom of every page), set margins, change the page orientation, etc. In this case, we want to force the worksheet to print on only one page. Open the drop-down list box labeled Size and choose "Fit all to page." Click the OK button to set the options and return to the Print dialog.

Before actually printing a worksheet, it is good practice to preview the output to make sure that it looks exactly as we want. This will save both time and paper. From the Print dialog click on the Preview button (or, from the File menu select

Print Pre_view). 1-2-3 will now display, on the screen, a likeness of the actual printed page.

At this point, everything should be ready for printing, so click the printer icon at the top of the preview page, or return to the print dialog and press the OK button. Your page should look nearly identical to the on-screen version.

To print the chart on a separate page, first click anywhere in the chart to select it for printing. Now, to print the chart simply select **File** **P**rint then from the print dialog box press the OK button. Presto! The chart prints out on its own page. Of course, you can use Print Pre_view and Page Set_up for charts just as we did for the worksheet.

What if you wanted to print the chart on the same page as the worksheet? Simple, just select the entire range that you want to print, including the chart. Now repeat the steps from above, and the worksheet and chart will print on the same page. An easier alternative is to select the range to print, choose **File** **P**rint, and make sure that Selectio**n** is selected in the Print What section of the print dialog box. Now, press the OK button.

Saving and Opening Files

Now that we have created a worksheet, you should save it so that it will be available to use at a later time. To save this file, choose **File** Save **A**s... from the menus. This will cause a dialog box to be displayed which allows you to supply a name for the file and the location where you would like it stored. For example, to save the file as MSOFT.WK4 on a floppy disk in the A: drive, you would type: `a:msoft.wk4` in the File **N**ame edit box.

After saving a file, you can open it at any time by choosing **File** **O**pen... from the menus. This will cause a dialog box to be displayed from which you may select the file. Once a file has been named and saved the first time you may save further changes by choosing **File** **S**ave.

Quitting 1-2-3

To exit from 1-2-3 you can select File Exit from the menus, or double-click on the system menu box in the upper left corner of the 1-2-3 window. Note that if you attempt to exit 1-2-3 without saving your work, 1-2-3 will warn you and ask if you would like to save the file.

Summary

In this chapter we have discussed the basics of Lotus 1-2-3. You should have gained a basic understanding of such topics as entering text and numbers, entering formulas, formatting, graphics, and printing. In the chapters ahead, we will cover many of these topics in more depth. We will, at the same time, introduce you to financial analysis and how 1-2-3 can make this analysis easier and more productive. Along the way, we hope to help you develop the reasoning and critical thinking skills which are necessary in the field of finance.

TABLE 1-3
FUNCTIONS INTRODUCED IN THIS CHAPTER

Purpose	Function	Page
Calculate the geometric mean	GEOMEAN(*LIST*)	19

CHAPTER 2

The Basic Financial Statements

After studying this chapter, you should be able to:

1. *Explain the purpose and understand the format of the firm's three basic financial statements: the income statement, the balance sheet, and the statement of cash flows.*

2. *Construct each of these statements in 1-2-3 with data for any company.*

3. *Link worksheets together so that formulas in one worksheet can reference data in another.*

Much of financial analysis takes as its starting point the basic financial statements of the firm. It is therefore crucial that the analyst have a strong fundamental understanding of these statements. There are three basic financial statements:

1. The *income statement* summarizes the results of the firm's operations over a period of time. The income statement tells us the total revenues and expenses for the time period, and also contains several different measures of the profits earned by the firm. Typically, income statements are prepared for different time periods, usually monthly, quarterly, and annually.

2. The *balance sheet* describes the assets, liabilities and equity of the firm at a specific point in time. Assets are the tangible or intangible things that a firm owns. Liabilities are the debts of the firm. Equity is the difference between what the firm owns and what it owes to others. Because the balance sheet is specific to a point in time, it is much like a photograph. What it shows was true when the snapshot was taken, but is not necessarily true when it is viewed.

3. The *statement of cash flows* outlines the sources of the firm's cash flows and where the cash flows went. Activities which bring cash into the firm are referred to as *sources* of cash, while those that take cash out of the firm are referred to as *uses* of cash.

In this chapter we will build each of these three statements for Elvis Products International, a small producer of Elvis paraphernalia. Each financial statement will be created in its own worksheet in the workbook, and we will create links between the sheets as necessary. Before beginning, open a new workbook.

The Income Statement

The income statement is a fairly simple document that begins by listing a firm's revenues (perhaps by sources or in total) followed by all of the firm's expenses. The result of the income statement is the net income for the period. Net income represents the cash left over from sales after all expenses have been paid.

Building an Income Statement in 1-2-3

Exhibit 2-1 presents the income statement for Elvis Products International (EPI) for the year ending December 31, 1997. We will build this income statement first, and then use it as a base for creating the 1996 income statement.

EXHIBIT 2-1
EPI'S INCOME STATEMENT FOR 1997

	A	B	C
1	Elvis Products International		
2	Income Statement		
3	For the Year Ended Dec. 31, 1997		
4		*1997*	*1996*
5	Sales	3850.00	3432.00
6	Cost of Goods Sold	3250.00	2864.00
7	*Gross Profit*	*600.00*	*568.00*
8	Selling and G&A Expenses	330.30	240.00
9	Fixed Expenses	100.00	100.00
10	Depreciation Expense	20.00	18.90
11	*EBIT*	*149.70*	*209.10*
12	Interest Expense	76.00	62.50
13	*Earnings Before Taxes*	*73.70*	*146.60*
14	Taxes @ 40%	29.48	58.64
15	*Net Income*	*44.22*	*87.96*

Principle 1:
Make 1-2-3 do as much of the work as possible. Whenever possible, a formula should be used rather than entering numbers. In the long run this will minimize errors.

Principle 2:
Format the worksheet so that it is easy to understand. Borders, shading, and font choices are more than just decorations. Properly chosen, they can make important numbers stand out and get the attention they deserve.

While we are building the income statement, we want to keep a couple of general principles in mind. Principle 1 says that we want to make 1-2-3 do as much of the work as possible. Any time a value can be calculated, it should be calculated. The reasoning behind this principle is that we want to avoid mistakes and increase productivity. A little thought before beginning the design of a worksheet can help to minimize data entry errors, and increase productivity by reducing the amount of data that needs to be entered. Principle 2 says that we should format the worksheet in such a way as to make it easy to comprehend. There are many times that you will be creating a worksheet for others to use, or for your use at a later date. Properly organizing the cells and judicious use of color and fonts can make the worksheet easier to use and modify.[1]

It is usually helpful when working with multiple worksheets in a workbook for each sheet to be given a name other than the default. Double-click on the sheet tab labeled "A" and then type Inc Statement when the tab blanks out and widens.

---

1. We would like to emphasize the word "judicious." Many people to whom fonts are a new idea end up producing documents with a ransom note appearance. Do yourself, and others, a favor by limiting your use of fonts to one or two per document.

This step is important because when we later begin referencing data on this sheet, the references require the name of the sheet. Note that we abbreviate the name because 1-2-3 limits worksheet names to 15 characters.

We will begin building the income statement with the titles in cells A1 to A3. Remember, if the need arises, we can always insert new rows or columns into the worksheet at a later time. In A1 type: Elvis Products International; in A2: Income Statement; in A3: For the Year Ended Dec. 31, 1997. The first line of the title identifies the company, the second identifies the type of statement, and the third identifies the time period that the statement covers. Now center the titles by selecting A1..C3, choose Style Alignment, then Center horizontally and Across columns.

How to proceed from this point is largely a matter of preference. We could move line by line through the income statement, entering a label followed by the value. An alternative is to enter all of the labels and then all of the numbers. The second method is preferable at this point so that we may concentrate on the numbers. The labels are going to be stored in column A, and the numbers will be in column B. It is good practice to enter a label indicating the end of the period above the data, so move to B4 and type: 1997.

Beginning in A5, enter the labels exactly as they appear in Exhibit 2-1. Once you have entered the labels, it is likely that you will find that some of these labels are too long to fit in only one cell. To remedy this problem, we need to change the width of column A. There are several ways to accomplish this in 1-2-3. The most cumbersome method is to select the column (click on the column header) choose Style Column Width and enter: 17 in the "Set width to" edit box. If you are using some font other than 12 point Times New Roman, you will have to experiment with different numbers to find the appropriate width for the column. Instead of entering a specific number for the column width, we can also let 1-2-3 determine the appropriate width. In the Column Width dialog box simply click "Fit widest entry" and 1-2-3 will automatically make the column wide enough to accommodate the longest text in the column.

As usual, there is an alternative for mouse users. If you slowly move the mouse pointer over the column headers, you will notice that the pointer changes its shape (to that pictured at left) as it passes over the boundary between columns. Press the left mouse button while the pointer is over this boundary, and drag until the column is wide enough to accommodate the text.

When entering data for large companies, it is often preferable to display the numbers in thousands or millions of dollars, rather than the full amount. For EPI, we will enter the numbers in thousands, since they are small. Move to B5 and enter: 3,850.[2] Keeping principle 2 in mind, we would like the numbers to display with commas and two decimal places. Since each cell can maintain a number format, regardless of whether it contains any numbers or not, we will pre-format the cells that we are going to use. Select cells B5..C15, choose Style Number format from the menus, and then choose the ",Comma" format with 2 decimal places. When we enter numbers into these cells, they will automatically take on this format.

Move to B6 and type: 3,250. Notice that, as promised, the number in B6 appears with commas. Note that the manner in which 1-2-3 displays numbers will not affect any calculations. Regardless of the format, 1-2-3 always stores numbers at their full precision. The format merely changes what we see on the screen, not what is kept in memory.

Gross profit is the amount that is left over after paying for the goods that were sold. To calculate gross profit, we subtract cost of goods sold from sales. Again, we want 1-2-3 to make all of the calculations, so in B7 type: +B5-B6. Selling, General and Administrative (S,G&A) Expense is an input, so enter: 330.3 in B8. Fixed expenses (rent, salaries, etc.) for the period are an input so enter: 100 in B9. Depreciation is also an input in this case, so in B10 enter: 20.

Earnings Before Interest and Taxes (EBIT) is exactly what it sounds like. Any of several formulas could be used for this calculation, but we will use: +B7-B8-B9-B10. We could simplify this equation somewhat by making use of the SUM function. The new function would be: +B7-@Sum(B8..10). @SUM is a built-in 1-2-3 function which returns the summation of the arguments. @SUM is defined:

$$@\textsc{Sum}(\textit{LIST})$$

where *LIST* is the range of numbers that are to be summed. 1-2-3 will also accept a list of cell addresses separated by commas. @SUM is one of the more commonly used built-in functions, so common that Lotus included a SmartIcon (pictured at left) on the toolbar to automate the summation of rows or columns of numbers. To use the Sum button, simply select the cell where you want the formula to be placed and then click the button. 1-2-3 will make an intelligent guess about which cells

---

2. There is no need for you to type the commas. We are showing them here for clarity. However, 1-2-3 will accept the numbers with commas if you wish to type them in.

you want included, and it is usually correct. If it guesses wrong, highlight the incorrect range in the edit line and then select the correct range on the worksheet. Note that the Sum button does not work when you are already in edit mode.

In B12 enter 76 for the interest expense. Next, we will calculate *Earnings Before Taxes* with the formula: +B11-B12 in cell B13. EPI pays taxes at the rate of 40% on taxable income. We will calculate this in B14 with: +B13*0.40. Finally, *Net Income* is the profit earned by the firm after all revenues and expenses have been taken into account. To calculate net income, enter +B13-B14 in cell B15.

As you can see, EPI's net income for the fiscal year 1997 was $44.22. However, for analysis purposes, we normally are not overly concerned with net income. Net income does not accurately represent the funds that a firm has available to spend. In the calculation of net income, we include depreciation expense (and/or other non-cash expenses such as depletion or amortization) which ostensibly accounts for the decline in the value of the long-term assets of the firm. Since nobody actually wrote a check for the depreciation expense, it should be added back to the net income number to give a better picture of the cash flow for the period. Cash flow is the number one concern to financial analysts.

To create EPI's income statement for 1996 doesn't take nearly as much work. First, select B5..B15 and copy the cells using Edit Copy or the Copy SmartIcon. Select C5 and choose Edit Paste. Now you have an exact copy of the 1997 income statement. Enter the numbers from Table 2-1 into the appropriate cells.

TABLE 2-1
EPI's 1996 INCOME AND EXPENSES

Category	Value
Sales	3,432
Cost of Goods Sold	2,864
S,G&A Expenses	240
Depreciation Expense	18.9
Interest Expense	62.5

Notice that you only had to enter the new numbers. The formulas are updated and recalculated automatically. So instead of entering 11 cells of formulas or numbers, you only had to enter 5 numbers. Your worksheet should now resemble the one in Exhibit 2-1 (page 31).

Common-Size Income Statements

A common technique among financial analysts is to examine *common-size financial statements*. Common-size financial statements display the data not as dollar amounts, but as percentages. These statements provide the analyst with two key benefits:

1. They allow for easy comparisons between firms which are different sizes.

2. They can aid in spotting important trends which otherwise might be obscured by the dollar amounts.

A common-size income statement is one which shows all of the data as a percentage of the firm's total revenues. 1-2-3 makes the building of common-size financial statements easy, as we'll see with the EPI data.

To begin, we need to make room for the common-size income statements. Select the whole of column B by clicking on the column header. From the menus choose **Edit Insert** which will insert a new column to the left of the selected column. This new column will need to be resized so that it is approximately the same size as Column C. Now, repeat this process with column D (the 1996 data). In columns B and D enter the labels: 1997% and 1996% respectively.

We will start building our common-size income statements with the 1997 data. In B5, enter the formula: +C5/C$5.[3] Note that the formatting in the new column B is the same as that in column C. So change the number format (**Style Number** format) to "Percent" with two decimal places. You should now see that the result is 100.00%. Copy B5, select cells B6..B15, and then choose **Edit Paste**. You have now created a common-size income statement for 1997.

To create the common-size income statement for 1996, simply copy B5..B15 and then paste into D5. The resulting worksheet should appear like the one in Exhibit 2-2.

---

3. The $ in the formula will freeze the reference to a specific address. In this instance, C$5 will always refer to row 5, but the column reference will change if you copy the formula to the right or left. We could freeze only the column address with $C5. However, that would be counter-productive in this case. Here, we always want the divisor to be sales, but it should be the appropriate sales figure.

EXHIBIT 2-2
EPI'S COMMON-SIZE INCOME STATEMENTS

	A	B	C	D	E
1	Elvis Products International				
2	Common-size Income Statement				
3	For the Year Ended Dec. 31, 1997				
4		*1997%*	*1997*	*1996%*	*1996*
5	Sales	100.00%	3850.00	100.00%	3432.00
6	Cost of Goods Sold	84.42%	3250.00	83.45%	2864.00
7	*Gross Profit*	*15.58%*	600.00	*16.55%*	568.00
8	Selling and G&A Expenses	8.58%	330.30	6.99%	240.00
9	Fixed Expenses	2.60%	100.00	2.91%	100.00
10	Depreciation Expense	0.52%	20.00	0.55%	18.90
11	*EBIT*	*3.89%*	149.70	*6.09%*	209.10
12	Interest Expense	1.97%	76.00	1.82%	62.50
13	*Earnings Before Taxes*	*1.91%*	73.70	*4.27%*	146.60
14	Taxes @ 40%	0.77%	29.48	1.71%	58.64
15	*Net Income*	*1.15%*	44.22	*2.56%*	87.96

The Balance Sheet

The balance sheet is usually depicted in two sections: the assets section at the top or left side, and the liabilities and owner's equity section at the bottom or right side. It is important to realize that the balance sheet must balance (hence, the name.) That is, total assets must equal the sum of total liabilities and total owner's equity. Each of these sections is usually further divided into subsections.

On the asset side, there are two subsections. The *current assets* section describes the value of the firm's short-term assets. Short-term, in this case, is defined as one year or the time it takes for the asset to go through one cash flow cycle (e.g., from purchase to sale.) Typical current assets are cash, accounts receivable, and inventories. *Fixed assets* are those assets with lives longer than one year. Examples of fixed assets include vehicles, property, buildings, etc.

Like assets, liabilities can be subdivided into two sections. *Current liabilities* are those liabilities that are expected to be retired within one year. Examples are items such as accounts payable, wages payable, etc. *Long-term liabilities* are those that will not be paid off within the current year. Generally, long-term liabilities are made up of various types of bonds, bank loans, etc.

Owner's equity represents the difference between the value of the total assets and liabilities of the firm. This part of the balance sheet is subdivided into contributed capital and retained earnings. *Contributed capital* is the investment made by the common and preferred stockholders of the firm. *Retained earnings* is the accumulation of the undistributed profits of the firm.

Building a Balance Sheet in 1-2-3

The process of building a balance sheet in 1-2-3 is very similar to building the income statement. We will build EPI's 1997 and 1996 balance sheets, as shown in Exhibit 2-3, for an example.

We will keep EPI's balance sheets in the same workbook as the income statement but on a different worksheet. Keeping related data in the same workbook allows for easy referencing. Using separate worksheets allows us to keep the worksheets uncluttered and makes it easier to design worksheets. If necessary, insert a new worksheet by clicking on the New Sheet button. Next, double-click on the "B" tab and type `Balance Sheet` as the new name for this worksheet.

Enter the labels from Exhibit 2-3 into the blank worksheet. Notice that many of the labels in the balance sheet are indented. The easiest way to indent is to simply type several spaces before enter the label. The number of spaces is your choice, but usually three or four is sufficient. This is the method we have used. The alternative is to insert the indented labels into column B instead of column A. This way by controlling the width of column A, we can control the depth of the indentation. The labels in column A will simply overlap into column B as long as there is no text in the cell to the right.

To achieve the underlining and shading effects pictured in the Exhibits, select the cells and then choose Style Lines & Color from the menus. To set the type of border, first click on the line type in the Border section of the dialog box, and then click on the location of the line (**O**utline, **L**eft, **R**ight, **T**op, or Botto**m**). If you want to shade the selection, choose a **B**ackground color and shading **P**attern from the Interior section of the dialog. Shading can be accomplished on most printers, but the effect looks best with laser printers. It is usually best to make the text in a shaded cell bold so that it can be clearly seen.

EXHIBIT 2-3
EPI'S BALANCE SHEET

	A	B	C
1	**Elvis Products International**		
2	**Balance Sheet**		
3	**As of Dec. 31, 1997**		
4	*Assets*	*1997*	*1996*
5	Cash and Equivalents	52.00	57.60
6	Accounts Receivable	402.00	351.20
7	Inventory	836.00	715.20
8	*Total Current Assets*	*1290.00*	*1124.00*
9	Plant & Equipment	527.00	491.00
10	Accumulated Depreciation	166.20	146.20
11	*Net Fixed Assets*	*360.80*	*344.80*
12	**Total Assets**	**1650.80**	**1468.80**
14	*Liabilities and Owner's Equity*		
15	Accounts Payable	175.20	145.60
16	Short-term Notes Payable	225.00	200.00
17	Other Current Liabilities	140.00	136.00
18	*Total Current Liabilities*	*540.20*	*481.60*
19	Long-term Debt	424.61	323.43
20	*Total Liabilities*	*964.81*	*805.03*
21	Common Stock	460.00	460.00
22	Retained Earnings	225.99	203.77
23	*Total Shareholder's Equity*	*685.99*	*663.77*
24	**Total Liabilities and Owner's Equity**	**1650.80**	**1468.80**

In EPI's balance sheet, nearly everything is a direct input so we won't discuss every cell. Enter the numbers which are not italicized. The italicized entries are formulas which we will discuss for 1997. The formulas for the 1996 balance sheet can be copied directly from the 1997 balance sheet.

On the asset section, the first formula is for total current assets in B8. This is simply the sum of all of the current asset accounts, so the formula is: @SUM(B5..B7). Next, we calculate EPI's net fixed assets. This is equal to plant and equipment less accumulated depreciation so in B11 enter: +B9-B10. Finally, calculate total assets by adding the current assets and net fixed assets with the formula: +B8+B11.

The liabilities and owner's equity section is similar. We will calculate several subtotals and then a grand total in B24. Total current liabilities in B18 is calculated with: `@SUM(B15..B17)`. Total liabilities are calculated with the formula: `+B18+B19` in B20. Total shareholder's equity is calculated in B23 with: `+B21+B22`. And, finally, we calculate the total liabilities and owner's equity in B24 with: `+B20+B23`.

Copy these formulas into the appropriate cells in column C to create the 1996 balance sheet. Before continuing, make sure that your worksheet looks like the one in Exhibit 2-3.

Creating a Common-Size Balance Sheet

You can create a common-size balance sheet in the same way as we did for the income statement. The only difference is that the balance sheet entries are displayed as a percentage of the firm's total assets instead of total revenues.

To create the common-size balance sheets for EPI, proceed in the same manner as for the common-size income statements. Remember, insert a column to the left of column B and another to the left of column C. Your "Common-Size" view should look like that in Exhibit 2-4.

NEXT PAGE

Building a Statement of Cash Flows

Boiled down to its essence, a firm participates in two kinds of financial transactions: those that increase the cash balance (cash inflows, or *sources* of funds) and those that decrease the cash balance (cash outflows, or *uses* of funds).

One way that a financial analyst can determine how well a firm's management is performing is to examine how they are managing the shareholders' money. The accounting profession has developed a tool which is useful for this type of analysis.

The tool is known as the *Statement of Cash Flows*.[4] The statement of cash flows

---

4. Prior to the November 1987 release of FASB standard 95, this statement was known as the Statement of Changes in Financial Position. The Sources and Uses of Funds statement, as it was also known, contained the same information but was organized differently.

EXHIBIT 2-4
EPI'S COMMON-SIZE BALANCE SHEET

	A	B	C	D	E
	Elvis Products International				
1					
2	*Common-size Balance Sheet*				
3	*As of Dec. 31, 1997*				
4	*Assets*	*1997%*	*1997*	*1996%*	*1996*
5	Cash and Equivalents	3.15%	52.00	3.92%	57.60
6	Accounts Receivable	24.35%	402.00	23.91%	351.20
7	Inventory	50.64%	836.00	48.69%	715.20
8	*Total Current Assets*	*78.14%*	*1290.00*	*76.53%*	*1124.00*
9	Plant & Equipment	31.92%	527.00	33.43%	491.00
10	Accumulated Depreciation	10.07%	166.20	9.95%	146.20
11	*Net Fixed Assets*	*21.86%*	*360.80*	*23.47%*	*344.80*
12	*Total Assets*	**100.00%**	**1650.80**	**100.00%**	**1468.80**
14	*Liabilities and Owner's Equity*				
15	Accounts Payable	10.61%	175.20	9.91%	145.60
16	Short-term Notes Payable	13.63%	225.00	13.62%	200.00
17	Other Current Liabilities	8.48%	140.00	9.26%	136.00
18	*Total Current Liabilities*	*32.72%*	*540.20*	*32.79%*	*481.60*
19	Long-term Debt	25.72%	424.61	22.02%	323.43
20	*Total Liabilities*	*58.45%*	*964.81*	*54.81%*	*805.03*
21	Common Stock	27.87%	460.00	31.32%	460.00
22	Retained Earnings	13.69%	225.99	13.87%	203.77
23	*Total Shareholder's Equity*	*41.55%*	*685.99*	*45.19%*	*663.77*
24	**Total Liabilities and Owner's Equity**	**100.00%**	**1650.80**	**100.00%**	**1468.80**

summarizes the changes in the firm's cash balance. Changes in the cash balance can be determined as follows:

TABLE 2-2
DETERMINING THE CHANGE IN THE CASH BALANCE

	Beginning Cash Balance
+	Cash inflows (sources)
-	Cash outflows (uses)
=	Ending Cash Balance

The statement of cash flows is organized into three sections according to how the cash flows were generated. The first section is "Cash Flows from Operations" which describes the cash flows generated by the firm in the ordinary course of conducting its business. The next section, "Cash Flows from Investing," describes cash flows due to purchasing or selling long-term fixed assets. The final section, "Cash Flows from Financing," describes the cash flows that are generated in the course of financing the firm.

It is important that you recognize that the statement of cash flows consists primarily of *changes* in balance sheet accounts. In order to calculate those changes, we must have balance sheets from two periods. Other than balance sheet changes, we also need the latest income statement, where the most important operational cash flows (net income and depreciation expense) come from.

Unlike the income statement and balance sheet, which are mostly exercises in data entry, the statement of cash flows is primarily composed of formulas. Since these formulas reference many different cells in the worksheet it is generally easiest to use 1-2-3's pointer mode when entering them. To begin, rename sheet "C" to Cash Flows and enter the labels as shown in Exhibit 2-5.

The first two items under Cash Flows from Operations are Net Income and Depreciation Expense. These are unique items because they are the only ones on the statement of cash flows that come from the income statement and are also the only items that are not represented as changes from a previous period.[5] To enter the net income first type an + in B5 and then (before pressing the Enter key) click on the sheet tab for the Income Statement. 1-2-3 will change to the worksheet containing the income statement. Now click on C15 and press Enter. At this point, 1-2-3 will switch back to the Statement of Cash Flows worksheet and your formula in B5 should read: +Inc Statement:C15. This formula directs 1-2-3 to put the value from cell C15 on the Income Statement worksheet into B5. If we should change some values in the income statement, any change in net income will automatically be reflected in the statement of cash flows. This type of cell linking works across workbooks as well as within workbooks.

---

5. Actually, we could calculate depreciation expense as the change in accumulated depreciation.

EXHIBIT 2-5
STATEMENT OF CASH FLOWS FOR EPI

	A	B	C
1	Elvis Products International		
2	Statement of Cash Flows		
3	For the Year Ended Dec. 31, 1997		
4	**Cash Flows from Operations**		
5	Net Income	44.22	
6	Depreciation Expense	20.00	
7	Change in Accounts Receivable	-50.80	
8	Change in Inventories	-120.80	
9	Change in Accounts Payable	29.60	
10	Change in Short-term Notes Payable	25.00	
11	Change in Other Current Liabilities	4.00	
12	**Total Cash Flows from Operations**		**-48.78**
13	**Cash Flows from Investing**		
14	Change in Plant & Equipment	-36.00	
15	**Total Cash Flows from Investing**		**-36.00**
16	**Cash Flows from Financing**		
17	Change in Long-term Debt	101.18	
18	Cash Dividends Paid to Shareholders	-22.00	
19	**Total Cash Flows from Financing**		**79.18**
20	**Net Change in Cash Balance**		**-5.60**

In B6, type + and then change to the Income Statement. Now scroll down so that cell C10 is visible and click on it and press the Enter key. The formula in B6 of the Statement of Cash Flows should read: `+Inc Statement:C10,` and the value should be 20. The rest of the statement of cash flows can be completed in a similar manner, except that we will be referencing the Balance Sheet.

At this point, we must be careful with respect to the signs of the numbers entered into the statement of cash flows. In general, when an asset account increases that represents a cash outflow (i.e., a *use* of funds). An asset account which decreases represents a cash inflow (i.e., a *source* of funds). Liability and equity accounts are exactly the opposite. We represent uses of funds as negative numbers and sources of funds as positive numbers on the statement of cash flows.

TABLE 2-3
SIGNS OF CASH FLOWS FOR THE STATEMENT OF CASH FLOWS

Type of Account	Direction of Change	
	Increase	Decrease
Asset	- (use)	+ (source)
Liability or Equity	+ (source)	- (use)

Table 2-3 summarizes this point. For example, EPI's accounts receivable balance increased from $351.20 in 1996 to $402.00 in 1997. This represents a use of funds and should be indicated with a negative sign on the statement of cash flows. On the other hand, their accounts payable balance increased and, because it is a liability account, represents a source of funds.

The formula for the change in accounts receivable in B7 should be: `+Balance Sheet:E6 - Balance Sheet:C6`. We can get the change in inventories by simply copying this formula down to B8. Note that for these asset accounts, the direction of the subtraction is 1996 value - 1997 value. For liability and equity accounts the direction of the subtraction is reversed. This will ensure that the correct sign is used.

The formula to calculate the change in accounts payable in B9 is: `+Balance Sheet:C15 - Balance Sheet:E15`. We can copy this down to B10 and B11 to get the next two values. Now we calculate the total cash flows from operations in C12 with: `@SUM(B5..B11)`.

Cash flows from investing are those cash flows generated from investments in long-term assets. In the case of EPI, that means plant and equipment. This change can be calculated in B14 by the formula: `+Balance Sheet:E9 - Balance Sheet:C9`. For consistency, we will calculate the total cash flows from investing in C15 with: `+B14`.

For the final section, we can calculate the change in long-term debt with the formula: `+Balance Sheet:C19 - Balance Sheet:E19`. Cash dividends paid to shareholders in 1997 were $22.00 (a use of funds). This is calculated with the formula:

Dividends Paid = Net Income – Change in Retained Earnings ,

so in B18 enter the formula: `-(Inc Statement:C15 - (Balance Sheet:C22 - Balance Sheet:E22))`. Note that the parentheses are important in this case, and that the result should be -22.00. Again, we can total the cash flows from financing in C19 with: `@SUM(B17..B18)`.

Finally, we calculate the net change in the cash balance by totalling up the subtotals, so the formula is: `@SUM(C12..C19)`. Note that this should exactly equal the actual change in the cash balance from 1996 to 1997, otherwise you have made an error. The most common errors are likely to be either a wrong sign or an omitted account. Make sure that your worksheet resembles that pictured in Exhibit 2-5 (page 42).

Summary

In this chapter we discussed the three primary financial statements: the income statement, the balance sheet, and the statement of cash flows. You should have a basic understanding of the purpose of each of these statements and know how to build them in 1-2-3. We demonstrated how worksheets can be linked so that formulas in one worksheet can reference data on another sheet.

Make sure that you have saved a copy of the EPI workbook because we will be making use of this data in future chapters.

TABLE 2-4
FUNCTIONS INTRODUCED IN THIS CHAPTER

Purpose	Function	Page
Totals numbers or a range of numbers	@SUM(*LIST*)	33

CHAPTER 3

The Cash Budget

After studying this chapter, you should be able to:

1. *Explain the purpose of the cash budget and how it is different from an income statement.*

2. *Calculate a firm's expected total cash collections and disbursements for a particular month.*

3. *Calculate a firm's expected ending cash balance and short-term borrowing needs.*

4. *Determine the optimal timing of major cash expenditures using 1-2-3.*

Of all the topics covered in this book, perhaps no other benefits so much from the use of spreadsheets as the cash budget. As we'll see, the cash budget can be a complex document with many inter-related entries. Manually updating a cash budget, especially for a large firm, is not a chore for which one volunteers. However, once the initial cash budget is set up on a spreadsheet, updating becomes very easy.

A *cash budget* is simply a listing of the firm's anticipated cash inflows and outflows over a specified period. Unlike a pro forma income statement (discussed in chapter 5), the cash budget includes only actual cash flows (e.g., depreciation expense does not appear on the cash budget). Because of its emphasis on cash income and expenditures, the cash budget is particularly useful for planning short-term borrowing and the timing of expenditures. As with all budgets, another important benefit of the cash budget comes from reconciling actual income and expenses with those from the forecast.

We'll see that a cash budget is composed of three parts:

1. The worksheet area;
2. A listing of each of the cash inflows (collections) and outflows (disbursements);
3. Calculation of the ending cash balance and borrowing requirements.

Throughout the chapter, we will create a complete cash budget with these three parts for Bithlo Barbecues, a small manufacturer of barbecue grills. The financial staff of the firm has compiled the following set of assumptions and forecasts to be used in the cash budgeting process:

1. Expected sales through September are as given in Exhibit 3-1.
2. 40% of sales are for cash. Of the remaining sales, 60% are collected in the following month and 40% are collected two months after the sale.
3. Inventory purchases are equal to 50% of the following month's sales (i.e., April purchases are 50% of May sales). 60% of purchases are paid for in the month following the purchase, and the remainder are paid for in the following month.
4. Wages are equal to 20% of sales.
5. Leasing expense for the property, plant, and equipment is $10,000 per month.
6. Interest payments of $30,000 on long-term debt are due in June and September.
7. A $50,000 dividend will be paid to common shareholders in June.
8. Taxes of $25,000 are expected to be paid in June and September.
9. A $200,000 capital improvement is scheduled to be paid in July, but management is flexible on the scheduling of this outlay.
10. Bithlo Barbecues must keep a minimum cash balance of $15,000 by agreement with its bank.

The Worksheet Area

The worksheet area is not necessarily a part of the cash budget. However, it is useful because it summarizes some of the most important calculations in the budget. This section includes a breakdown of expected sales, accounts receivable collections, and payments for materials (inventory) purchases.

Open a new workbook and rename sheet 'A' to Cash Budget. Like any other financial statement, we begin the cash budget with the titles. Enter the titles from Exhibit 3-1 into A1..A3 and center them across columns A..I. Next, enter the names of the months in B4..I4 using the Drag and Fill feature (see page 10).

The starting point for a cash budget is the sales forecast. Many of the other forecasts in the cash budget are driven (at least indirectly) by this forecast. The sales forecast has been provided for us in Exhibit 3-1. Copy the expected sales to C5..I5 in your worksheet.

EXHIBIT 3-1
THE WORKSHEET AREA OF A CASH BUDGET

	A	B	C	D	E	F	G	H	I
1	Bithlo Barbeques								
2	Cash Budget								
3	For the Period June to September 1998								
4			April	May	June	July	August	September	October
5	Sales		291,000	365,000	387,000	329,000	238,000	145,000	92,000
6	Collections:								
7	Cash	40%			154,800	131,600	95,200	58,000	
8	First Month	45%			164,250	174,150	148,050	107,100	
9	Second Month	15%			43,650	54,750	58,050	49,350	
10	Total Collections				362,700	360,500	301,300	214,450	
11	Purchases	50%	182,500	193,500	164,500	119,000	72,500	46,000	
12	Payments:								
13	First Month	60%			116,100	98,700	71,400	43,500	
14	Second Month	40%			73,000	77,400	65,800	47,600	
15	Total Payments				189,100	176,100	137,200	91,100	

Collections

For most firms, at least a portion of sales are made on credit. It is therefore important that the firm knows how quickly it can expect to collect on those sales. In the case of Bithlo Barbecues, experience has shown that about 40% of its sales are cash and 60% are on credit. Of the 60% of sales made on credit, about 75% will be collected within the month following the sale and the remaining 25% will be collected two months after the sale. In other words, 45% (= 0.60 x 0.75) of total sales in any month will be collected during the following month, and 15% (= 0.60 x 0.25) will be collected within two months.[1]

Our goal is to determine the total collections in each month. In A7 enter the label: `Cash`. This will indicate the cash sales for the month. In A8 enter: `First Month` to indicate collections from the previous month. In A9 enter: `Second Month` to indicate collections on sales made two months previously. Since our estimates of the collection percentages may change, it is important that they not be entered directly into formulas. Instead, enter these percentages in A7..A9.

Since the budget is for June to September we will begin our estimates of collections in E7. (Note that April and May sales are included here only because we need to reference sales from the two previous months to determine the collections from credit sales.) To calculate the cash collections for June we multiply the expected June sales by the percentage of cash sales, so enter: `+E5*$B7` into E7. To calculate collections from cash sales for the other months, simply copy this formula to F7..H7.

Collections on credit sales can be calculated similarly. In E8, we will calculate June collections from May sales with the formula: `+D5*$B8`. Copy this formula to F8..H8. Finally, collections from sales two months ago can be calculated with the formula: `+C5*$B9`. After copying this formula to E9..H9, calculate the total collections for each month by using the @SUM function. Check your numbers against those in Exhibit 3-1.

Purchases and Payments

In this section of the worksheet area we calculate the payments that are made for inventory purchases. Bithlo Barbecues purchases inventory (equal to 50% of sales) the month before the sale is made. For example, April inventory purchases will be 50% of expected May sales. However, it does not pay for the inventory immediately. Instead, 60% of the purchase is paid for in the following month, and the other 40% is paid for two months after the purchase.

---

1. For simplicity, we assume that 100% of sales will be collected. Most firms would include an allowance for "bad debts."

We first need to calculate the amount of inventory purchased in each month. As noted, this is 50% of the following month's sales. So in A11 type: Purchases and in B11 enter: 50%. We will calculate April purchases in C11 with the formula: +$B11*D5. Copying this formula to D11..H11 completes the calculation of purchases.

Next, we need to calculate the actual cash payments for inventory in each month. This is very similar to the way we calculated total cash collections. First, enter labels. In A12 type: Payments:. In A13 and A14 enter: First Month and Second Month respectively. Finally, enter: Total Payments in A15. In June Bithlo Barbecues will pay for 60% of purchases made in May. So the formula in E13 is: +$B13*D11. Copy this to F13..H13 to complete the first month's payments. To calculate the June payment for April purchases in E14, use the formula: +$B14*C11. Copy this to F14..H14 and then calculate the total payments for each month.

At this point your worksheet should look like the one in Exhibit 3-1. Check your numbers carefully to make sure that they agree with those in the exhibit. To clarify the logic of these formulas, examine Exhibit 3-2 which shows the references for June.

EXHIBIT 3-2
THE WORKSHEET AREA OF A CASH BUDGET

	A	B	C	D	E	F	G	H	I
1					Bithlo Barbeques				
2					Cash Budget				
3					For the Period June to September 1998				
4			April	May	June	July	August	September	October
5	Sales		291,000	365,000	387,000	329,000	238,000	145,000	92,000
6	Collections:								
7	Cash	40%			154,800	131,600	95,200	58,000	
8	First Month	45%			164,250	174,150	148,050	107,100	
9	Second Month	15%			43,650	54,750	58,050	49,350	
10	Total Collections				362,700	360,500	301,300	214,450	
11	Purchases	50%	182,500	193,500	164,500	119,000	72,500	46,000	
12	Payments:								
13	First Month	60%			116,100	98,700	71,400	43,500	
14	Second Month	40%			73,000	77,400	65,800	47,600	
15	Total Payments				189,100	176,100	137,200	91,100	

Collections And Disbursements

This section of the cash budget is the easiest to set up in a spreadsheet because there are no complex relationships between the cells as there are in the worksheet area. The collections and disbursements area is very much like a cash-based income statement (i.e., there are no non-cash expenses). We simply list the cash inflows and outflows that are expected for each month.

We will begin by summarizing the cash collections for each month. Enter the label: Collections in A17. In E17..H17 the formulas simply reference the total collections that were calculated in E10..H10. So, for example, the formula in E17 is: +E10. Copy this formula to F17..H17.

In A18, enter the label: Less Disbursements: . The first cash outflow that we will enter is the inventory payment which was calculated in the worksheet area. Enter Inventory Payments as the label in A19 and the formula, in E19, is: +E15. Wages are assumed to be equal to 20% of sales. In A20 add the label: Wages and in B20 type: 20% which will be used to calculate the monthly wage expense. The formula to calculate wages in E20 is: +$B20*E5. Now copy this formula to F20..H20. By now, you should be able to finish this section by entering the remaining labels and numbers as pictured in Exhibit 3-3.

EXHIBIT 3-3
COLLECTIONS AND DISBURSEMENTS

	A	B	C	D	E	F	G	H
17	Collections				362,700	360,500	301,300	214,450
18	*Less Disbursements:*							
19	Inventory Payments				189,100	176,100	137,200	91,100
20	Wages	20%			77,400	65,800	47,600	29,000
21	Lease Payment				10,000	10,000	10,000	10,000
22	Interest				30,000	0	0	30,000
23	Dividend (Common)				50,000	0	0	0
24	Taxes				25,000	0	0	25,000
25	Capital Outlays				0	200,000	0	0
26	**Total Disbursements**				**381,500**	**451,900**	**194,800**	**185,100**

There are a couple of points to note about this portion of the cash budget. First, we have assumed that the only cash inflows are from selling the firm's products. In other cases, however, it is possible that the firm might plan to sell some assets or bonds or stock. Any of these actions would bring cash into the firm and should be included under collections.

Second, we have included dividends which do not appear on the income statement. The reason that they are on the cash budget is that dividends represent a very real cash expenditure for the firm. They don't appear on the income statement because dividends are paid from after-tax dollars.

Finally, Bithlo Barbecues has scheduled capital outlays of $200,000 in July. Even though they are paying the full cost in July, it is unlikely that they would be allowed to expense this entire amount during 1998. Instead, the income statement would reflect the depreciation of these assets over a longer period of time. Regardless of tax laws or accounting conventions, it is important to include all expected cash inflows and outflows on the cash budget.

Calculating The Ending Cash Balance

This last section of the cash budget calculates the expected ending cash balance at the end of each month. This is the most important part of the cash budget because is helps the manager understand the firm's short-term borrowing requirements. Knowing the borrowing requirements in advance allows managers to arrange for financing when they need it and provides the time necessary to evaluate possible alternatives. Managers can also use this information to determine the best timing for major expenditures.

TABLE 3-1
CALCULATING THE ENDING CASH BALANCE

	Beginning Cash Balance
+	Total Collections
-	Total Disbursements
=	Unadjusted Cash Balance
+	Current Borrowing
=	Ending Cash Balance

Table 3-1 shows the series of calculations necessary to determine the firm's ending cash balance. Essentially, this is the same procedure we saw in Table 2-2 on page 40. In the next section we will add a few steps to this calculation, but the basic procedure is always as outlined in Table 3-1.

We have already made most of the calculations that are necessary to complete the cash budget. Before we finish this last section, however, we need to add another detail. The management of Bithlo Barbecues has decided that they would like to keep a minimum cash balance of $15,000. If the projected cash balance falls below this amount, they will need to borrow to bring the balance back to this minimum. In A32 enter the label: Notes. We will use cells below A32 to indicate important assumptions about our cash budget. The first of these is the minimum cash balance requirement. In A33 enter the label: Minimum Acceptable Cash and in B33 enter: 15,000.

In cells A27..A31 enter the labels as shown in Exhibit 3-4. (Notice that this is exactly the same as was outlined in Table 3-1.) We start with the unadjusted cash balance in May. Enter: $20,000 into D29. In D30 enter: 0 because the firm had no short-term borrowing needs in May. The ending cash balance for the month is simply the unadjusted cash balance plus current borrowing, so the formula in D31 is: +D29+D30. This formula will be the same for each month, so copy it across to E31..H31.

EXHIBIT 3-4
ENDING CASH BALANCE CALCULATION

	A	B	C	D	E	F	G	H
27	Beginning Cash Balance				20,000	15,000	15,000	121,500
28	Collections - Disbursements				(18,800)	(91,400)	106,500	29,350
29	Unadjusted Cash Balance			20,000	1,200	(76,400)	121,500	150,850
30	Current Borrowing			0	13,800	91,400	0	0
31	**Ending Cash Balance**			**20,000**	**15,000**	**15,000**	**121,500**	**150,850**
32	Notes:							
33	Minimum Acceptable Cash	15,000						

The beginning cash balance for any month is the same as the ending cash balance from the previous month. Therefore, we can simply reference the previous month's ending cash balance calculation. In E27 enter the formula: +D31 and copy this across to F27..H27. At this point, your beginning cash balance for each month, except June, will be 0 because we have not yet entered any data.

Since we have already calculated the total collections and total disbursements, there is no need to have separate rows for those calculations in this section. Instead, we will calculate the net collections for June in E28 with the formula: +E17-E26. For June, the result is -18,800 which indicates that the firm expects to spend more than it will collect. In other words, the cash balance is expected to decline by $18,800 in June. This decline will be reflected in the unadjusted cash balance.

The unadjusted cash balance is what the cash balance would be if the firm did not have any short-term borrowing during the month. We simply add the beginning cash balance and the net collections for the month. The formula in E29 is: +E27+E28. The result is $1,200 which is less than the firm's minimum acceptable cash balance of $15,000. Therefore, Bithlo Barbecues will need to borrow $13,800 to bring the balance up to this minimum.

How did we determine that the firm needs to borrow $13,800? We could use the following equation:

$$\text{Current Borrowing} = \text{Minimum Cash} - \text{Unadjusted Cash.} \qquad (3\text{-}1)$$

In this case we find that Bithlo Barbecues needs to borrow:

$$\$13,800 = \$15,000 - \$1,200$$

Unfortunately, Equation 3-1 is not appropriate in all circumstances. Suppose, for example, that the unadjusted cash balance had been $20,000. This would suggest that the firm needs to borrow -$5,000, which is absurd.[2] In a case such as this, we would like to see current borrowing at 0.

The calculation that we need can be stated as follows: "If the unadjusted cash balance is less than the minimum, then we borrow an amount equal to minimum cash - unadjusted cash. Otherwise, current borrowing is zero." With the formulas that we have used so far, this type of calculation is impossible. However, 1-2-3 has a built in function that can handle situations where the result depends on some condition — the @IF statement.

The @IF statement returns one of two values, depending on whether a statement is true or false:

$$\text{@IF}(\textit{CONDITION}, X, Y).$$

CONDITION is any statement which can be evaluated as true or false, and X and Y are the return values which depend on whether CONDITION was true or false. If you

---

2. Unless, of course, you assume that negative borrowing is the same as investing. But we will consider investing excess funds in the next section.

are familiar with computer programming, you will recognize this as the equivalent of the If-Then-Else construct that is supported by most programming languages.

The formula to calculate Bithlo Barbecues's borrowing needs from June, in E30, is: `@IF(E29<$B33,$B33-E29,0)`. Since the unadjusted cash balance is only $1,200, the result should indicate the need to borrow $13,800 as we found earlier. Copy this formula to F30..H30 to complete the calculation of current borrowing. Notice that, because of large positive net collections, the firm does not need to borrow funds in August or September.

We have already entered formulas for the ending cash balance in each month. You should now check your numbers against those in Exhibit 3-5.

Using the Cash Budget for Timing Large Expenditures

Besides being useful for planning the firm's short-term borrowing needs, the cash budget can be useful in planning for large capital expenditures. As an example, consider Bithlo Barbecues's $200,000 expenditure currently planned for July 1998. This expenditure is the primary cause of the borrowing need in July. Indeed, without this $200,000 outlay, the firm wouldn't need to borrow in July.

Assuming that there is some flexibility in scheduling this outlay, in which month should the expenditure be made? The answer, of course, depends on a number of factors, but we might decide to make the decision based on minimizing borrowing needs. That is, schedule the project such that the firm's short-term borrowing needs are minimized. This might be especially important if the firm expected borrowing needs in excess of its line of credit in a given month.

EXHIBIT 3-5
A COMPLETED SIMPLE CASH BUDGET

	A	B	C	D	E	F	G	H	I
1	Bithlo Barbeques								
2	Cash Budget								
3	For the Period June to September 1998								
4			April	May	June	July	August	September	October
5	Sales		291,000	365,000	387,000	329,000	238,000	145,000	92,000
6	Collections:								
7	Cash	40%			154,800	131,600	95,200	58,000	
8	First Month	45%			164,250	174,150	148,050	107,100	
9	Second Month	15%			43,650	54,750	58,050	49,350	
10	Total Collections				362,700	360,500	301,300	214,450	
11	Purchases	50%	182,500	193,500	164,500	119,000	72,500	46,000	
12	Payments:								
13	First Month	60%			116,100	98,700	71,400	43,500	
14	Second Month	40%			73,000	77,400	65,800	47,600	
15	Total Payments				189,100	176,100	137,200	91,100	
16									
17	Collections				362,700	360,500	301,300	214,450	
18	Less Disbursements:								
19	Inventory Payments				189,100	176,100	137,200	91,100	
20	Wages	20%			77,400	65,800	47,600	29,000	
21	Lease Payment				10,000	10,000	10,000	10,000	
22	Interest				30,000	0	0	30,000	
23	Dividend (Common)				50,000	0	0	0	
24	Taxes				25,000	0	0	25,000	
25	Capital Outlays				0	200,000	0	0	
26	Total Disbursement				381,500	451,900	194,800	185,100	
27	Beginning Cash Balance				20,000	15,000	15,000	121,500	
28	Collections - Disbursements				(18,800)	(91,400)	106,500	29,350	
29	Unadjusted Cash Balance			20,000	1,200	(76,400)	121,500	150,850	
30	Current Borrowing			0	13,800	91,400	0	0	
31	Ending Cash Balance			20,000	15,000	15,000	121,500	150,850	
32	Notes:								
33	Minimum Acceptable Cash	15,000							

You can experiment a bit by changing the month in which the capital expenditure is made. First, however, it would be helpful to know the total expected borrowing for the four-month period. In I30, enter the formula: `@Sum(E30..H30)` to calculate total borrowing. Now, by moving the capital expenditure to different months, you should be able to verify the numbers in Table 3-2.

TABLE 3-2
OPTIMAL SCHEDULING FOR A CAPITAL EXPENDITURE

Month of Outlay	Total Four-month Borrowing
June	$ 213,800
July	$ 105,200
August	$ 13,800
September	$ 13,800

Obviously, by this criteria, the best time to schedule the outlay would be in either August or September.

Adding Interest and Investment of Excess Cash[3]

In the previous section you created a basic cash budget for Bithlo Barbecues. In this section we will refine the calculation of the ending cash balance by considering two additional factors. First, we will add interest payments on borrowed funds. Then, we will consider the investment of excess cash.

Before beginning let's create a copy of the previous cash budget in the same worksheet. Right click the tab label "Cash Budget" and select Copy from the menu. Click the New Sheet button and then paste the data onto the new sheet. Now rename the new sheet as Complex CB (we have to abbreviate the name).

Next, we will need to make a few additions to the notes at the bottom of the worksheet. We will now assume that Bithlo Barbecues will invest any cash in excess of $40,000. In A33 add the label: Maximum Acceptable Cash and in B33 enter: 40,000. Furthermore, the firm will have to pay interest on its short-term borrowings and will earn interest on invested funds. In A34 type: Borrowing Rate (Annual) and in B34 enter: 8%. In A35 add the label: Lending Rate (Annual) and enter: 6% in B35.

---

3. This section is considerably more complex than the previous sections. Some instructors may wish to omit this material.

Since we are working with monthly time periods, we need to convert these annual rates into monthly rates of interest. So, in C34 and C35 enter the label: Monthly. We will convert the annual rate to a monthly rate by dividing by 12. In D34 enter the formula: +B34/12, and copy this to D35. You should see that the monthly borrowing rate is 0.67% and the monthly lending rate is 0.50%.

We are now ready to expand the cash budget to include borrowing and lending and the interest expense and income. Before entering any new formulas we need to insert a few new rows. Select row 29 (the unadjusted cash balance), and then choose **E**dit **I**nsert **R**ow from the menu. This will insert a row above the selection. In A29 enter the label: Short-Term Interest Income (Exp.). Next, select row 32 (the ending cash balance), insert a row, and enter: Current Investing into A32. Finally, select rows 34 and 35 and choose **E**dit **I**nsert **R**ow from the menu. This will insert two rows above the selection. In A34 type: Cumulative Investing (Borrowing) and in A35 type: Cumulative Interest Income (Exp.).

We will start by entering the formulas to calculate the cumulative amount of investing (borrowing) in D34. Negative numbers will represent borrowing while positive numbers will represent investing. In order to calculate the *cumulative* amount, we need to add the previous period's cumulative amount to current investing and subtract current borrowing. For May, in D34, the formula is: +C34+D32-D31, and the result should be 0. Copy this formula to E34..H34. Note that at this point the result for each month should be equal to the negative of the cumulative current borrowing.

Short-term interest income (expense) can now be calculated by multiplying the cumulative amount of investing (borrowing) from the previous month by the appropriate interest rate. So, in E29 we will use an **@IF** statement to determine which rate to use. If the cumulative amount of investing (borrowing) is negative, we will multiply it by the borrowing rate. Otherwise, use the lending rate. The formula for June, E29, is: @IF(D34<0,$D$39*D34,$D$40*D34). In June, since the firm has not previous borrowing or lending, the result should be 0. Copy this across to F29..H29.

We can now calculate the cumulative interest income (expense) in E35. To do this we simply add the previous month's interest income (expense) to the current month's interest income (expense). For June, the formula is: +D35+E29. This formula should be copied across to F35..H35.

Calculating Current Borrowing

Determining the amount of current borrowing and current investing is the most complex part of this cash budget. We have already calculated current borrowing, but since we are now considering investing and interest, the formula will need to be changed. For current borrowing, the logic can be explained this way: "If the unadjusted cash balance is less than the minimum acceptable cash, then borrow enough to bring the balance to the minimum. However, if the firm has some investments, reduce the amount of borrowing by the amount of the investments (or total borrowing needs, whichever is less). If the unadjusted cash balance is greater than the minimum and the firm has previous borrowing, then use the cash above the minimum to reduce the outstanding borrowing."

Writing a formula to implement this logic requires the use of nested **IF** statements. That is, we embed a second **IF** statement within the first. In pseudocode this is:

```
If unadjusted Cash < Minimum Cash then {Need to raise funds}
      If Cumulative Investing > 0 then {Firm has investments it can sell}
            Current Borrowing = Minimum Cash - Unadjusted Cash - Cumulative Investing
      Else Current Borrowing = Minimum Cash - Unadjusted Cash {Must Borrow}
Else {Firm has excess cash}
      If Cumulative Investing < 0 then {Use funds to reduce previous borrowings}
            Current Borrowing = Minimum(-Cumulative Investing, Unadjusted Cash- Minimum Cash)
      Else Current Borrowing = 0
End
```

The formula to calculate current borrowing in July, E31, is: `@IF (E30<$B$37, @IF(D34>0, $B$37-D34-E30, $B$37-E30), @IF (D34<0, -@MIN(-D34, E30 - $B$37),0))`. Type this formula carefully, and then copy it to F31..H31. Note that we have also used the built-in **@MIN** function. **@MIN** returns the smallest of the parameters, and is defined as:

$$\textbf{@M\textsc{in}\textit{(List)}}$$

In this function, *LIST* is the set of up to 30 arguments from which the function chooses the minimum value.[4] In our formula, we are trying to find the minimum of either (1) the cumulative amount of investing, or (2) the difference between the unadjusted cash balance and the minimum acceptable cash balance. Note that we had to use the negative of cumulative investing in the **@MIN** function in order to get the correct result.

---

4. In other situations, you might wish to determine the maximum of a list of arguments. The **@MAX** function, which is defined the same as **@MIN**, will handle these situations.

Calculating Current Investing

If Bithlo Barbecues has cash in excess of the maximum ($40,000 in this case) the cash should be invested in short-term securities. This is the essential idea behind the current investing item.

The current borrowing formula was constructed so that the firm will first sell any existing short-term investments before borrowing. Therefore, if the sum of the unadjusted cash balance and current borrowing is less than the minimum required cash, the firm needs to sell some investments. Otherwise, if the unadjusted cash balance plus current borrowing is greater than the maximum acceptable cash, the firm must invest the excess.

To implement this logic we will again use the nested **@IF** statements. We also need to use the **AND** statement which returns true only if all of the arguments are true. We will use this statement to determine if both of the following conditions are true: (1) unadjusted cash + current borrowing is less than the minimum cash, and (2) cumulative investing is positive. To use the And statement, it must be enclosed in pound signs (#) as you will see in the formula.

The formula to calculate the amount of current investing, in E32, is: `@IF(E30+E31<$B$37 #and# D34>0,E30+ E31-$B$37,@IF(E30+ E31> $B$38,E30+E31-$B$38,0))`. Enter this formula and copy it across to F32..H32. Again, this is a complex formula, but it can be broken down into more understandable components:

If Unadjusted Cash + Borrowing < Minimum Cash **and** Current Investing > 0 then
    Current Investing = Unadjusted Cash + Borrowing - Minimum Cash
Else
    If Unadjusted Cash + Borrowing > Maximum Cash then
        Current Investing = Unadjusted Cash + Borrowing - Maximum Cash
    Else Current Investing = 0
End.

At this point, this portion of your cash budget should resemble that in Exhibit 3-6.

Working Through the Example

In order to understand the complex cash budget, you must work through it line-by-line. In this section, we will do just that. Follow along in Exhibit 3-6.

EXHIBIT 3-6
CALCULATING THE CASH BALANCE WITH BORROWING AND INVESTING

	A	B	C	D	E	F	G	H
27	Beginning Cash Balance				20,000	15,000	15,000	15,506
28	Collections - Disbursements				(18,800)	(91,400)	106,500	29,350
29	Short-Term Interest Income (Exp.)				0	(92)	(702)	0
30	Unadjusted Cash Balance			20,000	1,200	(76,492)	120,798	44,856
31	Current Borrowing			0	13,800	91,492	(105,292)	0
32	Current Investing			0	0	0	0	4,856
33	**Ending Cash Balance**			**20,000**	**15,000**	**15,000**	**15,506**	**40,000**
34	Cumulative Investing (Borrowing)			0	(13,800)	(105,292)	0	4,856
35	Cumulative Interest Income (Exp.)				0	(92)	(794)	(794)
36	Notes:							
37	Minimum Acceptable Cash	15,000						
38	Maximum Acceptable Cash	40,000						
39	Borrowing Rate (Annual)	8.00%	Monthly	0.67%				
40	Lending Rate (Annual)	6.00%	Monthly	0.50%				

June: The unadjusted cash balance in June is projected to be only $1,200. Since this is less than the $15,000 minimum, the firm needs to raise funds. In this case it has no investments to sell, so it must borrow $13,800 to bring the ending cash balance to $15,000.

July: The firm is projecting that it will be overdrawn by $76,492. Again, it has no investments to sell and must borrow $91,492. Note that its cumulative borrowing is now $105,292.

August: The firm is projecting an unadjusted cash balance of $120,798, well in excess of the maximum allowable cash. Before investing the excess however, it needs to pay off the $105, 292 of existing short-term debt. In this case, the firm can pay off the entire balance and still remain above the minimum cash requirement. However, its cash balance is not high enough to demand investment of excess funds.

September: The firm is projecting that the unadjusted cash balance will be $44,856. In this case, there is no borrowing balance, so the $4,856 is excess of the maximum allowable cash can be invested.

In any complex worksheet such as this one, it is important that you work through the calculations by hand to check the results. Never accept the output until you are sure that it is absolutely correct. With this in mind, let's change the maximum acceptable cash in B38 to $15,000 and work through this alternative scenario. First, make sure that this portion of your worksheet is the same as that in Exhibit 3-7.

EXHIBIT 3-7
CASH BALANCE AFTER CHANGING MAXIMUM CASH TO $15,000

	A	B	C	D	E	F	G	H
27	Beginning Cash Balance				15,000	15,000	15,000	15,000
28	Collections - Disbursements				(18,800)	(91,400)	106,500	29,350
29	Short-Term Interest Income (Exp.)				25	(92)	(702)	3
30	Unadjusted Cash Balance			20,000	(3,775)	(76,492)	120,798	44,353
31	Current Borrowing				0	13,775	91,492	(105,267)	0
32	Current Investing			5,000	(5,000)	0	531	29,353
33	**Ending Cash Balance**			15,000	15,000	15,000	15,000	15,000
34	Cumulative Investing (Borrowing)			5,000	(13,775)	(105,267)	531	29,884
35	Cumulative Interest Income (Exp.)				25	(67)	(769)	(766)
36	Notes:							
37	Minimum Acceptable Cash	15,000						
38	Maximum Acceptable Cash	15,000						
39	Borrowing Rate (Annual)	8.00%	Monthly	0.67%				
40	Lending Rate (Annual)	6.00%	Monthly	0.50%				

June: The firm is projecting the unadjusted cash balance to be -$3,775, but it does not borrow $18,775 (+$15,000 - [-$3,775]) because it has $5,000 in investments from May that reduce the borrowing need to only $13,775.

July: The unadjusted cash balance is projected to be -$76,492 and there are no investments that can be sold. Therefore the firm must borrow $91,492. The cumulative borrowing is now $105,267.

August: The firm is expected to have a large surplus of funds which can be used to pay off the entire loan balance. Furthermore, it will have $531 in excess of the maximum allowable cash which is available to invest.

September: The unadjusted cash balance is expected to be $44,353 which is $29,353 in excess of the maximum. This amount can be invested.

You are encouraged to experiment by changing values throughout the cash budget to see what happens. In particular, changing the projected sales and/or the payment schedule can be very enlightening. For example, suppose that Bithlo Barbecues's management decides to slow down payments for inventory purchases. Specifically, assume that it decides to pay only 40% in the month after the purchase, and 60% two months after the purchase. You should find that this is not as good an idea as it sounds. Table 3-3 shows Cumulative Investing (Borrowing) before and after the change, assuming that the maximum cash is $40,000.

TABLE 3-3
CUMULATIVE INVESTING (BORROWING)

Month	Before	After
June	(13,800)	(11,600)
July	(105,292)	(108,877)
August	0	(12,203)
September	4,856	0
Total	(114,236)	(132,680)

Summary

In this chapter we have seen that the cash budget is simply a listing of the firm's expected *cash* inflows and outflows over a period of time. Cash budgets are useful in determining the firm's short-term borrowing and investing needs, as well as scheduling transactions. The cash budget is composed of three sections: (1) the worksheet area; (2) collections and disbursements; and (3) the ending cash balance.

TABLE 3-4
FUNCTIONS INTRODUCED IN THIS CHAPTER

Purpose	Function	Page
Returns a value based on a logical test	@IF(*CONDITION*, *X*, *Y*)	53
Determines the minimum of a list of arguments	@MIN(*LIST*)	58
Returns true only if all arguments are true	#AND#	59

CHAPTER 4

Evaluating Performance with Financial Ratios

After studying this chapter, you should be able to:

1. *Describe what financial ratios are, who uses them, and why they are used.*

2. *Define the five major categories of ratios (liquidity, efficiency, leverage, coverage and profitability).*

3. *Calculate the common ratios for any firm by using income statement and balance sheet data.*

4. *Use financial ratios to assess a firm's past performance, identify its current problems, and suggest future strategies for dealing with these problems.*

In previous chapters we have seen how the firm's basic financial statements are constructed. In this chapter we will see how financial analysts can use the information contained in the income statement and balance sheet for various purposes.

There are several tools that you can use to evaluate a company, but one of the most valuable is financial ratios. Ratios are an analyst's microscope; they provide a better view of the firm's financial health than just looking at the raw financial statements. Ratios are useful both to internal and external analysts of the firm. For internal purposes, ratios can be useful in planning for the future and for evaluating the performance of managers. External analysts use ratios to decide whether to grant credit, to monitor performance, and to decide whether to invest in the company.

We will look at many different ratios, but you should be aware that these are, of necessity, only a sampling of the ratios that might be useful. Furthermore, different analysts may calculate ratios slightly differently, so you will need to know exactly how the ratios are calculated in a given situation. The keys to understanding ratio analysis are experience and an analytical mind.

We will divide our discussion of the ratios into five categories:

High
1. *Liquidity ratios* describe the ability of a firm to meets its current obligations.

High
2. *Efficiency ratios* describe how well the firm is using its investment in assets to produce sales.

Low
3. *Leverage ratios* reveal the degree to which debt has been used to finance the firm's asset purchases.

High
4. *Coverage ratios* are similar to liquidity ratios in that they describe the ability of a firm to pay certain expenses.

High
5. *Profitability ratios* provide indications of how profitable a firm has been over a period of time.

Before we begin the discussion of individual financial ratios, open your Elvis Products International workbook (from Chapter 2) and add a new worksheet named "Ratios."

Liquidity Ratios

The term "liquidity" refers to the speed with which an asset can be converted into cash without large discounts to its value. Some assets such as accounts receivable can easily be converted to cash with only small discounts. Other assets, such as buildings, can be converted into cash very quickly only if large discounts are given. We therefore say that accounts receivable are more liquid than buildings.

All other things being equal, a firm with more liquid assets will be more able to meet its maturing obligations (i.e., its bills) than a firm with fewer liquid assets. As you might imagine, creditors are particularly concerned with a firm's ability to pay its bills. To assess this ability, it is common to use the current ratio and/or the quick ratio.

The Current Ratio

Generally, a firm's bills (its current liabilities) are paid from its current assets. Therefore, it is logical to assess its ability to pay its bills by comparing the size of its current assets to the size of its current liabilities. The current ratio does exactly this. It is defined as:

$$\text{Current Ratio} = \frac{\text{Current Assets}}{\text{Current Liabilities}} \qquad (4\text{-}1)$$

Obviously, the higher the current ratio, the higher the likelihood that a firm will be able to pay its bills. So, from the creditor's point of view, higher is better. However, from a shareholder's point of view this is not always the case. Current assets usually have a lower expected return than do fixed assets, so the shareholders would like to see that only the minimum amount of the company's capital is invested in current assets. Of course, too little investment in current assets could be disastrous for both creditors and owners of the firm.

We can calculate the current ratio for 1997 for EPI by looking at the balance sheet (Exhibit 2-3, page 38). In this case, we have:

$$\text{Current Ratio} = \frac{1290.00}{540.20} = 2.39 \text{ times}$$

meaning that EPI has 2.39 times as many current assets as current liabilities. We will determine later whether this is sufficient or not.

Exhibit 4-1 shows the beginnings of our "Ratios" worksheet. Enter the labels as shown. We can calculate the current ratio for 1997 in C3 with the formula: `+Balance Sheet:C8/Balance Sheet:C18`. After formatting to show two decimal places, you will see that the current ratio is 2.39. We have temporarily left column D blank so that we can simply copy the formulas from column C to column E to get the 1996 ratios. We can later delete column D and the formulas will automatically adjust. This is much more efficient than re-entering the formulas for 1996.

EXHIBIT 4-1
RATIO WORKSHEET FOR EPI

	A	B	C	D	E
1	Ratio		1997		1996
2	Liquidity Ratios				
3	Current		2.39		2.33
4					

The Quick Ratio

Inventories are often the least liquid of the firm's current assets.[1] For this reason, many believe that a better measure of liquidity can be obtained by ignoring inventories. The result is known as the quick ratio (sometimes called the acid-test ratio), and is calculated as:

$$\text{Quick Ratio} = \frac{\text{Current Assets} - \text{Inventories}}{\text{Current Liabilities}}. \tag{4-2}$$

For EPI in 1997 the quick ratio is:

$$\text{Quick Ratio} = \frac{1290.00 - 836.00}{540.20} = 0.84 \text{ times}.$$

Notice that the quick ratio will always be less than the current ratio. This is by design. However, a quick ratio that is too low relative to the current ratio may indicate that inventories are higher than they should be.

We can calculate EPI's 1997 quick ratio in C4 with the formula: `+(Balance Sheet:C8-Balance Sheet:C7)/Balance Sheet:C18`. Copying this formula to E3 reveals that the 1996 quick ratio was 0.85.

---

1. That is why you so often see 50% off sales when firms are going out of business.

Efficiency Ratios

Efficiency ratios, as the name implies, provide information about how well the company is using its assets to generate sales. For example, if two firms have the same level of sales, but one firm has a lower investment in inventories, we would say that the firm with lower inventories is more efficient with respect to its inventory investment.

There are many different types of efficiency ratios that could be defined. However, we will illustrate five of the most common.

Inventory Turnover Ratio

The inventory turnover ratio measures the number of dollars of sales that are generated per dollar of inventory. It also tells us the number of times that a firm replaces its inventories during a year. It is calculated as:

$$\text{Inventory Turnover Ratio} = \frac{\text{Cost of Goods Sold}}{\text{Inventory}}. \qquad \text{(4-3)}$$

Note that it is also common to use sales in the numerator. Since the only difference between sales and cost of goods sold is a markup this causes no problems. However, it does point to the need to be aware of the method of calculation whenever using ratios.

For 1997, EPI's inventory turnover ratio was:

$$\text{Inventory Turnover Ratio} = \frac{3,250.00}{836.00} = 3.89 \text{ times}$$

meaning that EPI replaced its inventories about 3.89 times during the year. Alternatively, we could say that EPI generated $3.89 in sales for each dollar invested in inventories.

To calculate the inventory turnover ratio for EPI, enter the formula: `+Inc Statement:C6/Balance Sheet:C7` into C6 and copy this formula to E6. Notice that this ratio has deteriorated somewhat from 4 times in 1996 to 3.89 times in 1997. Generally, high inventory turnover is considered to be good, but if it is too high the firm may be risking outages and the loss of customers. Also, high inventory turnover might indicate that the firm is spending too much on the ordering process.

Accounts Receivable Turnover Ratio

Businesses grant credit for one main reason: to increase sales. It is important, therefore, to know how well the firm is managing its accounts receivable. The accounts receivable turnover ratio (and the average collection period, below) provides us with this information. It is calculated by:

$$\text{Accounts Receivable Turnover Ratio} = \frac{\text{Credit Sales}}{\text{Accounts Receivable}} . \qquad (4\text{-}4)$$

For EPI, the 1997 accounts receivable turnover ratio is (assuming that all sales are credit sales):

$$\text{Accounts Receivable Turnover Ratio} = \frac{3,850.00}{402.00} = 9.58 \text{ times} .$$

So each dollar invested in accounts receivable generated $9.58 in sales. In cell C7 of your worksheet enter: `+Inc Statement:C5/Balance Sheet:C6`. The result is 9.58 which is the same as we found above. Copy this formula to E7 to get the 1996 accounts receivable turnover.

Whether or not 9.58 is a good accounts receivable turnover ratio is difficult to know at this point. We can say that higher is generally better, but too high might indicate that the firm is denying credit to creditworthy customers (thereby losing sales).

Average Collection Period

The average collection period tells us, on average, how many days it takes to collect on a credit sale.[2]

$$\text{Average Collection Period} = \frac{\text{Accounts Receivable}}{\text{Annual Credit Sales}/360} . \qquad (4\text{-}5)$$

In 1997, it took EPI an average of 37.59 days to collect on its credit sales:

$$\text{Average Collection Period} = \frac{402.00}{3,850.00/360} = 37.59 \text{ days} .$$

---

2. Following convention, we assume that there are 360 days per year (12 months with each having 30 days).

We can calculate the 1997 average collection period in C8 with the formula: `+Balance Sheet:C6/(Inc Statement:C5/360)`. Copy this to E8 to find that in 1996 the average collection period was 36.84 days which was slightly better than 1997.

Note that this ratio actually provides us with the same information as the accounts receivable turnover ratio. In fact, it can easily be demonstrated by simple algebraic manipulation that:

$$\text{Accounts Receivable Turnover Ratio} = \frac{360}{\text{Average Collection Period}},$$

or alternatively:

$$\text{Average Collection Period} = \frac{360}{\text{Accounts Receivable Turnover Ratio}}$$

Since the average collection period is (in a sense) the inverse of the accounts receivable turnover ratio, it should be apparent that the inverse criteria apply to judging this ratio. In other words, lower is usually better, but too low may indicate lost sales.

Fixed Asset Turnover Ratio

The fixed asset turnover ratio describes the dollar amount of sales that are generated by each dollar invested in fixed assets. It is given by:

$$\text{Fixed Asset Turnover} = \frac{\text{Sales}}{\text{Net Fixed Assets}}. \qquad (4\text{-}6)$$

For EPI, the 1997 fixed asset turnover is:

$$\text{Fixed Asset Turnover} = \frac{3,850.00}{360.80} = 10.67 \text{ times}$$

so, EPI generated $10.67 for each dollar invested in fixed assets. In your "Ratios" worksheet, entering: `+Inc Statement:C5/Balance Sheet:C11` into C9 will confirm that the fixed asset turnover was 10.67 times in 1997. Again, copy this formula to E9 to get the 1996 ratio.

Total Asset Turnover Ratio

Like the other ratios discussed in this section, the total asset turnover ratio describes how efficiently the firm is using its assets to generate sales. In this case, we look at the firm's total asset investment:

$$\text{Total Asset Turnover} = \frac{\text{Sales}}{\text{Total Assets}}. \qquad (4\text{-}7)$$

In 1997, EPI generated $2.33 in sales for each dollar invested in total assets:

$$\text{Total Asset Turnover} = \frac{3,850.00}{1,650.80} = 2.33 \text{ times}.$$

This ratio can be calculated in C10 on your worksheet with: `+Inc Statement:C5/Balance Sheet:C12`. After copying this formula to E10, you should see that the 1996 value was 2.34, essentially the same as 1997.

We can interpret the asset turnover ratios as follows: higher is better. However, you should be aware that some industries will naturally have lower turnover ratios than others. For example, a consulting business will almost surely have a very low investment in fixed assets, and therefore a high fixed asset turnover ratio. On the other hand, an electric utility will have a large investment in fixed assets and a low fixed asset turnover ratio. This does not mean, necessarily, that the utility company is more poorly managed than the consulting firm. Rather, each is simply responding to the demands of their choice of business.

At this point your worksheet should resemble Exhibit 4-2.

Leverage Ratios

In physics, leverage refers to a multiplication of force. Using a lever and fulcrum, you can press down on one end of a lever with a given force, and get a larger force at the other end. The amount of leverage depends on the length of the lever and the position of the fulcrum. In finance, leverage refers to a multiplication of changes in profitability measures. For example, a 10% increase in sales might lead to a 20% increase in net income. The amount of leverage depends on the amount of debt that a firm uses to finance its operations.

EXHIBIT 4-2
EPI'S FINANCIAL RATIOS

	A	B	C	D	E
1	Ratio		1997		1996
2	Liquidity Ratios				
3	Current		2.39		2.33
4	Quick		0.84		0.85
5	Efficiency Ratios				
6	Inventory Turnover		3.89		4.00
7	A/R Turnover		9.58		9.77
8	Average Collection Period		37.59		36.84
9	Fixed Asset Turnover		10.67		9.95
10	Total Asset Turnover		2.33		2.34

Leverage ratios describe the degree to which the firm uses debt in its capital structure. This is important information for creditors and investors in the firm. Creditors might be concerned that a firm has too much debt and will therefore have difficulty in repaying loans. Investors might be concerned because a large amount of debt can lead to a large amount of volatility in the firm's earnings. However, most firms use some debt. This is because the tax deductibility of interest can increase the wealth of the firm's shareholders. We will examine several ratios which help to determine the amount of debt that a firm is using. How much is too much will depend on the nature of the business.

The Total Debt Ratio

The total debt ratio measures the total amount of debt (long-term and short-term) that the firm uses to finance its assets:

$$\text{Total Debt Ratio} = \frac{\text{Total Debt}}{\text{Total Assets}} = \frac{\text{Total Assets} - \text{Total Equity}}{\text{Total Assets}} . \qquad (4\text{-}8)$$

Calculating the total debt ratio for EPI, we find that debt makes up about 58.4% of its capital structure:

$$\text{Total Debt Ratio} = \frac{964.81}{1,650.80} = 58.45\% .$$

The formula to calculate the total debt ratio in your worksheet is: `+Balance Sheet:C20/Balance Sheet:C12`. The result for 1997 is 58.45% which is higher than the 54.81% in 1996.

The Long-term Debt Ratio

Many analysts believe that it is more useful to focus on just the long-term debt (LTD) instead of total debt. The long-term debt ratio is the same as the total debt ratio, except that the numerator includes only long-term debt:

$$\text{Long-term Debt Ratio} = \frac{\text{Long-term Debt}}{\text{Total Assets}} \qquad (4\text{-}9)$$

EPI's long-term debt ratio is:

$$\text{Long-term Debt Ratio} = \frac{424.61}{1,650.80} = 25.72\%.$$

In C13, the formula to calculate the long-term debt ratio for 1997 is : `+Balance Sheet:C19/Balance Sheet:C12`. Copying this formula to E13 reveals that in 1996 the ratio was only 22.02%.

The Long-term Debt to Total Capitalization Ratio

Similar to the previous two ratios, the long-term debt to total capitalization ratio tells us the percentage of long-term sources of capital that is provided by long-term debt. It is calculated by:

$$\text{LTD to Total Capitalization} = \frac{\text{LTD}}{\text{LTD} + \text{Preferred Equity} + \text{Common Equity}}. \quad (4\text{-}10)$$

For EPI, we have:

$$\text{LTD to Total Capitalization} = \frac{424.61}{424.61 + 685.99} = 38.23\%.$$

Since EPI has no preferred equity, its total capitalization consists of long-term debt and common equity. Note that common equity is the total of common stock and retained earnings. We can calculate this ratio in C14 of the worksheet with: `+Balance Sheet:C19/(Balance Sheet:C21+Balance Sheet:C22 +Balance Sheet:C19)`. In 1996 this ratio was only 32.76%.

The Debt to Equity Ratio

The debt to equity ratio provides exactly the same information as the total debt ratio, but in a slightly different form that some analysts prefer:

$$\text{Debt to Equity} = \frac{\text{Total Debt}}{\text{Total Equity}}.$$

(4-11)

For EPI the debt to equity ratio is:

$$\text{Debt to Equity} = \frac{964.81}{685.99} = 1.41 \text{ times}.$$

In C15, this is calculated as: `+Balance Sheet:C20/Balance Sheet:C23.`
Copy this to E15 to find that the debt to equity ratio in 1996 was 1.21 times.

To see that the total debt ratio and the debt to equity ratio provide the same information, realize that:

$$\frac{\text{Total Debt}}{\text{Total Equity}} = \frac{\text{Total Debt}}{\text{Total Assets}} \times \frac{\text{Total Assets}}{\text{Total Equity}}$$

but

$$\frac{\text{Total Assets}}{\text{Total Equity}} = \frac{1}{1 - \text{Total Debt Ratio}}$$

so, by substitution we have:

$$\frac{\text{Total Debt}}{\text{Total Equity}} = \frac{\text{Total Debt}}{\text{Total Assets}} \times \frac{1}{1 - \dfrac{\text{Total Debt}}{\text{Total Assets}}}.$$

The Long-term Debt to Equity Ratio

Once again, many analysts prefer to focus on the amount of long-term debt that a firm carries. For this reason, many analysts like to use the long-term debt to total equity ratio:

$$\text{Long-term Debt to Equity} = \frac{\text{LTD}}{\text{Preferred Equity} + \text{Common Equity}}.$$

(4-12)

EPI's long-term debt to equity ratio is:

$$\text{Long-term Debt to Equity} = \frac{424.61}{685.99} = 61.90\%.$$

The formula to calculate EPI's 1997 long-term debt to equity ratio in C16 is: `+Balance Sheet:C19/Balance Sheet:C23`. After copying this formula to E16, note that the ratio was only 48.73% in 1996.

At this point, your worksheet should look like the one in Exhibit 4-3.

EXHIBIT 4-3
EPI'S FINANCIAL RATIOS WITH THE LEVERAGE RATIOS

	A	B	C	D	E
1	Ratio		1997		1996
2	Liquidity Ratios				
3	Current		2.39		2.33
4	Quick		0.84		0.85
5	Efficiency Ratios				
6	Inventory Turnover		3.89		4.00
7	A/R Turnover		9.58		9.77
8	Average Collection Period		37.59		36.84
9	Fixed Asset Turnover		10.67		9.95
10	Total Asset Turnover		2.33		2.34
11	Leverage Ratios				
12	Total Debt Ratio		58.45%		54.81%
13	Long-term Debt Ratio		25.72%		22.02%
14	LTD to Total Capitalization		38.23%		32.76%
15	Debt to Equity		1.41		1.21
16	LTD to Equity		61.90%		48.73%

Coverage Ratios

The coverage ratios are similar to liquidity ratios in that they describe the quantity of funds available to "cover" certain expenses. We will examine two very similar ratios which describe the firm's ability to meet its interest payment obligations. In both cases, higher ratios are desirable to a degree. However, if they are too high, it may indicate that the firm is under-utilizing its debt capacity, and therefore not maximizing shareholder wealth.

The Times Interest Earned Ratio

The times interest earned ratio measures the ability of the firm to pay its interest obligations by comparing earnings before interest and taxes (EBIT) to interest expense:

$$\text{Times Interest Earned} = \frac{\text{EBIT}}{\text{Interest Expense}} . \qquad (4\text{-}13)$$

For EPI in 1997 the times interest earned ratio is:

$$\text{Times Interest Earned} = \frac{149.70}{76.00} = 1.97 \text{ times}.$$

In your worksheet, the times interest earned ratio can be calculated in C18 with the formula: `+Inc Statement:C11/Inc Statement:C12`. Notice that this ratio has declined from 3.35 times in 1996.

The Cash Coverage Ratio

EBIT does not really reflect the cash that is available to pay the firm's interest expense. That is because a non-cash expense (depreciation) has been subtracted in the calculation of EBIT. To correct for this deficiency, many analysts like to use the cash coverage ratio instead of times interest earned. The cash coverage ratio is calculated as:

$$\text{Cash Coverage Ratio} = \frac{\text{EBIT} + \text{Non-cash Expenses}}{\text{Interest Expense}} . \qquad (4\text{-}14)$$

The calculation for EPI in 1997 is:

$$\text{Cash Coverage Ratio} = \frac{149.70 + 20.00}{76.00} = 2.23 \text{ times}.$$

Note that the cash coverage ratio will always be higher than the times interest earned ratio. The difference depends on the amount of depreciation expense, and therefore the investment in fixed assets.

The cash coverage ratio can be calculated in cell C19 of your "Ratios" worksheet with: +(Inc Statement:C11 + Inc Statement:C10)/Inc Statement:C12. In 1996, the ratio was 3.65 times.

Profitability Ratios

Investors, and therefore managers, are particularly interested in the profitability of the firms that they own. As we'll see, there are many ways to measure profits. Profitability ratios provide an easy way to compare profits to earlier periods or to other firms. Furthermore, by simultaneously examining the first three profitability ratios, an analyst can discover categories of expenses which may be out of line.

Profitability ratios are the easiest of all of the ratios to analyze. Without exception, high ratios are preferred. However, the definition of high is dependent on the industry in which the firm operates. Generally, firms in mature industries with lots of competition will have lower profitability measures than firms in younger industries with less competition. For example, grocery stores will have lower profit margins than do computer software companies. In the grocery business, a net profit margin of 3% would be considered quite high, but that would be abysmal in the software business.

The Gross Profit Margin

The gross profit margin measures the gross profit relative to sales. It indicates the amount of funds available to pay the firm's expenses other than its cost of sales. The gross profit margin is calculated by:

$$\text{Gross Profit Margin} = \frac{\text{Gross Profit}}{\text{Sales}}. \tag{4-15}$$

In 1997, EPI's gross profit margin was:

$$\text{Gross Profit Margin} = \frac{600.00}{3,850.00} = 15.58\%,$$

which means that cost of goods sold consumed about 84.42% (= $1 - 0.1558$) of sales revenue. We can calculate this ratio in C21 with: +Inc Statement:C7/Inc Statement:C5. After copying this formula to E21, you will see that the gross profit margin has declined from 16.55% in 1996.

The Operating Profit Margin

Moving down the income statement, we can calculate the profits that remain after the firm has paid all of its usual (non-financial) expenses. The operating profit margin is calculated as:

$$\text{Operating Profit Margin} = \frac{\text{Net Operating Income}}{\text{Sales}}. \qquad (4\text{-}16)$$

For EPI in 1997:

$$\text{Operating Profit Margin} = \frac{149.70}{3,850.00} = 3.89\%.$$

The operating profit margin can be calculated in C22 with the formula: `+Inc Statement:C11/Inc Statement:C5`. Note that this is significantly lower than the 6.09% from 1996, indicating that EPI seems to be having problems controlling its costs.

The Net Profit Margin

The net profit margin relates net income to sales. Since net income is profit after all expenses, the net profit margin tells us the percentage of sales that remains for the shareholders of the firm:

$$\text{Net Profit Margin} = \frac{\text{Net Income}}{\text{Sales}}. \qquad (4\text{-}17)$$

The net profit margin for EPI in 1997 is:

$$\text{Net Profit Margin} = \frac{44.22}{3,850.00} = 1.15\%,$$

which can be calculated on your worksheet in C23 with: `+Inc Statement:C15/Inc Statement:C5`. This is lower than the 2.56% in 1996.

Taken together, the three profit margin ratios that we have examined show a company which may be losing control over its costs. Of course, high expenses mean lower returns, and we'll see this confirmed by the next three profitability ratios.

Return on Total Assets

The total assets of a firm are the investment that the shareholders have made. Much like you might be interested in the returns generated by your investments, analysts are often interested in the return that a firm is able to get from its investments. The return on total assets is:

$$\text{Return on Total Assets} = \frac{\text{Net Income}}{\text{Total Assets}} \cdot \qquad (4\text{-}18)$$

In 1997, EPI earned about 2.68% on its assets:

$$\text{Return on Total Assets} = \frac{44.22}{1650.80} = 2.68\% \cdot$$

For 1997, we can calculate the return on total assets in cell C24 with the formula: `+Inc Statement:C15/Balance Sheet:C12`. Notice that this is more than 50% lower than the 5.99% recorded in 1996. EPI's total assets obviously increased in 1997 at a faster rate than did its net income, which actually declined.

Return on Equity

While total assets represent the total investment in the firm, the owners' own funds usually represent only a portion of this amount. For this reason it is useful to calculate the rate of return on the shareholder's invested funds. We can calculate the return on (total) equity as:

$$\text{Return on Equity} = \frac{\text{Net Income}}{\text{Total Equity}} \cdot \qquad (4\text{-}19)$$

For EPI in 1997 this was:

$$\text{Return on Equity} = \frac{44.22}{685.99} = 6.45\% \,,$$

which can be calculated in your worksheet with: `+Inc Statement:C15/ Balance Sheet:C23`. Again, copying this formula to E25 reveals that this ratio has declined from 13.25% in 1996.

Return on Common Equity

For firm's which have issued preferred stock in addition to common stock, it is often helpful to determine the rate of return on just the common stockholders' investment:

$$\text{Return on Common Equity} = \frac{\text{Net Income Available to Common}}{\text{Common Equity}}. \qquad (4\text{-}20)$$

Net income available to common is net income less preferred dividends. In the case of EPI, this ratio is the same as the return on equity because it has no preferred shareholders:

$$\text{Return on Common Equity} = \frac{44.22}{685.99} = 6.45\%.$$

For EPI, the worksheet formula for the return on common equity is exactly the same as for the return on equity.

Analysis of EPI's Profitability Ratios

Obviously, EPI's profitability has slipped rather dramatically in the past year. The sources of these declines can be seen most clearly if we look at all of EPI's ratios. Before continuing, remember that we left column D in the worksheet blank. We did this so that we could easily calculate the 1996 ratios by simply copying formulas from column C to column E. Now that calculation of the ratios has been completed, we can delete column D to get a better look for the worksheet. At this point your worksheet should resemble that in Exhibit 4-4.

The gross profit margin in 1997 is lower than in 1996, but not significantly (at least as compared to the declines in the other ratios). The operating profit margin, however, is significantly lower in 1997 than in 1996. This indicates potential problems in controlling the firm's operating expenses. The other profitability ratios are lower than in 1996 partly because of the "trickle down" effect of the increase in operating expenses. However, they are also lower because EPI has taken on a lot of extra debt in 1997, resulting in interest expense increasing faster than sales. This can be confirmed by examining EPI's common-size income statement (Exhibit 2-2, page 36).

EXHIBIT 4-4
COMPLETED RATIO WORKSHEET FOR EPI

	A	B	C	D
1	Ratio		1997	1996
2	Liquidity Ratios			
3	Current		2.39	2.33
4	Quick		0.84	0.85
5	Efficiency Ratios			
6	Inventory Turnover		3.89	4.00
7	A/R Turnover		9.58	9.77
8	Average Collection Period		37.59	36.84
9	Fixed Asset Turnover		10.67	9.95
10	Total Asset Turnover		2.33	2.34
11	Leverage Ratios			
12	Total Debt Ratio		58.45%	54.81%
13	Long-term Debt Ratio		25.72%	22.02%
14	LTD to Total Capitalization		38.23%	32.76%
15	Debt to Equity		1.41	1.21
16	LTD to Equity		61.90%	48.73%
17	Coverage Ratios			
18	Times Interest Earned		1.97	3.35
19	Cash Coverage Ratio		2.23	3.65
20	Profitability Ratios			
21	Gross Profit Margin		15.58%	16.55%
22	Operating Profit Margin		3.89%	6.09%
23	Net Profit Margin		1.15%	2.56%
24	Return on Total Assets		2.68%	5.99%
25	Return on Equity		6.45%	13.25%
26	Return on Common Equity		6.45%	13.25%

Using Financial Ratios

Calculating financial ratios is a pointless exercise unless you understand how to use them. One overriding rule of ratio analysis is this: *a single ratio provides very little information and may be misleading.* You should never draw conclusions from a single ratio. Instead, several ratios should support any conclusions that are made.

With that precaution in mind, there are several ways that ratios can be used to draw important conclusions.

Trend Analysis

Trend analysis involves the examination of ratios over time. Trends, or lack of trends, can help managers gauge their progress towards a goal. Furthermore, trends can highlight areas in need of attention. While we don't really have enough information on Elvis Products International to perform a trend analysis, it is obvious that many of its ratios are moving in the wrong direction.

For example, all of EPI's profitability ratios have declined in 1997 relative to 1996, some rather precipitously. Management should immediately try to isolate the problem areas. For example, the gross profit margin has declined only slightly, indicating that increasing materials costs are not a major problem (though a price increase may be called for). The operating profit margin has fallen by about 36%, and since we can't blame increasing costs of materials, we must conclude that operating costs have increased at a more rapid rate than revenues. This increase in operating costs has led, to a large degree, to the decline in the other profitability ratios.

One potential problem area for trend analysis is seasonality. We must be careful to compare similar time periods. For example, many firms generate most of their sales during the holidays in the fourth quarter of the year. For this reason they may begin building inventories in the third quarter when sales are low. In this situation, comparing the third quarter inventory turnover ratio to the fourth quarter inventory turnover would be misleading.

Comparing to Industry Averages

Aside from trend analysis, one of the most beneficial uses of financial ratios is to compare similar firms. Most often this is done by comparing a company's ratios with the industry average ratios which are published by organizations such as

Robert Morris Associates, Standard & Poor's, and Dunn & Bradstreet. These industry averages provide a standard of comparison so that we can determine how well a firm is performing in relation to its peers.

As an example of the use of industry averages, consider Exhibit 4-5 which shows EPI's financial ratios and the industry averages for 1997. You can enter the industry averages from Exhibit 4-5 into your worksheet starting in B1 with the label: Industry 1997. In order to get the text to wrap, as we have done, choose Style Alignment and then click on Wrap Text. To enter the numbers, first select B3..B26, and notice that B3 will not be darkened. Type 2.70 into B3 and then press the enter key. Notice that the active cell will change to B4 as soon as the enter key is pressed. This may be a more efficient method of entering a lot of numbers because your fingers never have to leave the number keypad.

It should be obvious that EPI is not being managed as well as the average firm in the industry. From the liquidity ratios we can see that EPI is less able to meet its short-term obligations than the average firm, though it is probably not in imminent danger of missing payments. The efficiency ratios show us that EPI is not managing its assets as well as would be expected, especially its inventories. It is also obvious that EPI is using substantially more debt than its peers. The coverage ratios indicate that EPI has less cash to pay its interest expense than the industry average. This may be due to its carrying more debt than average. Finally, all of these problems have led to sub-par profitability measures which seem to be getting worse, rather than better.

Company Goals and Debt Covenants

Financial ratios are often the basis of company goal setting. For example, a CEO might decide that one goal of the firm should be to earn at least 15% on equity (ROE = 15%). Obviously, whether or not this goal is achieved can be determined by calculating the return on equity. Further, by using trend analysis managers can gauge progress towards meeting goals, and they can determine whether goals are realistic or not.

Another use of financial ratios can be found in covenants to loan contracts. Very often when companies borrow money the lenders place restrictions on the values of certain ratios. For example, the lender may require that the borrowing firm maintain a current ratio of at least 2.0. Or, they may require that the firm's total debt ratio not exceed 40%. Whatever the restriction, it is important that the firm monitor its ratios for compliance, or the loan may be due immediately.

EXHIBIT 4-5
EPI'S RATIOS VS. INDUSTRY AVERAGES

	A	B	C	D
1	Ratio	Industry 1997	1997	1996
2	Liquidity Ratios			
3	Current	2.70	2.39	2.33
4	Quick	1.00	0.84	0.85
5	Efficiency Ratios			
6	Inventory Turnover	7.00	3.89	4.00
7	A/R Turnover	10.70	9.58	9.77
8	Average Collection Period	33.64	37.59	36.84
9	Fixed Asset Turnover	11.20	10.67	9.95
10	Total Asset Turnover	2.60	2.33	2.34
11	Leverage Ratios			
12	Total Debt Ratio	50.00%	58.45%	54.81%
13	Long-term Debt Ratio	20.00%	25.72%	22.02%
14	LTD to Total Capitalization	28.57%	38.23%	32.76%
15	Debt to Equity	1.00	1.41	1.21
16	LTD to Equity	40.00%	61.90%	48.73%
17	Coverage Ratios			
18	Times Interest Earned	2.50	1.97	3.35
19	Cash Coverage Ratio	2.80	2.23	3.65
20	Profitability Ratios			
21	Gross Profit Margin	17.50%	15.58%	16.55%
22	Operating Profit Margin	6.25%	3.89%	6.09%
23	Net Profit Margin	3.50%	1.15%	2.56%
24	Return on Total Assets	9.10%	2.68%	5.99%
25	Return on Equity	18.20%	6.45%	13.25%
26	Return on Common Equity	18.20%	6.45%	13.25%

Automating Ratio Analysis

Ratio analysis is a very subjective endeavor. Different analysts are likely to render somewhat different judgements on a firm. Nonetheless, you can have 1-2-3 do a rudimentary analysis for you. Actually, the analysis could be made quite sophisticated if you are willing to put in the effort. The technique that we will illustrate is analogous to creating an expert system, though we wouldn't call it a true expert system at this point.

An *expert system* is a computer program that can diagnose problems or provide an analysis by using the same techniques as an expert in the field. For example, a medical doctor might use an expert system to diagnose a patient's illness. The doctor would tell the system about the symptoms and the expert system would consult its list of rules to generate a likely diagnosis.

Building a true ratio analysis expert system in 1-2-3 would be very time consuming, and there are better tools available. However, we can build a very simple system using only a few functions. Our system will analyze each ratio separately and will only determine whether a ratio is either "Good," "Ok," or "Bad." To be really useful, the system would need to consider the inter-relationships between the ratios, the industry that the company is in, etc. We leave it to you to improve the system.

As a first step in developing our expert system we need to specify the rules that will be used to categorize the ratios. In most cases, we have seen that the higher the ratio the better. Therefore, we would like to see that the ratio is higher in 1997 than in 1996, and that the 1997 ratio is greater than the industry average.

We can use 1-2-3's **@IF** function to implement our automatic analysis. We actually want to make two tests to determine whether a ratio is "Good," "Ok," or "Bad." First, we will test to see if the 1997 ratio is greater than the 1996 ratio. To do this, we divide the 1997 value by the 1996 value. If the result is greater than one, then the 1997 ratio is greater than the 1996 ratio. Using only this test, our formula for the current ratio would be: `@IF(C4/D4>=1,"Good","Bad")` in E3. In this case the result should be "Good" since the 1997 value is greater than the 1996 value. If you copy this formula to E4, the result will be "Bad" since the 1997 quick ratio is lower than the 1996 quick ratio.

We can modify this formula to also take account of the industry average. If the 1997 ratio is greater than the 1996 ratio **and** the 1997 ratio is greater than the industry average, then the ratio is "Good". To accomplish this we need to use the **AND** statement which was introduced on page 59. The modified function in E3 is now: `@IF(C3/D3>=1 #and# C3/B3>=1,"Good","Bad")`. Now, the ratio will only be judged as "Good" if both conditions are true, which they are not for the current ratio.

One final improvement can be made by adding "Ok" to the possible outcomes. We will say that the ratio is "Ok" if the 1997 value is greater than the 1996 value, **or** the 1997 value is greater than the industry average. We can accomplish this by nesting a second **@IF** function inside the first in place of "Bad." For the second **@IF** statement, we need to use 1-2-3's **OR** statement.

This statement is identical to the **AND** statement, except that it returns true if any of its arguments are true. The final form of our equation is: `@IF(C3/D3>=1 #and# C3/B3>=1,"Good",IF(C3/D3>=1 #or# C3/B3>=1,"Ok", "Bad"))`. For the current ratio, this will evaluate to "Ok." You can now evaluate all of EPI's ratios by copying this formula to E4..E26 and erasing the unnecessary copies in E11, E17, and E20.

One more change is necessary. Recall that for leverage ratios lower is generally better. Therefore, change all of the ">=" to "<=" in E12..E16. You also need to make the same change in E8 for the average collection period. Your worksheet should now resemble that in Exhibit 4-6.

You should see that nearly all of EPI's ratios are judged to be "Bad." This is exactly what our previous analysis has determined, except that 1-2-3 has done it automatically. There are many changes that could be made to improve on this simple ratio analyzer, but we will leave that job as an exercise for you.

Summary

In this chapter we have seen how various financial ratios can be used to evaluate the financial health of a company, and therefore the performance of the managers of the firm. You have also seen how 1-2-3 can make the calculation of ratios quicker and easier than doing it by hand. We looked at five categories of ratios: *Liquidity ratios* measure the ability of a firm to pays its bills; *efficiency ratios* measure how well the firm is making use of its assets to generate sales; *leverage ratios* describe how much debt the firm is using to finance its assets; *coverage ratios* tell how much cash the firm has available to pay specific expenses; and *profitability ratios* measure how profitable the firm has been over a period of time.

We have also seen how 1-2-3 can be programed to do a rudimentary ratio analysis automatically, using only a few of the built-in logical statements. Table 4-1 provides a summary of the ratio formulas that were presented in this chapter.

EXHIBIT 4-6
EPI'S RATIOS WITH AUTOMATIC ANALYSIS

	A	B	C	D	E
1	Ratio	Industry 1997	1997	1996	Analysis
2	Liquidity Ratios				
3	Current	2.70	2.39	2.33	Ok
4	Quick	1.00	0.84	0.85	Bad
5	Efficiency Ratios				
6	Inventory Turnover	7.00	3.89	4.00	Bad
7	A/R Turnover	10.70	9.58	9.77	Bad
8	Average Collection Period	33.64	37.59	36.84	Bad
9	Fixed Asset Turnover	11.20	10.67	9.95	Ok
10	Total Asset Turnover	2.60	2.33	2.34	Bad
11	Leverage Ratios				
12	Total Debt Ratio	50.00%	58.45%	54.81%	Bad
13	Long-term Debt Ratio	20.00%	25.72%	22.02%	Bad
14	LTD to Total Capitalization	28.57%	38.23%	32.76%	Bad
15	Debt to Equity	1.00	1.41	1.21	Bad
16	LTD to Equity	40.00%	61.90%	48.73%	Bad
17	Coverage Ratios				
18	Times Interest Earned	2.50	1.97	3.35	Bad
19	Cash Coverage Ratio	2.80	2.23	3.65	Bad
20	Profitability Ratios				
21	Gross Profit Margin	17.50%	15.58%	16.55%	Bad
22	Operating Profit Margin	6.25%	3.89%	6.09%	Bad
23	Net Profit Margin	3.50%	1.15%	2.56%	Bad
24	Return on Total Assets	9.10%	2.68%	5.99%	Bad
25	Return on Equity	18.20%	6.45%	13.25%	Bad
26	Return on Common Equity	18.20%	6.45%	13.25%	Bad

TABLE 4-1
SUMMARY OF FINANCIAL RATIOS

Name of Ratio	Formula
Liquidity Ratios	
Current Ratio	$\dfrac{\text{Current Assets}}{\text{Current Liabilities}}$
Quick Ratio	$\dfrac{\text{Current Assets} - \text{Inventories}}{\text{Current Liabilities}}$
Efficiency Ratios	
Inventory Turnover	$\dfrac{\text{Cost of Goods Sold}}{\text{Inventory}}$
A/R Turnover	$\dfrac{\text{Credit Sales}}{\text{Accounts Receivable}}$
Average Collection Period	$\dfrac{\text{Accounts Receivable}}{\text{Annual Credit Sales}/360}$
Fixed Asset Turnover	$\dfrac{\text{Sales}}{\text{Net Fixed Assets}}$
Total Asset Turnover	$\dfrac{\text{Sales}}{\text{Total Assets}}$
Leverage Ratios	
Total Debt Ratio	$\dfrac{\text{Total Debt}}{\text{Total Assets}}$
Long-term Debt Ratio	$\dfrac{\text{Long-term Debt}}{\text{Total Assets}}$
LTD to Total Capitalization	$\dfrac{\text{LTD}}{\text{LTD} + \text{Preferred Equity} + \text{Common Equity}}$
Debt to Equity	$\dfrac{\text{Total Debt}}{\text{Total Equity}}$
LTD to Equity	$\dfrac{\text{LTD}}{\text{Preferred Equity} + \text{Common Equity}}$

TABLE 4-1 (CONTINUED)
SUMMARY OF FINANCIAL RATIOS

Name of Ratio	Formula
Coverage Ratios	
Times Interest Earned	$\dfrac{\text{EBIT}}{\text{Interest Expense}}$
Cash Coverage Ratio	$\dfrac{\text{EBIT + Non-cash Expenses}}{\text{Interest Expense}}$
Profitability Ratios	
Gross Profit Margin	$\dfrac{\text{Gross Profit}}{\text{Sales}}$
Operating Profit Margin	$\dfrac{\text{Net Operating Income}}{\text{Sales}}$
Net Profit Margin	$\dfrac{\text{Net Income}}{\text{Sales}}$
Return on Total Assets	$\dfrac{\text{Net Income}}{\text{Total Assets}}$
Return on Equity	$\dfrac{\text{Net Income}}{\text{Total Equity}}$
Return on Common Equity	$\dfrac{\text{Net Income Available to Common}}{\text{Common Equity}}$

TABLE 4-2
FUNCTIONS INTRODUCED IN THIS CHAPTER

Purpose	Function	Page
Returns true if one argument is true	#OR#	85

CHAPTER 5 — *Financial Forecasting*

After studying this chapter, you should be able to:

1. *Explain how the "Percent of Sales" method is used to develop pro-forma financial statements, and construct such statements in 1-2-3.*

2. *Use the @Regression function for forecasting sales or any other trending variables.*

3. *Perform a regression analysis with 1-2-3's built-in regression tools .*

4. *Explain "systematic risk" and calculate a firm's beta (β) coefficient using regression analysis.*

Forecasting is an important activity for a wide variety of business people. Nearly all of the decisions by financial managers are made on the basis of forecasts of one kind or another. In this chapter we will examine several methods of forecasting. The first, the percent of sales method, is the most simplistic. We will also look at more advanced techniques such as regression analysis.

The Percent of Sales Method

Forecasting financial statements is important for a number of reasons. Among these reasons are planning for the future and providing information to the company's investors. The simplest method of forecasting income statements and balance sheets is the percent of sales method. This method has the added advantage of requiring relatively little data to make a forecast.

The fundamental premise of the percent of sales method is that many (but not all) income statement and balance sheet items maintain a constant relationship to the level of sales. For example, if the cost of goods sold has averaged 65% of sales over the last several years, we would assume that this relationship would hold for the next year. If sales were expected to be $10 million next year, our cost of goods forecast would be $6.5 million (10 million × 0.65 = 6.5 million). Of course, this method assumes that the sales forecast is provided by others.

Forecasting the Income Statement

As an example of income statement forecasting, consider the Elvis Products International statements that you originally created in Exhibit 2-1. The income statement is recreated here in Exhibit 5-1 (we are showing only the original dollar amounts, but we will be making use of the common-size income statement).

The level of detail that you have in an income statement will affect how many items will fluctuate directly with sales. In general, we will proceed through the income statement line by line asking the question, "is it likely that this item will change directly with sales?" If the answer is yes, then we calculate the percentage of sales and multiply the result by the sales forecast for the next period. Otherwise, we will take one of two actions: Leave the item unchanged, or use other information to change the item.[1]

For EPI only one income statement item will clearly change with sales: the cost of goods sold. One other item, selling, general and administrative expense (SG&A), is a conglomeration of many accounts, some of which will probably change with

---

1. Realize that you may have important information regarding one or more of these items. For example, if you know that the lease for the company's headquarters building has a scheduled increase, then you should be sure to include this information in your forecast for fixed costs.

sales and some which won't. For our purposes we choose to believe that, on balance, SG&A will change along with sales.

EXHIBIT 5-1
EPI'S INCOME STATEMENTS FOR 1997 AND 1996

	A	B	C
1	Elvis Products International		
2	Income Statement		
3	For the Year Ended Dec. 31, 1997		
4		1997	1996
5	Sales	3,850.00	3,432.00
6	Cost of Goods Sold	3,250.00	2,864.00
7	*Gross Profit*	*600.00*	*568.00*
8	Selling and G&A Expenses	330.30	240.00
9	Fixed Expenses	100.00	100.00
10	Depreciation Expense	20.00	18.90
11	*EBIT*	*149.70*	*209.10*
12	Interest Expense	76.00	62.50
13	*Earnings Before Taxes*	*73.70*	*146.60*
14	Taxes @ 40%	29.48	58.64
15	*Net Income*	*44.22*	*87.96*

The other items don't change as a result of a change in sales. Depreciation expense, for example, depends on the amount and age of the firm's fixed assets. Interest expense is a function of the amount and maturity structure of debt in the firm's capital structure. Taxes depend directly on the firm's taxable income, though this indirectly depends on the level of sales. All of the other items on the income statement are calculated.

To generate our income statement forecast, we first determine the percentage of sales for each of the prior years for each item that changes. In this case for 1997 we have:

Cost of Goods Sold 1997 % of Sales $\frac{3,250,000}{3,850,000} = 0.8442 = 84.42\%$

Selling and G&A Expense 1997 % of Sales $\frac{330,300}{3,850,000} = 0.0858 = 8.58\%$

The 1996 percentages (83.45% and 6.99%, respectively) can be found in exactly the same manner. We now calculate the average of these percentages and use this average as our estimate of the 1998 percentage of sales. The forecast is then found by multiplying these percentages by next year's sales forecast. Assuming that sales are forecasted to be $4,300,000 then for 1998 we have:

Cost of Goods Sold 1998 forecast	$4,300,000 \times 0.8393 = 3,609,108$
S,G&A Expense 1998 forecast	$4,300,000 \times 0.0779 = 334,803$

Exhibit 5-2 shows a completed forecast for the 1998 income statement. To create this forecast in your worksheet, begin by selecting columns B and C and then choose Edit Insert Column. This will create two blank columns into which we will enter our forecasts for 1996. In B4 enter: 1998%* and in C4 enter: 1998*. (The * indicates a footnote that will inform the reader that these are forecasts.) Because the 1998 income statement will be calculated in exactly the same way as 1997, the easiest way to proceed is to copy E5..E15 into C5..C15. In column B we will calculate the average percentage of sales for each item. In B5 enter the formula: @AVG(D5,F5) and copy this formula down through the range B6..B15. Note that we are making use of the common-size data we previously created.[2] Next change the 1998 sales in C5 to: 4,300. All that remains is to enter the formulas for forecasting cost of goods sold and SG&A. In C6 we enter the formula to calculate the cost of goods sold forecast as: +B6*C$5 and copy this to C8 so that it reads: +B8*C$5. Your worksheet should now look like the one in Exhibit 5-2.

Forecasting Assets on the Balance Sheet

We can forecast the balance sheet in exactly the same way as the income statement. The main difference in this case is that we cannot make use of the common-size information that we created in Chapter 2. This is because the common-size balance sheet calculates the percentages based on total assets not on sales. If necessary, open your EPI workbook and switch to the Balance Sheet worksheet before continuing.

---

2. If we didn't already have the common-size information, we could have achieved an identical result with the formula: @Avg(E5/E$5,G5/G$5).

Exhibit 5-2
Percent of Sales Forecast for 1998

	A	B	C	D	E	F	G
1		Elvis Products International					
2		Income Statement					
3		For the Year Ended Dec. 31, 1997 ($ 000's)					
4		1998%*	1998*	1997%	1997	1996%	1996
5	Sales	100.00%	4,300.00	100.00%	3,850.00	100.00%	3,432.00
6	Cost of Goods Sold	83.93%	3,609.11	84.42%	3,250.00	83.45%	2,864.00
7	*Gross Profit*	16.07%	*690.89*	15.58%	*600.00*	16.55%	*568.00*
8	Selling and G&A Expenses	7.79%	334.80	8.58%	330.30	6.99%	240.00
9	Fixed Expenses	2.76%	100.00	2.60%	100.00	2.91%	100.00
10	Depreciation Expense	0.54%	20.00	0.52%	20.00	0.55%	18.90
11	*EBIT*	4.99%	*236.09*	3.89%	*149.70*	6.09%	*209.10*
12	Interest Expense	1.90%	76.00	1.97%	76.00	1.82%	62.50
13	*Earnings Before Taxes*	3.09%	*160.09*	1.91%	*73.70*	4.27%	*146.60*
14	Taxes @ 40%	1.24%	64.04	0.77%	29.48	1.71%	58.64
15	*Net Income*	1.86%	*96.05*	1.15%	*44.22*	2.56%	*87.96*
17	*Forecasted						

Because we cannot make use of the common-size information, our formulas will be somewhat more complex than for the income statement. However, this should pose no difficulty if you follow along carefully and keep in mind the general premise of the percent of sales method.

Create the percent of sales balance sheet for 1998 by selecting column B and inserting a new column (Edit Insert Column). In B4 type the label: 1998*. As before, the star indicates a footnote we'll add which says that the information is a forecast. Like we did with the income statement, we will move, line by line, through the balance sheet to determine which items will vary with sales.

The firm's cash balance is the first, and perhaps most difficult, item with which we need to work. Does the cash balance vary, in constant proportion, with sales? Your first response might be, "Of course it does. As the firm sells more goods it accumulates cash." This line of reasoning neglects two important facts. The firm has other things to do with its cash aside from accumulating it, and, because cash is a low-return (perhaps negative-return when inflation is considered) asset, firms should seek to minimize the amount of their cash balance.[3] For these reasons, even though the cash balance will probably change, it probably will not change by the same percentage as sales. Therefore, we will simply use the cash balance from 1997 as our forecast, so enter: +D5 into cell B5.

The next two items, accounts receivable and inventory, are much easier. Both of these accounts are likely to fluctuate roughly in proportion to sales. Using the same methodology that we used for the pro-forma income statement, we will find the average percentage of sales for the past two years and multiply that amount by our sales forecast for 1998. For the accounts receivable, the formula in B6 is: `@Avg(D6/Inc Statement:E$5, F6/Inc Statement:G$5)* Inc Statement:C$5`. Remember, instead of typing the references to the income statement, it is easier to switch to the income statement and select the appropriate cells with the mouse. Since we will use the same formula for Inventory, we can simply copy this formula down to B7. Total Current Assets in B8 is a calculated value, so we can copy the formula directly from cell D8.

In cell B9 we have the 1998 gross Plant and Equipment. This is the historical purchase price of the buildings and equipment that the firm owns. Even though the firm will probably buy and sell (or otherwise dispose of) many pieces of equipment, there is no reason to believe that these actions are directly related to the level of sales. Furthermore, no firm builds new plants (or other buildings) every time sales increase. For these reasons we will leave the Plant and Equipment unchanged from 1997. Only if we know of plans to increase Plant and Equipment should we enter a different number in B9. In this case we will simply insert the formula: `+D9` into this cell.

Accumulated Depreciation will definitely increase in 1998, but not because of the forecasted change in sales. Instead, Accumulated Depreciation will increase by the amount of the Depreciation Expense for 1996. To determine the accumulated depreciation for 1998 we will add 1998's depreciation expense to 1997's accumulated depreciation. The formula is: `+D10 + Inc Statement:E10`.

To complete the asset side of the balance sheet, we note that both Net Fixed Assets and Total Assets are calculated values. We can simply copy the formulas from D11:D12 and paste them into B11:B12.

Forecasting Liabilities on the Balance Sheet

Once the assets are completed the rest of the balance sheet is comparatively simple because we can mostly copy formulas already entered. Before continuing however,

---

3. Within reason, of course. Firms need some amount of cash to operate, but the amount needed does not necessarily vary directly with the level of sales.

we need to distinguish among the types of financing sources. We have already seen that the types of financing that a firm uses can be divided into three categories:

- Current liabilities
- Long-term liabilities
- Owner's equity

These categories are not sufficiently distinguished for our purposes here. Instead, we will divide the liabilities and equity of a firm into two categories:

- *Spontaneous sources of financing* — these are the sources of financing that arise in the ordinary course of doing business. An example is the firm's accounts payable. Once the credit account is established with a supplier, no additional work is required to obtain credit; it just happens spontaneously when the firm makes a purchase.

- *Discretionary source of financing* — these are the financing sources which require a large effort on the part of the firm to obtain. In other words, the firm must make a conscious decision to obtain these funds. Furthermore, the firm's upper-level management will use its discretion to determine the appropriate type of financing to use. Examples of this type of financing include any type of bank loan, bonds, and common and preferred stock.

Generally speaking, spontaneous sources of financing can be expected to vary directly with sales. Changes in discretionary sources, on the other hand, will not have a direct relationship to changes in sales.

Returning now to our forecasting problem, the first item to consider is accounts payable. As noted above, accounts payable is a spontaneous source of financing and will, therefore, change directly with sales. To enter the formula, all that is necessary is to copy the formula from one of the other items that we have already completed. Copy the contents of B6 (or B7, it doesn't matter which) and paste it into B15. The result should indicate a forecasted accounts payable of 189.05.

The next item to consider is the short-term notes payable. Since this is a discretionary source of financing, we will leave it unchanged from 1997. In reality, we might handle this item differently if we had more information. For example, if we knew that the notes would be retired before the end of 1998, we would change our forecast to zero. Alternatively, if the payments on the notes include both principal and interest, our forecast would be the 1997 amount less principal payments that we expect to make in 1998. Since we are leaving it unchanged, the formula in B16 is: +D16.

If we assume that the "other current liabilities" account represents accrued expenses, then it is a spontaneous source of financing. We can, therefore, simply copy the formula from B15 and paste it into B17. The forecasted amount is 163.38.

Long-term debt, in B19, and common stock, in B21, are both discretionary sources of financing. We will leave these balances unchanged from 1997. In B19 the formula is +D19 and in B21 the formula is +D21.

The final item which we must consider is the retained earnings balance. Recall that retained earnings is an accumulation account. That is, the balance in any year is the accumulated amount that has been added in previous years. The amount which will be added to retained earnings is given by:

$$\text{Change in Retained Earnings} = \text{Net Income} - \text{Dividends}$$

where the dividends are those which are paid to both the common and preferred stockholders. The formula for the retained earnings balance requires that we reference forecasted 1998 net income from the income statement and the dividends from statement of cash flows. Note that we are assuming that 1998 dividends will be the same as the 1997 dividends. We can reference these cells in exactly the same way as before, so the formula is: +D22 + Inc Statement:C15 + Cash Flows:B18. The results should show that we are forecasting retained earnings to be $300.04 in 1998.

At this point, you should go back and calculate the subtotals in B18, B20, and B23. Finally, we calculate the total liabilities and owner's equity in B24 with +B20+B23.

Discretionary Financing Needed

Sharp-eyed readers will notice that our *pro-forma* balance sheet does not balance. While this appears to be a serious problem, it actually represents one of the purposes of the *pro-forma* balance sheet. The difference between total assets and total liabilities and owner's equity is referred to as *discretionary financing needed*. In other words, this is the amount of discretionary financing that the firm thinks it will need to raise in the next year. Because of the amount of time and effort required to raise these funds, it is important that the firm be aware of its needs well in advance. The *pro-forma* balance sheet fills this need.

We should add an extra line at the bottom of the pro-forma balance sheet to calculate the discretionary financing needed. In B26 add the formula +B12-B24. This calculation tells us that EPI expects to have $9,880.50 more in discretionary funds than are needed to support its forecasted level of assets. In this case, EPI is forecasting a surplus of discretionary funds. It is also possible for the forecasted level of assets to be greater than the forecasted liabilities and equity. In this case we would say that EPI had a deficit of discretionary funds.

To make this clear, we can have 1-2-3 inform us whether we will have a surplus or deficit of discretionary funds by using an **@IF** function. Realize that if the discretionary financing needed is a positive number, then we have a deficit; otherwise we have a surplus. So the formula in C26 is: @IF(B26>0,"Deficit","Surplus"). Your balance sheet should now resemble that in Exhibit 5-3.

Other Forecasting Methods

The primary advantage of the percent of sales forecasting method is its simplicity. There are many other more sophisticated forecasting techniques that can be implemented in a spreadsheet program. In this section we will look at two of these which are particularly useful.

Linear Trend Extrapolation

Suppose that you were asked to perform the percent of sales forecast for EPI. The first step in that analysis requires a sales forecast. Since EPI is a small company, there is nobody who regularly makes such forecasts and you will have to generate your own. Where do you start?

EXHIBIT 5-3
EPI'S PRO-FORMA BALANCE SHEET FOR 1998

	A	B	C	D	E	F
1	Elvis Products International					
2	Balance Sheet					
3	As of Dec. 31, 1997					
4	*Assets*	*1998**	*1997%*	*1997*	*1996%*	*1996*
5	Cash and Equivalents	52.00	3.15%	52.00	3.92%	57.60
6	Accounts Receivable	444.51	24.35%	402.00	23.91%	351.20
7	Inventory	914.90	50.64%	836.00	48.69%	715.20
8	*Total Current Assets*	*1411.40*	*78.14%*	*1290.00*	*76.53%*	*1124.00*
9	Plant & Equipment	527.00	31.92%	527.00	33.43%	491.00
10	Accumulated Depreciation	186.20	10.07%	166.20	9.95%	146.20
11	*Net Fixed Assets*	*340.80*	*21.86%*	*360.80*	*23.47%*	*344.80*
12	*Total Assets*	**1752.20**	**100.00%**	**1650.80**	**100.00%**	**1468.80**
14	*Liabilities and Owner's Equity*					
15	Accounts Payable	189.05	10.61%	175.20	9.91%	145.60
16	Short-term Notes Payable	225.00	13.63%	225.00	13.62%	200.00
17	Other Current Liabilities	163.38	8.48%	140.00	9.26%	136.00
18	*Total Current Liabilities*	*577.43*	*32.72%*	*540.20*	*32.79%*	*481.60*
19	Long-term Debt	424.61	25.72%	424.61	22.02%	323.43
20	*Total Liabilities*	*1002.04*	*58.45%*	*964.81*	*54.81%*	*805.03*
21	Common Stock	460.00	27.87%	460.00	31.32%	460.00
22	Retained Earnings	300.04	13.69%	225.99	13.87%	203.77
23	*Total Shareholder's Equity*	*760.04*	*41.55%*	*685.99*	*45.19%*	*663.77*
24	*Total Liabilities and Owner's Equity*	**1762.08**	**100.00%**	**1650.80**	**100.00%**	**1468.80**
26	Discretionary Financing Needed	-9.88	Surplus			
27	* Forecasted					

Your first idea might be to see if there has been a clear trend in sales over the past several years and to extrapolate that trend, if it exists, to 1998. To see if there has been a trend, you first gather data on sales for EPI for the past five years. Table 5-1 presents the data that you have gathered.

Add a new worksheet to you EPI workbook, and rename it "Trend Forecast" so that it can be easily identified. Enter the labels and data from Table 5-1 into your worksheet beginning in A1.

TABLE 5-1
EPI SALES FOR 1993 TO 1997

Year	Sales
1993	1,890,532
1994	2,098,490
1995	2,350,308
1996	3,432,000
1997	3,850,000

The easiest way to see if there has been a trend in sales is to create a chart which plots the sales data versus the years. Create this chart using the Chart Wizard by first selecting A1:B6. Make sure to select an XY chart and to enter the title as "EPI Sales for 1993 to 1997." Your worksheet should resemble that in Exhibit 5-4.

EXHIBIT 5-4
EPI TREND FORECAST WORKSHEET

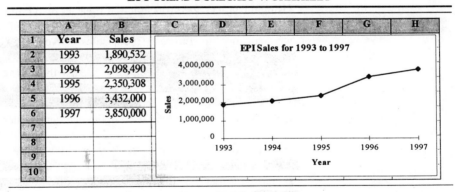

Examining the chart leads to the conclusion that sales have definitely been increasing over the past five years, but not at a constant rate. There are several ways to generate a forecast from this data, even though the sales are not increasing at a constant rate.

One of these methods is to let 1-2-3 determine a linear trend. That is, let 1-2-3 fit a straight line to the data and extrapolate that line to 1998 (or beyond). The line that is generated is in the form of:

$$Y = mX + b$$

which you should recognize as the same equation used in algebra courses to describe a straight line. In this equation, m is the slope and b is the intercept.

To determine the parameters for this line (m and b), 1-2-3 uses regression analysis which we will examine in more detail later. To generate a forecast based on the trend, we need to use the **@REGRESSION** function which is defined as:

@REGRESSION(*X-RANGE, Y-RANGE, ATTRIBUTE, COMPUTE*).

In the **@REGRESSION** function definition, *X-RANGE* is the range of the data (the independent variable) that we want to use to determine the trend in the dependent variable. *Y-RANGE* is the range that we wish to forecast (the dependent variable). In this situation, the *X-RANGE* is the years, and the *Y-RANGE* is the sales data. *ATTRIBUTE* tells 1-2-3 which parameter of the regression equation to calculate (consult the on-line help for more information on acceptable values). *COMPUTE* is an optional variable that tells 1-2-3 whether to use 0 as the intercept or to calculate it (usually this can be safely omitted and 1-2-3 will calculate the intercept).

Using the **@REGRESSION** function is easier than it may at first seem. To generate a forecast for 1998, first enter `1998` into A7. This will provide us with a value that we will use to forecast 1998 sales. Next, in B7 enter the equation as: `@REGRESSION($A$2..$A$6,$B$2..$B$6,1)+@REGRESSION($A$2..$A$6,$B$2..$B$6,101)*A7`. We use the **@REGRESSION** function twice: the first calculates the intercept and the second calculates the slope which is multiplied by the x-value (1998). The result is a sales forecast of $4,300,000 which is the same sales forecast that we used in the percent of sales forecast.

We can extend our forecast to 1999 and 2000 quite easily. To do this, first enter `1999` into A8 and `2000` into A9. Now copy the formula from B7 to B8..B9. You should see that the forecasted sales for 1999 and 2000 are $4,825,244 and $5,350,489 respectively.

A trendline can be added to the chart by first calculating the predicted value for each year from 1993 to 2000 using our regression equation. In C1 enter the label: `Trend`, and then copy the formula from B7 to C2..C9. Now, select the chart and then choose **Chart Ranges** from the menus. In the dialog box click on series B and then click in the **R**ange edit box. Now, on the worksheet, select the C2..C9 range and then click the OK button. Your worksheet should now look like the one in Exhibit 5-5.

Regression Analysis

The term *regression analysis* is a sophisticated-sounding term for a rather simple concept: fitting the best line to a data set. As simple as it sounds, the mathematics behind regression analysis are beyond the scope of this book. However, 1-2-3 can easily handle quite complex regression models with minimal knowledge on your part. We will make use of 1-2-3's regression tools without delving too deeply into the underlying mathematics.

EXHIBIT 5-5
EPI TREND FORECAST WORKSHEET

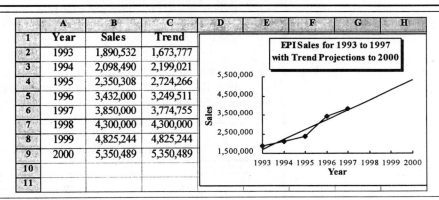

	A	B	C	D	E	F	G	H
1	Year	Sales	Trend					
2	1993	1,890,532	1,673,777					
3	1994	2,098,490	2,199,021					
4	1995	2,350,308	2,724,266					
5	1996	3,432,000	3,249,511					
6	1997	3,850,000	3,774,755					
7	1998	4,300,000	4,300,000					
8	1999	4,825,244	4,825,244					
9	2000	5,350,489	5,350,489					
10								
11								

EPI Sales for 1993 to 1997 with Trend Projections to 2000

As we've noted, regression analysis is a technique for fitting the best line to a data set; a very powerful tool for determining the relationship between variables and for forecasting. You could, for example, simply plot the data and draw in what appears to be the line which best fits the data, but there is no guarantee that the line you choose is actually the best line. In regression analysis, the best line is defined as the one which minimizes the sum of the squared errors. The errors are the difference between the actual data point and that predicted by the model.

In our previous example, we used regression analysis to forecast EPI's level of sales for 1998 to 2000. Aside from forecasting, the second major use of regression analysis is to understand the relationship between variables. In this section we will use 1-2-3's regression tool to perform a regression analysis.[4]

---

4. The regression tool is not a built-in function in the same sense as **@REGRESSION**. Instead, it is a part of the data analysis tools included with 1-2-3. This tool is easier to use, and provides more information than **@REGRESSION**, though it performs the same set of calculations.

Consider the following example in which we will make use of regression analysis to gain an understanding of the relationship between changes in the stock market (proxied by the S&P 500 Index) and changes in the price of an individual stock. The line we will fit is known as the *characteristic line,* and the slope (beta) plays an important part in the models discussed in Chapter 8.

Suppose that you are considering an investment in Microsoft (MSFT). Before purchasing the stock, you are interested in knowing how it responds to changes in the overall market. In other words, if the market is up will MSFT, on average, be up or down? To answer this question you decide to plot the monthly returns for MSFT over the past five years against those of the market, as measured by the Standard & Poor's 500 index (S&P 500).

Because of the size of this data set, we have included the data in the file: SP_vs_MS.WK4. The data are percentage returns calculated from monthly closing prices (not including dividends).

FIGURE 5-1
MONTHLY RETURNS FOR MSFT VS. S&P 500

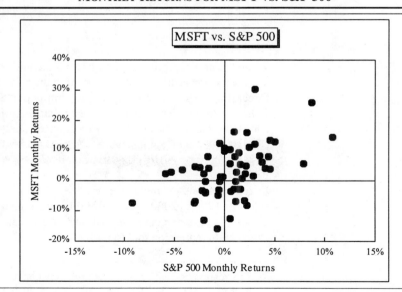

Open the SP_vs_MS.WK4 file. To create the chart, first select B2..C61 and then choose **T**ools **C**hart and change the type to an XY plot. Once the chart is created, you can make it look like Figure 5-1 by entering the titles and formatting the axis numbers. Upon inspection, you may find that the chart is difficult to interpret. You can probably detect a vaguely positive relationship between the two data sets. That is, it appears that when the market is up, MSFT is usually up as well. One way to clarify this relationship is to use regression analysis.

Before running the analysis, we need to determine the theoretical relationship between the variables of interest. In this case, it seems more likely that changes in the overall market cause changes in MSFT, rather than the other way around. Therefore, we will make the returns on the S&P 500 the independent (x) variable, and the returns on MSFT common will be the dependent (y) variable. Our hypothesized equation is:

$$MSFT\% = \alpha + \beta(S\&P500\%) + e$$

where α is the intercept, β is the slope of the line, and e is the random error term.

To run the regression analysis, select **R**ange **A**nalyze **R**egression from the main menus. This will bring up the Regression dialog box, which is pictured (with the inputs for this problem) in Figure 5-2.

There are only a few options on this dialog box. First, we need to tell 1-2-3 where the independent (X) variable data are located. In the "**X** Range" edit box enter B2..B61, or merely select this range with the mouse. In the "**Y** Range" edit box enter C2..C61. (We have not included the labels in these ranges because 1-2-3 expects only numerical data.) Next, we need to tell 1-2-3 where on the worksheet to place the output. We chose E21 because it is below the chart, but you are free to choose any convenient location. The last option (Y-intercept) tells 1-2-3 whether to calculate the intercept or to force it to zero. In the majority of cases you will want to calculate the intercept.

FIGURE 5-2
1-2-3'S REGRESSION DIALOG BOX

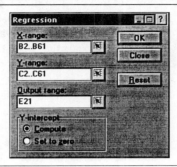

Make sure that you have set up the dialog box exactly as pictured in Figure 5-2 and then press the OK button. After a few seconds of calculating, the data will appear as they do in Exhibit 5-6. (Note that we have reformatted the numbers.) The output may appear to be complex if you are not familiar with regression analysis. However, we are only concerned with the output which gives the parameters of the regression line. The rest of the output is primarily concerned with the success of the equation for forecasting purposes, and the amount of confidence we have in the values of the parameters.[5]

The parameters of interest are in H22 and G28. The intercept (α) is 0.0245, listed as the constant, and the slope of the line (β) is 1.2529, listed as the x coefficient. Therefore, the line of best fit is given by the equation:

$$\text{MSFT\%} = 0.0245 + 1.2529(\text{SP500\%})$$

---

5. We are not trying to minimize the importance of this other output. On the contrary, it would be foolish to attempt to use regression methods for any important purpose without understanding the model completely. We are merely trying to illustrate how 1-2-3 can be used for this type of analysis in as simple a way as possible.

EXHIBIT 5-6
REGRESSION OUTPUT

	E	F	G	H
21		Regression Output:		
22	Constant			0.0245
23	Std Err of Y Est			0.0773
24	R Squared			0.2301
25	No. of Observations			60
26	Degrees of Freedom			58
27				
28	X Coefficient(s)		1.2529	
29	Std Err of Coef.		0.3009	

What this equation tells us is that, on average, if the market is up 1%, Microsoft common stock will be up about 1.25%. Similarly, if the market is down 1%, MSFT will be down about 1.25%. In other words, MSFT is about 1.25 times as volatile as the market.[6]

There is no reason to think that the market is the sole factor which explains changes in Microsoft's common stock. There are likely to be many others. Regression analysis is not restricted to a single explanatory (i.e., independent) variable. 1-2-3 can handle regression models with as many explanatory variables as you are likely to want to use. All that is required is that you enter multiple ranges for the "**X** Range."

One final point is that we can display this regression line on our chart (Figure 5-3) in the same way we did for the trend line. To do this, we first need to add the predicted values from the regression equation. In D1 enter the label: Regression, and in D2 enter the equation: `+$H$22+$G$28*B2`. This equation uses the intercept and slope from the regression and the first S&P 500 return to generate the predicted return for Microsoft. Copy D2 down over the range D3..D61. Now select the chart and choose **C**hart **R**anges. After selecting series C in the dialog box, enter D2..D61 in the **R**anges edit box. Finally, make sure that the **M**ixed type

---

6. We should note, for the statistically inclined, that we do not have a large degree of confidence in this result. The R^2 indicates that the market only explains about 23% of the variability of Microsoft returns.

for this series is set to Line and then click the OK button. Your chart will resemble that in Figure 5-3.

FIGURE 5-3
MSFT VS. S&P 500 WITH REGRESSION LINE

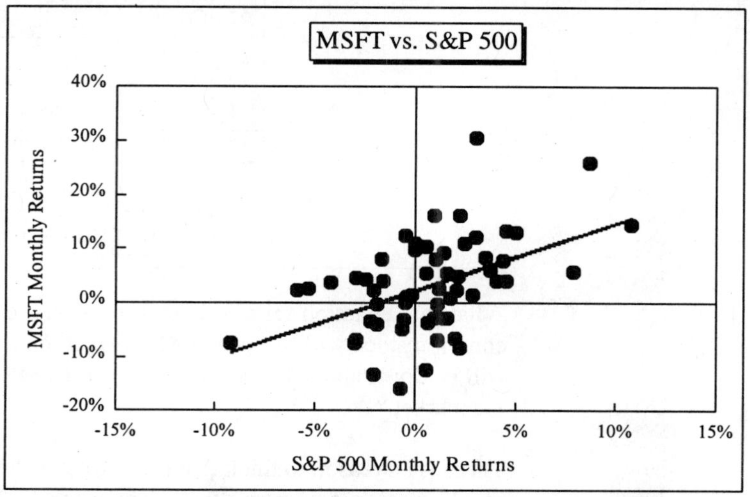

Summary

In this chapter we have examined three methods of forecasting financial statements and variables. We used the percent of sales technique to forecast the firm's income statement and balance sheet based upon an estimated level of sales. We used a time-trend technique to forecast sales as an input to the percent of sales method. Finally, we looked at regression analysis to help understand how the movements of an individual stock relate to overall market movements.

We have barely scratched the surface of forecasting methodologies. However, we hope that this chapter has stimulated an interest in this important subject. If so, be assured that 1-2-3, either alone or through an add-in program, can be made to handle nearly all of your forecasting problems.

TABLE 5-2
FUNCTIONS INTRODUCED IN THIS CHAPTER

Purpose	Function	Page
Forecasts future outcomes based on a time-trend	@REGRESSION(*X-RANGE, Y-RANGE, ATTRIBUTE, COMPUTE*)	100

CHAPTER 6

Break-even and Leverage Analysis

After studying this chapter, you should be able to:

1. *Differentiate between fixed and variable costs.*

2. *Calculate the operating and cash break-even points, and find the number of units that need to be sold to reach a target level of EBIT.*

3. *Define the terms "business risk" and "financial risk," and describe how each of these risks originate.*

4. *Use 1-2-3 to calculate the DOL ,DFL, and DCL and explain the significance of each of these risk measures.*

5. *Explain how the DOL, DFL, and DCL change as the firm's level of sales changes.*

In this chapter we will consider the decisions that managers make regarding the cost structure of the firm. These decisions will, in turn, impact the decisions they make regarding methods of financing the firm's assets and pricing the firm's products.

In general, we will assume that there are two kinds of costs that a firm faces:

1. *Variable costs* are those costs which are expected to change at the same rate as the firm's level of sales. Variable costs are constant per unit, so as more units are sold the total variable cost will rise.

Examples of variable costs include sales commissions, costs of raw materials, hourly wages, etc.

2. *Fixed costs* are those costs that are constant, regardless of the quantity produced, over some relevant range of production. Total fixed cost per unit will decline as the number of units increases. Examples of fixed costs include rent, salaries, depreciation, etc.

Figure 6-1 illustrates these costs.

FIGURE 6-1
TOTAL FIXED AND TOTAL VARIABLE COSTS

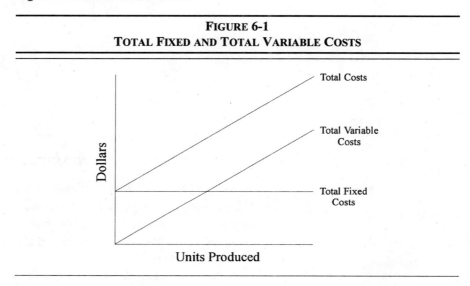

Break-even Points

We can define the *break-even point* as the level of sales (either units or dollars) which causes profits (however measured) to be equal to zero. Most commonly, we define the break-even point as the unit sales required for earnings before interest and taxes (EBIT) to be equal to zero. This point is often referred to as the *operating break-even point*.

Define Q as the quantity sold, P is the price per unit, V is the variable cost per unit, and F as total fixed costs. With these definitions, we can say:

$$Q(P-V) - F = \text{EBIT} \qquad \text{(6-1)}$$

If we set EBIT in equation (6-1) to zero, we can solve for the break-even quantity (Q^*):

$$Q^* = \frac{F}{P-V} \qquad \text{(6-2)}$$

Assume, for example, that a firm is selling widgets for $30 per unit, while variable costs are $20 per unit and fixed costs total $100,000. In this situation, the firm must sell 10,000 units to break-even:

$$Q^* = \frac{100,000}{30-20} = 10,000 \text{ units}.$$

The quantity $P - V$ is often referred to as the *contribution margin* (CM) per unit. This is because this is the amount that each unit sold contributes to coverage of the firm's fixed costs. Using equation (6-1) you can verify that the firm will break-even if it sells 10,000 widgets:

$$10,000(30-20) - 100,000 = 0.$$

We can now calculate the firm's break-even point in dollars by simply multiplying Q^* by the price per unit:

$$\$BE = P \times Q^* \qquad \text{(6-3)}$$

In this example, the result shows that the firm must sell $300,000 worth of widgets to break-even.

Note that we can substitute equation (6-2) into (6-3):

$$\$BE = P \times \frac{F}{(P-V)} = \frac{F}{(P-V)/P} = \frac{F}{CM\%}. \qquad \text{(6-4)}$$

So, if we know the contribution margin as a percentage of the selling price (*CM*%), we can easily calculate the break-even point in dollars. In the previous example, *CM*% is 33.33%, so the break-even point in dollars must be:

$$\$BE = \frac{100,000}{0.3333} = \$300,000$$

which confirms our earlier result.

Calculating Break-even Points in 1-2-3

We can, of course, calculate break-even points in 1-2-3. Consider the income statement for Spuds and Suds, a very popular sports bar which serves only one product: a plate of gourmet french fries and a pitcher of imported beer for $16 per serving. The income statement is presented in Exhibit 6-1.

EXHIBIT 6-1
INCOME STATEMENT FOR SPUDS AND SUDS

	A	B
1	Spuds and Suds	
2	Income Statement	
3	For the Year Ended Dec. 31, 1997	
4		1997
5	Sales	$ 2,500,000
6	Less: Variable Costs (60%)	1,500,000
7	Less: Fixed Costs	400,000
8	*Earnings Before Interest and Taxes*	*600,000*
9	Less: Interest Expense	100,000
10	*Earnings Before Taxes*	*500,000*
11	Taxes (@ 40%)	200,000
12	*Net Income*	*300,000*
13		
14	Less: Preferred Dividends	100,000
15	*Net Income Available to Common*	*200,000*
16	Common Shares Outstanding	1,000,000
17	*Earnings per Share*	*$ 0.20*
18		
19	Price per Unit	$ 16.00
20	Unit Sales	156,250

Before calculating the break-even point, enter the labels into a new worksheet as shown in the Exhibit. Since we will be expanding this example, it is important that you enter formulas where they are appropriate.

We will first calculate the dollar amount of sales, in B5, by multiplying the per unit price by the number of units sold. The formula is: +B19*B20, though the result will be zero until we enter the price and unit sales information. Variable costs are always 60% of sales, so the formula in B6 is: `+0.60*B5`. Both Fixed Costs, in B7, and Interest Expense, in B9, are constants so they are simply entered directly. The simple subtraction and multiplication required to complete the income statement through B12 should be obvious.

In B14..B17 we have added information that is not immediately useful, but it will be when we discuss operating and financial leverage. In cell B14 we have added preferred dividends which will be subtracted from net income. The result, in B15, is net income available to the common shareholders. Preferred dividends are simply input into B14, and the formula in B15 is: `+B12-B14`. In B16, enter the number of common shares outstanding: `1,000,000`. Earnings per share is then calculated as: `+B15/B16` in cell B17. Finally, enter the price per unit and unit sales information into B19 and B20. Make sure that your numbers match those in Exhibit 6-1.

We can now calculate the break-even points. In cell A22 enter the label: `Break-even Point (Units)`. Next, copy this label to A23, and change the word "Units" to $. In B22, we can calculate the break-even point in units using equation (6-2). The formula is: `+B7/(B19-B6/B20)`. Notice that we have to calculate the variable cost per unit by dividing total variable costs (B6) by the number of units sold (B20). You can see that Spuds and Suds must sell 62,500 units in order to break-even and that they are well above this level.

Other Break-even Points

Recall that we found the break-even point by setting EBIT in equation (6-1) equal to zero. However, there is no reason that we can't set EBIT equal to any amount that we might desire. For example, if we define $EBIT_{Target}$ as the target level of EBIT, we find that we can earn the target EBIT by selling:

$$Q^*_{Target} = \frac{F + EBIT_{Target}}{P - V}.$$

(6-5)

Consider that Spuds and Suds might want to know the number of units that they need to sell in order to have EBIT equal $800,000. Mathematically, we can see that:

$$Q^*_{800,000} = \frac{400,000 + 800,000}{16 - 9.60} = 187,500 \text{ units}$$

need to be sold to reach this target. You can verify that this number is correct by typing 187,500 into B20, and checking the value in B8. To return the worksheet to its original values, enter 156,250 into B20.

Recall from Chapter 2 that we defined cash flow as net income plus non-cash expenses. We do this because the presence of non-cash expenses (principally depreciation) distort the accounting numbers. We can make a similar adjustment to our break-even calculations by setting $EBIT_{Target}$ equal to the negative of the depreciation expense. This results in a type of break-even that we refer to as the *cash break-even point*:

$$Q^*_{Cash} = \frac{F - \text{Depreciation}}{P - V}. \tag{6-6}$$

Note that the cash break-even point will always be lower than the operating break-even point because we don't have to cover the depreciation expense.

Leverage Analysis

In Chapter 4 (page 70) we defined leverage as a multiplication of changes in sales resulting in even larger changes in profitability measures. Firms which use large amounts of operating leverage will find that their earnings before interest and taxes will be more variable than those who do not. We would say that such a firm has high *business risk*. Business risk is one of the major risks faced by a firm, and can be defined as the variability of EBIT. The more variable a firm's revenues, relative to its costs, the more variable its EBIT will be. Also, the likelihood that the firm won't be able to pay its expenses will be higher.

Business risk results from the environment in which the firm operates. Such factors as the competitive position of the firm in its industry, the state of its labor relations, and the state of the economy all affect the amount of business risk a firm faces. In addition, as we will see, the degree to which the firm's costs are fixed (as opposed to variable) will affect the amount of business risk. To a large degree, these components of business risk are beyond the control of the firm's managers.

In contrast, the amount of *financial risk* is determined directly by management. Financial risk refers to the probability that the firm will be unable to meet its fixed financing obligations (which includes both interest and preferred dividends). Obviously, all other things being equal, the more debt a firm uses to finance its assets, the higher its interest cost will be. Higher interest costs lead directly to a higher probability that the firm won't be able to pay. Since the amount of debt is determined by managerial choice, the financial risk that a firm faces is also determined by management.

We will examine these concepts in more detail by continuing with our Spuds and Suds example.

The Degree of Operating Leverage

Earlier we mentioned that a firm's business risk can be measured by the variability of its earnings before interest and taxes. Obviously, if a firm's costs are all variable, then any percentage change in sales will be reflected by exactly the same percentage change in EBIT. However, if a firm has some fixed expenses, EBIT will change by more than sales. We refer to this concept as *operating leverage*.

We can measure operating leverage by comparing the percentage change in EBIT to a given percentage change in sales. This measure is called the *degree of operating leverage* (DOL):

$$DOL = \frac{\%\Delta \text{ in EBIT}}{\%\Delta \text{ in Sales}} \cdot \tag{6-7}$$

So, if a 10% change in sales results in a 20% change in EBIT, we would say that the degree of operating leverage is 2. As we will see, this is a symmetrical concept. As long as sales are increasing, a high DOL is desirable. However, if sales begin to decline, a high DOL will result in EBIT declining at an even faster pace than sales.

To make this concept more concrete, let's extend the Spuds and Suds example. Assume that management believes that unit sales will increase by 10% in 1998. Furthermore, they expect that variable costs will remain at 60% of sales and fixed costs will stay at $400,000. Copy B4..B23 to C4..C23, and enter: +B20*1.1 into C20. (Note that you have just created a percent of sales income statement forecast for 1998, just as we did in Chapter 5.) Change the label in C4 to 1998* and you have completed the changes.

Before continuing, notice that the operating break-even point (C22..C23) has not changed. This will always be the case if fixed costs are constant and variable costs are a constant percentage of sales. The break-even point is always driven by the level of fixed costs.

Since we wish to calculate the DOL for 1997, we first need to calculate the percentage changes in EBIT and Sales. In A25 enter the label: `% Change in Sales from Prior Year`, and in A26 enter: `% Change in EBIT from Prior Year`. To calculate the percentage changes enter: `+C5/B5 − 1` in cell C25 and then: `+C8/B8 − 1` in C26. You should see that sales increased by 10% while EBIT increased by 16.67%. According to equation (6-7), the DOL for Spuds and Suds in 1997 is:

$$DOL = \frac{16.67\%}{10.00\%} = 1.667 \,.$$

So, any change in sales will be multiplied by 1.667 times in EBIT. To see this, recall that the formula in C20 increased the 1997 unit sales by 10%. Temporarily, change this formula to: `+B20*1.20`. You should see that if sales increase by 20%, EBIT will increase by 33.33%. Recalculating the DOL, we see that it is unchanged:

$$DOL = \frac{33.33\%}{20.00\%} = 1.667 \,.$$

Furthermore, if we change the formula in C20 to `+B20*0.90` so that sales decline by 10%, we find that EBIT declines by 16.67%. In this case the DOL is:

$$DOL = \frac{-16.67\%}{-10.00\%} = 1.667 \,.$$

So leverage is indeed a double-edged sword. You can see that a high DOL would be desirable as long as sales are increasing, but very undesirable when sales are decreasing. Unfortunately, most businesses don't have the luxury of instantaneously altering their DOL.

Calculating the DOL with equation (6-7) is actually more cumbersome than is required. With this equation, we need to use two income statements. However, a more direct method of calculating the DOL is to use the following equation:

$$DOL = \frac{Q(P-V)}{Q(P-V)-F} = \frac{\text{Sales} - \text{Variable Costs}}{\text{EBIT}} \,. \tag{6-8}$$

For Spuds and Suds in 1997, we can calculate the DOL using equation (6-8):

$$DOL = \frac{2{,}500{,}000 - 1{,}500{,}000}{600{,}000} = 1.667$$

which is exactly as we found with equation (6-7).

Continuing with our example, enter the label: Degree of Operating Leverage in A29. In B29 we will calculate the DOL for 1997 with the formula: +(B5-B6)/B8. You should get the same result as before. If you copy the formula from B29 to C29, you will find that in 1998 the DOL will decline to 1.57. We will examine this decline in the DOL later. Your worksheet should now appear similar to the one in Exhibit 6-2.

The Degree of Financial Leverage

Financial leverage is similar to operating leverage, but the fixed costs that we are interested in are the fixed financing costs. These are the interest expense and preferred dividends.[1] We can measure financial leverage by relating percentage changes in earnings per share (EPS) to percentage changes in EBIT. This measure is referred to as the *degree of financial leverage* (DFL):

$$DFL = \frac{\%\Delta \text{ in EPS}}{\%\Delta \text{ in EBIT}}. \qquad\qquad (6\text{-}9)$$

For Spuds and Suds we have already calculated the percentage change in EBIT, so all that remains is to calculate the percentage change in EPS. In A27 add the label: % Change in EPS from Prior Year, and in C27 add the formula: +C17/ B17-1. Note that EPS is expected to increase by 30% in 1998 compared to only 16.67% for EBIT. Using equation (6-9) we find that the degree of financial leverage employed by Spuds and Suds in 1997 is:

$$DFL = \frac{30.00\%}{16.67\%} = 1.80.$$

Therefore, any change in EBIT will be multiplied by 1.80 times in earnings per share. Like operating leverage, financial leverage works both ways. When EBIT is increasing, EPS will increase even more. And, when EBIT decreases EPS will decline by a larger percentage.

---

1. Preferred stock, as we'll see in Chapter 8, is a hybrid security; part debt and part equity. How it is treated is determined by one's goals. When discussing financial leverage we treat preferred stock as if it were a debt security.

EXHIBIT 6-2
SPUDS AND SUDS BREAK-EVEN AND LEVERAGE WORKSHEET

	A	B	C
1	Spuds and Suds		
2	Income Statement		
3	For the Year Ended Dec. 31, 1997		
4		1997	1998*
5	Sales	$2,500,000	$2,750,000
6	Less: Variable Costs (60%)	1,500,000	1,650,000
7	Less: Fixed Costs	400,000	400,000
8	Earnings Before Interest and Taxes	600,000	700,000
9	Less: Interest Expense	100,000	100,000
10	Earnings Before Taxes	500,000	600,000
11	Taxes (@ 40%)	200,000	240,000
12	Net Income	300,000	360,000
13			
14	Less: Preferred Dividends	100,000	100,000
15	Net Income Available to Common	200,000	260,000
16	Common Shares Outstanding	1,000,000	1,000,000
17	Earnings per Share	$ 0.20	$ 0.26
18			
19	Price per Unit	$ 16.00	$ 16.00
20	Unit Sales	156,250	171,875
21			
22	Operating Break-even Point (Units)	62,500	62,500
23	Operating Break-even Point ($)	1,000,000	1,000,000
24			
25	% Change in Sales from Prior Year		10.00%
26	% Change in EBIT from Prior Year		16.67%
27	% Change in EPS from Prior Year		30.00%
28			
29	Degree of Operating Leverage	1.67	1.57

As with the DOL, there is a more direct method of calculating the degree of financial leverage:

$$DFL = \frac{EBIT}{EBT - \dfrac{PD}{(1-t)}} . \qquad (6\text{-}10)$$

In equation (6-10), PD is the preferred dividends paid by the firm, and t is the tax rate paid by the firm. The second term in the denominator, $PD/(1-t)$, requires some explanation. Since preferred dividends are paid out of after-tax dollars, we must determine how many *pre-tax* dollars are required to meet this expense. In this case, Spuds and Suds pays taxes at a rate of 40%, so they require $166,666.67 in pre-tax dollars in order to pay $100,000 in preferred dividends:

$$\frac{100,000}{(1-0.40)} = 166,666.67 .$$

We can use equation (6-10) in the worksheet to calculate the DFL for Spuds and Suds. In cell A30, enter the label: Degree of Financial Leverage. In B30, enter: +B8/(B10-B14/(1-0.4)). You should find that the DFL is 1.80, which is the same as we found by using equation (6-9). Copying this formula to C30 reveals that in 1998 we expect the DFL to decline to 1.62.

The Degree of Combined Leverage

Most firms make use of both operating and financial leverage. Since they are using two kinds of leverage, it is useful to understand the combined effect. We can measure the total leverage employed by the firm by comparing the percentage change in sales to the percentage change in earnings per share. This measure is called the *degree of combined leverage* (DCL):[2]

$$DCL = \frac{\%\Delta \text{ in EPS}}{\%\Delta \text{ in Sales}} . \tag{6-11}$$

Since we have already calculated the relevant percentage changes, it is a simple matter to determine that the DCL for Spuds and Suds in 1997 was:

$$DCL = \frac{30.00\%}{10.00\%} = 3.00 .$$

Therefore, any change in sales will be multiplied three-fold in EPS. Recall that we earlier said that the DCL was a combination of operating and financial leverage. You can see this if we rewrite equation (6-11) as follows:

---

2. Some textbooks refer to this measure as the degree of total leverage.

$$DCL = \frac{\%\Delta \text{ in EBIT}}{\%\Delta \text{ in Sales}} \times \frac{\%\Delta \text{ in EPS}}{\%\Delta \text{ in EBIT}} = \frac{\%\Delta \text{ in EPS}}{\%\Delta \text{ in Sales}}.$$

Therefore, the combined effect of using both operating and financial leverage is multiplicative. Managers should take note of this and use caution in increasing one type of leverage while ignoring the other. They may end up with more total leverage than anticipated. As we have just seen, the DCL is the product of DOL and DFL, so we can rewrite equation (6-11) as:

$$DCL = DOL \times DFL. \qquad \text{(6-12)}$$

To calculate the DCL for Spuds and Suds in your worksheet, first enter the label: Degree of Combined Leverage into A31. In B31, enter the formula: +B29*B30, and copy this to C31 to find the expected DCL for 1998. At this point, your worksheet should look like the one in Exhibit 6-3.

Extending the Example

Comparing the three leverage measures for 1997 and 1998 shows that in all cases the firm will be using less leverage in 1998. Recall that the only change in 1998 was that sales were increased by 10% over their 1997 level. The reason for the decline in leverage is that fixed costs have become a smaller portion of the total costs of the firm. This will always be the case: *As sales increase above the break-even point, leverage will decline regardless of the measure which is used.*

We can see this by extending our Spuds and Suds example. Suppose that management is forecasting that sales will increase by 10% each year for the foreseeable future. Furthermore, because of contractual agreements, the firm's fixed costs will remain constant through at least 2001. In order to see the changes in the leverage measures under these conditions, copy C4..C31 and paste into D4..F31. This will create pro-forma income statements for three additional years. Change the labels in D4..F4 to 1999*, 2000* and 2001*.

You should see that the DOL, DFL and DCL are all decreasing as sales increase. This is easier to see if we create a chart. As a first step, enter the formula: +B4 into cell B28, and copy it to C28..F28. This will provide the X-axis labels for our chart. Now select A28..F31 and create a line chart of the data. You should end up with a chart that resembles the one in Figure 6-2.

EXHIBIT 6-3
SPUDS AND SUDS WORKSHEET WITH THREE MEASURES OF LEVERAGE

	A	B	C
1	Spuds and Suds		
2	Income Statement		
3	For the Year Ended Dec. 31, 1997		
4		1997	1998*
5	Sales	$2,500,000	$2,750,000
6	Less: Variable Costs (60%)	1,500,000	1,650,000
7	Less: Fixed Costs	400,000	400,000
8	*Earnings Before Interest and Taxes*	600,000	700,000
9	Less: Interest Expense	100,000	100,000
10	*Earnings Before Taxes*	500,000	600,000
11	Taxes (@ 40%)	200,000	240,000
12	*Net Income*	300,000	360,000
13			
14	Less: Preferred Dividends	100,000	100,000
15	*Net Income Available to Common*	200,000	260,000
16	Common Shares Outstanding	1,000,000	1,000,000
17	*Earnings per Share*	$ 0.20	$ 0.26
18			
19	Price per Unit	$ 16.00	$ 16.00
20	Unit Sales	156,250	171,875
21			
22	Operating Break-even Point (Units)	62,500	62,500
23	Operating Break-even Point ($)	1,000,000	1,000,000
24			
25	% Change in Sales from Prior Year		10.00%
26	% Change in EBIT from Prior Year		16.67%
27	% Change in EPS from Prior Year		30.00%
28			
29	Degree of Operating Leverage	1.67	1.57
30	Degree of Financial Leverage	1.80	1.62
31	Degree of Combined Leverage	3.00	2.54

Obviously, as we stated earlier, the amount of leverage declines as the sales level increases. One caveat to this is that in the real world, fixed costs are not necessarily the same year after year. Furthermore, variable costs do not always maintain an exact percentage of sales. For these reasons, leverage may not decline as smoothly as depicted in our example. However, the principle is sound and should be understood by all managers.

FIGURE 6-2
CHART OF VARIOUS LEVERAGE MEASURES AS SALES INCREASE

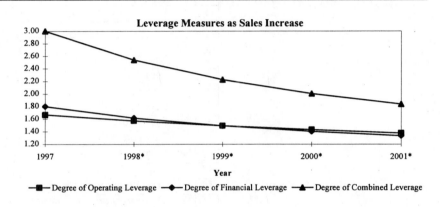

Summary

We started this chapter by discussing the firm's operating break-even point. The break-even point is determined by a product's price, and the amount of fixed and variable costs. The amount of fixed costs also played an important role in the determination of the amount of leverage a firm employs. We studied three measures of leverage:

1. The *degree of operating leverage* (DOL) measures the degree to which the presence of fixed costs multiplies changes in sales into even larger changes in EBIT.

2. The *degree of financial leverage* (DFL) measures the change in EPS relative to a change in EBIT. Financial leverage is a direct result of managerial decisions about how the firm should be financed.

3. The *degree of combined leverage* (DCL) provides a measure of the total leverage used by the firm. This is the product of the DOL and DFL.

TABLE 6-1
SUMMARY OF EQUATIONS

Name	Equation
Operating Break-even Level in Units	$Q^* = \dfrac{F}{P - V}$
Operating Break-even Level in Dollars	$\$BE = P \times Q^*$ or $\$BE = \dfrac{F}{CM\%}$
Cash Break-even Point in Units	$Q^*_{\text{Cash}} = \dfrac{F - \text{Depreciation}}{P - V}$
Degree of Operating Leverage (DOL)	$\text{DOL} = \dfrac{\%\Delta \text{ in EBIT}}{\%\Delta \text{ in Sales}}$ or $\text{DOL} = \dfrac{Q(P - V)}{Q(P - V) - F}$
Degree of Financial Leverage (DFL)	$\text{DFL} = \dfrac{\%\Delta \text{ in EPS}}{\%\Delta \text{ in EBIT}}$ or $\text{DFL} = \dfrac{\text{EBIT}}{\text{EBT} - \dfrac{\text{PD}}{(1 - t)}}$
Degree of Combined Leverage (DCL)	$\text{DCL} = \dfrac{\%\Delta \text{ in EPS}}{\%\Delta \text{ in Sales}}$ or $\text{DCL} = \text{DOL} \times \text{DFL}$

The Time Value of Money

After studying this chapter, you should be able to:

1. *Explain the concept of the time value of money.*

2. *Calculate the present value and future value of a stream of cash flows using 1-2-3.*

3. *Explain the types of cash flows encountered in financial analysis, and adjust for each type in making time value calculations in 1-2-3.*

4. *Differentiate between the alternative compounding periods, and use 1-2-3 to compare present and future values under different compounding schemes.*

"A bird in the hand is worth more than two in the bush." That old aphorism, when translated into the language of finance, becomes "A dollar today is worth more than a dollar tomorrow." Intuitively, it probably makes sense, but why? Stated very simply, you can take that dollar today and invest it with the expectation of having more than a dollar tomorrow.

Because money can be invested to grow to a larger amount, we say that money has a "time value." This concept of a time value of money underlies much of the theory of financial decision making.

Future Value

Imagine that you have $1,000 available to invest. If you earn interest at the rate of 10% per year, then you will have $1,100 at the end of one year. The mathematics behind this example is quite simple:

$$1,000 + 1,000(0.10) = 1,100$$

In other words, after one year you will have your original $1,000 (the *principal* amount) plus the interest earned. Since you won't have the $1,100 until one year in the future, we refer to this amount as the *future value*. The amount that you have today, $1,000, is referred to as the *present value*. If, at the end of the year, you choose to make the same investment again, then at the end of the second year you will have:

$$1,000 + 1,000(0.10) + 100(0.10) + 1,000(0.10) = 1,210$$

The $1,210 at the end of the second year can be broken down into its components: the original principal, the first year's interest, the interest earned in the second year on the first year's interest, and the second year's interest. Note that we could restate the second year calculation to be:

$$1,100 + 1,100(0.10) = 1,210$$

or, by factoring out the 1,100 we get:

$$1,100(1 + 0.10) = 1,210$$

Notice that in the second year the interest is earned on both the original principal and the interest earned during the first year. The idea of earning interest on previously earned interest is known as *compounding*. This is why the total interest earned in the second year is $110 versus only $100 the first year.

Returning to our original one-year example, we can generalize the formula for any one-year investment, as follows:

$$FV = PV + PV(i)$$

Where *FV* is the future value, *PV* is the present value, and *i* is the one-year interest rate (compounding rate). The above equation is not in its simplest form. We can factor *PV* from both terms on the right-hand side, simplifying the future value equation to:

$$FV = PV(1 + i)$$

Recall that in our two-year example, we earned interest on both the principal and interest from the first year. In other words, the first year *FV* became the second year *PV*. Symbolically, the second year *FV* is:

$$FV_2 = FV_1(1 + i)$$

Substituting *PV* for *FV₁* and simplifying, we have:

$$FV_2 = PV(1 + i)(1 + i) = PV(1 + i)^2$$

We can actually further generalize our future value equation. Realize that the exponent on the right-hand side is the same as the subscript on the left-hand side in the future value equation. When we were solving for the future value at the end of the first year, the exponent was 1. When we were solving for the future value at the end of the second year, the exponent was 2. In general, the exponent will be equal to the number of the year for which we wish to find the future value.

$$FV_N = PV(1 + i)^N \qquad \text{(7-1)}$$

Equation (7-1) is the basis for all of the time value equations which we will look at in the sections ahead. Using this version of the equation you can see that investing $1,000 for two years at 10% per year will leave you with $1,210 at the end of two years. In other words:

$$FV_2 = 1,000(1.10)^2 = 1,210$$

Using 1-2-3 to Find Future Values

It is easy enough to calculate future values with a hand calculator, especially a financial calculator. But, as we will see in the sections and chapters ahead, it is often necessary to use future values in worksheets. 1-2-3 makes these calculations easy with the use of the built-in function @FVAL.

@FVAL(*PAYMENTS*, *INTEREST*, *TERM*, *TYPE*, *PRESENT-VALUE*)

There are five parameters to the @FVAL function. *PAYMENTS* is an annual payment amount, *INTEREST* is the interest rate per period (year, month, day, etc.), *TERM* is the total number of periods. *PRESENT-VALUE* and *TYPE* are optional values. *PRESENT-VALUE* is the amount of money that we are investing today, and *TYPE* tells 1-2-3 whether the cash flow occurs at the beginning (1) or end (0, the default if *TYPE* is omitted) of a period. For problems of the type that we are currently solving, we will set both *PAYMENTS* and *TYPE* to 0.

Let's set up a simple worksheet to calculate the future value of a single sum. Starting with a blank worksheet, enter the labels and numbers as shown in Exhibit 7-1.

EXHIBIT 7-1
FUTURE VALUE OF A SINGLE CASH FLOW

	A	B
1	Future Value Calculations	
2	Present Value	1000.00
3	Years	1
4	Rate	10%
5	Future Value	

We want to use the @FVAL function to calculate the future value of $1,000 for one-year at 10% per year. In B5 enter the formula: @FVAL(0,B4,B3,0,B2). The result, $1,100, is exactly the same as we found earlier.

You can now experiment with different values for the parameters. Try replacing the 1 in B3 with a 2. 1-2-3 immediately updates the result in B5 with $1,210, just as we found in the second part of our example. To see just how powerful compounding can be, insert 30 into B3. The result, $17,449.40, indicates that each $1,000 invested at 10% per year will grow to $17,449.40 after just 30 years. If we double the investment, to $2,000, then we should double the future value. Try it; you should get a result of $34,898.80, exactly twice what we got with a $1,000 investment. In general, any money invested for 30 years at 10% per year will grow to 17.449 times its initial value. To see even more powerful examples of compounding, try changing the interest rate.

Present Value

Our future value equation can be solved for any of its variables. We may wish to turn our example problem around to solve for the present value. Suppose that our problem is restated as, "What initial investment is required so that you will accumulate $1,210 after two years if you earn an interest rate of 10% per year?" In this case, we want to solve for the present value — we already know the future value.

Mathematically, all we need to do is to solve the future value equation for the present value:

$$PV = \frac{FV_N}{(1 + i)^N} \qquad (7\text{-}2)$$

Of course, we already know that the answer must be $1,000:

$$PV = \frac{1,210}{(1.10)^2} = 1,000 \, .$$

In 1-2-3, we can solve problems of this type by using the built-in **@PVAL** function:

@PVAL(*PAYMENTS*, *INTEREST*, *TERM*, *TYPE*, *FUTURE-VALUE*)

The parameters to the **@PVAL** function are exactly the same as those for the **@FVAL** function, except that *PRESENT-VALUE* is replaced by *FUTURE-VALUE*. For this example, in cells D1..E5, set up the worksheet in Exhibit 7-2.

EXHIBIT 7-2
PRESENT VALUE OF A SINGLE CASH FLOW

	D	E
1	Present Value Calculations	
2	Future Value	$1,100.00
3	Years	1
4	Rate	10%
5	Present Value	

In cell E5 place the formula: `@PVAL(0,E4,E3,0,E2)`. Again, *PAYMENTS* and *TYPE* must be set to 0. The result will be $1,000, exactly as expected.

We have purposely constructed our future value and present value examples side-by-side in the worksheet to demonstrate that present value and future value are inverse functions. Let's change our worksheet to make this concept clear. We want to link the references in the present value function to the cells used in the future value function. This will allow changes in the future value parameters to change the present value parameters. First, select E2 and enter: +B5, in E3 type: +B3, and in E4 enter: +B4. Now, regardless of the changes made to the future value side of the worksheet, the present value should be equal to the value in B2. Try making some changes to the inputs in B2, B3, and B4. No matter what changes you make, the calculated present value (in E5) is always the same as the present value input in B2. This is because the present value and future value are inverse functions.

Annuities

Thus far we have examined the present and future values of single sums. These are powerful concepts which will allow us to deal with more complex cash flows. *Annuities* are a series of nominally equal cash flows, equally spaced in time. Examples of annuities abound. Your car payment is an annuity, so is your mortgage payment. If not already, you may someday own annuities as part of a retirement program. The cash flow pictured in Figure 7-1 is another example.

FIGURE 7-1
A TIMELINE FOR AN ANNUITY CASH FLOW

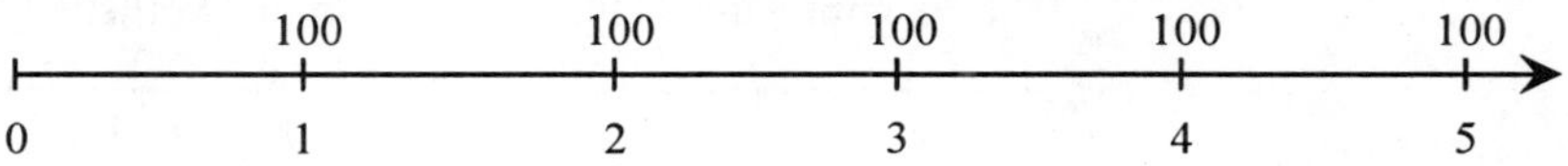

How do we find the value of a stream of cash flows such as that pictured in Figure 7-1? The answer involves the *principle of value additivity*. This principle says that, "the value of a stream of cash flows is equal to the sum of the values of the components." As long as the cash flows occur at the same time, they can be added together. Therefore, if we can move each of the cash flows to the same time period, we can add them to find the value as of that time period. Cash flows can be moved around in time by compounding (finding the future value) or discounting (finding the present value).

Present Value of an Annuity

One way to find the present value of an annuity is to find the present value of each of the cash flows separately and add them together. Equation (7-3) summarizes this method:

$$PV_A = \sum_{t=1}^{N} \frac{Pmt_t}{(1+i)^t} \qquad (7\text{-}3)$$

where PV_A is the present value of the annuity, t is the time period, N is the total number of payments, Pmt_t is the payment in period t, and i is the discount rate.

Of course, this equation works fine for any annuity (or any stream of cash flows), but it can be very tedious for annuities with more than just a few payments. Imagine finding the current balance (i.e., present value) of a mortgage with more than 300 payments to go before it is paid off! We can find a closed-form solution (the above equation is an "open-form" solution because the number of additions is indefinite) by taking the summation:

$$PV_A = Pmt \left[\frac{1 - \dfrac{1}{(1+i)^N}}{i} \right] \qquad (7\text{-}4)$$

where all terms are as previously defined. Notice that we have dropped the subscript, t, because this solution does not depend on our taking the present values separately. Instead, since each payment is the same, we can value the whole annuity in one step.

Let's find the present value of the cash flow pictured in Figure 7-1. Assuming that the discount rate for this cash flow is 8%, the equation is:

$$PV_A = 100 \left[\frac{1 - \dfrac{1}{(1.08)^5}}{0.08} \right] = 399.271$$

This means that if you were to deposit $399.27 into an account today which pays 8% interest per year, you could withdraw $100 at the end of each year for the next five years and be left with a balance of $0.00 at the end of the five years.

Recall from our earlier discussion of single cash flows that we can use 1-2-3's built-in **@PVAL** function to find present values. When dealing with single cash flows we set *PAYMENTS* and *TYPE* to 0. For annuities, *PAYMENTS* will be set to the dollar amount of the periodic payment. *TYPE* is an optional binary (0 or 1) variable which controls whether 1-2-3 assumes the payment occurs at the end (0) or the beginning (1) of the period. For this example, we'll assume this is a *regular* annuity, which means all payments occur at the end of the period.

EXHIBIT 7-3
PRESENT VALUE OF AN ANNUITY

	A	B
1	**Present Value of an Annuity**	
2	Payment	100
3	Interest Rate	8%
4	Number of Payments	5
5	Present Value	

Set up a worksheet with the data pictured in Exhibit 7-3 in cells A1..B5. In B5 we wish to find the present value of the annuity presented in Figure 7-1, so enter: @PVAL(B2,B3,B4,0,0). The result is $399.27.

1-2-3 also has another built-in function which can find the present value of an annuity. The **@PV** function works the same as **@PVAL** for regular annuities, but it is simpler to use. This function is defined as:

@PV(*PAYMENTS, INTEREST, TERM*).

where all of the parameters are as previously defined. To use **@PV**, change the equation in B5 to: @PV(B2,B3,B4). Of course, the answer is the same.

We can, of course, experiment with various parameters. For example, suppose that instead of five withdrawals of $100 each, you wanted to make ten withdrawals of $50 each. How much would you need to deposit into this account in order to deplete the account after 10 withdrawals? Change the number of payments in B4 to: 10, and the payment in B2 to: 50. After these changes, you will see that an initial deposit of only $335.50 will allow you to achieve your goal.

Returning now to our original example, reset the payment amount to 100 and the number of payments to 5. How much would you have to deposit if you want to make your first withdrawal today, rather than one year from today? To answer this question, realize that the only thing we have changed is the timing of the first withdrawal. In other words, we are now assuming that this is an *annuity due*. We will still make a total of five withdrawals of $100 each, but they occur at the beginning of each period. In B5, change the *TYPE* parameter to 1, from 0 originally, so that the formula is now: @PVAL(B2,B3,B4,1,0). The result is $431.21 indicating that, because the first withdrawal occurs immediately, you will have to make a larger initial deposit. The amount of the deposit must be larger because you will not earn the first year's interest before making the first withdrawal.

Another way to look at this is that we are effectively depositing $331.21 (= 431.21 deposit - 100 withdrawal) in order to be able to make four future withdrawals of $100 each. To see that this is the case, change the @PVAL formula back to its original form (*TYPE* = 0) and change the number of payments to 4. The present value is then shown to be $331.21 exactly as claimed.

Future Value of an Annuity

Imagine that you have recently begun planning for retirement. One of the attractive options available is to set up an Individual Retirement Account (IRA). What makes the IRA so attractive is that you can deposit up to $2,000 per year, and the investment gains will accrue tax-free until you begin to make withdrawals after age 59½. Furthermore, depending on your situation, the IRA deposits may reduce your taxable income.

To determine the amount that you will have accumulated in your IRA at retirement requires an understanding of the future value of an annuity. Recalling the principle of value additivity, we could simply find the future value of each year's investment and add them together at retirement. Mathematically this is:

$$FV_A = \sum_{t=1}^{N}[Pmt_t(1+i)^{N-t}] \qquad \text{(7-5)}$$

Alternatively, we could use the closed-form solution of Equation (7-5):

$$FV_A = Pmt\left[\frac{(1+i)^N - 1}{i}\right] \qquad \text{(7-6)}$$

Assume that you are planning on retirement in 30 years. If you deposit $2,000 each year into your IRA account which will earn an average of 7.5% per year, how much will you have after 30 years? Because of the large number of deposits, Equation (7-6) will be easier to use than Equation (7-5) though we could use either one. The solution is:

$$FV_A = 2,000\left[\frac{(1.075)^{30} - 1}{0.075}\right] = 206,798.81 \ .$$

As usual, 1-2-3 provides a built-in function to handle problems such as this one. The **@FVAL** function, which we used to find the future value of a single sum earlier, will also find the future value of an annuity. Set up the worksheet in Exhibit 7-4.

EXHIBIT 7-4
FUTURE VALUE OF AN ANNUITY

	A	B
1	Future Value of an Annuity	
2	Payment	2000
3	Interest Rate	7.50%
4	Number of Payments	30
5	Future Value	

In B5 place the formula: @FVAL(B2,B3,B4,0,0). The result, $206,798.81, agrees exactly with the result from the formula.

What if that amount is less than you had hoped for? One solution is to start making the investments this year, rather than next (i.e, the beginning of this period rather than the end of this period). To see the effect of this change all that needs to be done is to change the *TYPE* parameter to 1 so that the formula is now: @FVAL(B2,B3,B4,1,0). That minor change in your investment strategy will net you a little over $15,500 extra dollars at retirement. Perhaps a better alternative is to accept a little extra risk (we assume that you are young enough that this makes sense) by investing in stock mutual funds which will return an average of about 10% per year over the 30-year horizon. In this case, still assuming that you start investing this year, you will have $361,886.85 at retirement. Significantly better!

As with the **@PV** function, 1-2-3 also has a simpler function to calculate the future value of an annuity. The **@FV** function works the same as **@FVAL**, except that it only handles regular annuities (end of period cash flows). It is defined as:

@FV(*PAYMENTS, INTEREST, TERM*).

Solving for the Annuity Payment

Suppose that we want to know the amount that we have to deposit in order to accumulate a given sum after a number of years. For example, assume that you are planning to purchase a house five years from now. Since you are currently a student, you will begin saving for the $10,000 downpayment one year from today. How much will you need to save each year, if your savings will earn a rate of 4% per year? Figure 7-2 diagrams the problem.

FIGURE 7-2
A TIMELINE FOR ANNUAL SAVINGS TO OBTAIN $10,000 IN FIVE YEARS

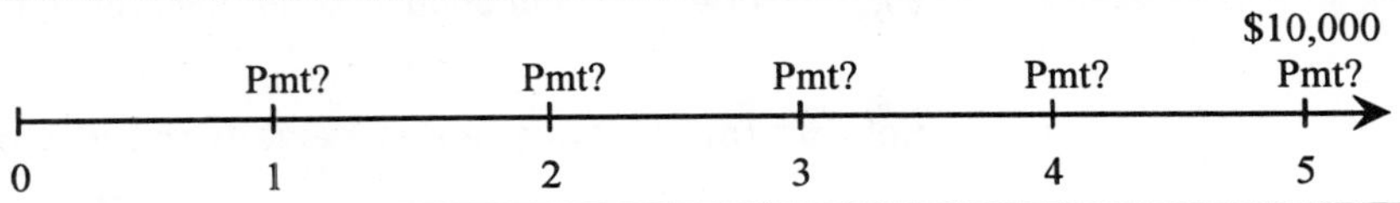

In this case, we wish to solve for the payment you would have to make each year. The future value of the annuity is already known, so the **@FVAL** function would be inappropriate. What we need is 1-2-3's **@PAYMT** function:

@PAYMT(*PRINCIPAL, INTEREST, TERM, TYPE, FUTURE-VALUE*)

The parameters for the **@PAYMT** function are similar to those for **@PVAL** and **@FVAL**, except that it has *PRINCIPAL* parameter in place of the *PAYMENTS* parameter.

EXHIBIT 7-5
ANNUITY PAYMENT WHEN PV OR FV IS KNOWN

	A	B
1	**Solving for an Annuity Payment**	
2	Present Value	0
3	Future Value	$10,000
4	Number of Payments	5
5	Interest Rate	4%
6	Annual Payment Amount	

Enter the information from Exhibit 7-5 into cells A1..B6 of a new worksheet. In cell B6 enter the equation: @PAYMT(B2,B5,B4,0,B3). The result indicates that you will have to save $1,846.27 per year in order to accumulate $10,000 for the downpayment in five years.

The **@PAYMT** function allows *both* the **PRINCIPAL** and **FUTURE-VALUE** to be inputs. In the previous example, it was assumed that **PRINCIPAL** was 0. However, let's presume that you have recently inherited $3,000 from your uncle, and that you want to use this money to begin saving now for that downpayment. Since the $3,000 will grow to only $3,649.96 after five years at 4% per year (this can be verified by using the worksheet created for Exhibit 7-1) you will still need to save some amount every year. How much will you need to save each year? To find out, simply set the present value, in B2, to 3000 leaving the other values unchanged. Because the initial investment *reduces* the total amount that you need to save to $6,350.04 (why?), your annual saving requirement is reduced to $1,172.39.

Solving for the Number of Periods in an Annuity

Solving for the present value, future value and payment for annuities are fairly simple problems. That is, the formulas are straightforward and easy to apply. Solving for the number of periods, N, is not as obvious mathematically. To do so requires knowledge of logarithms. If you know the present value of the annuity then solving Equation (7-4) for N we get:

$$N = \frac{\ln\left(\frac{-iPV_A}{Pmt} + 1\right)}{-\ln(1 + i)} \tag{7-7}$$

where $\ln(\cdot)$ is the natural logarithm operator. If you know the future value then solving Equation (7-6) for N results in:

$$N = \frac{\ln\left(\frac{iFV_A}{Pmt} + 1\right)}{\ln(1 + i)} \tag{7-8}$$

1-2-3 offers the built-in **@NPER** function to solve problems of this type. This function is defined as:

@NPER(*PAYMENTS, INTEREST, FUTURE-VALUE, TYPE, PRESENT-VALUE*)

where all of the parameters are as previously defined. To use this function, you must know the payment, per period interest rate, and either the present value or future value or both.

Return now to our example of saving for the downpayment for a house. Recall that it was determined that by saving $1,846.27 per year you could afford the downpayment after five years. Set up the worksheet in Exhibit 7-6.

EXHIBIT 7-6
NUMBER OF ANNUITY PAYMENTS WHEN PV OR FV IS KNOWN

	A	B
1	Solving for N in an Annuity	
2	Present Value	$0
3	Future Value	$10,000
4	Annual Payment	$1,846
5	Annual Rate	4.00%
6	Number of Years	

Since we want to solve for the number of periods, insert the **@NPER** function into B6: @NPER(B4,B5,B3,0,B2). The result is 5 years, exactly as we would expect.

Solving for the Interest Rate in an Annuity

Unlike the present value, future value, payment and number of periods, there is no closed-form solution for the rate of interest of an annuity. The only way to solve this problem is to use a trial and error approach, perhaps an intelligent one such as the bisection or Newton-Raphson methods.[1]

1-2-3, however, offers a built-in function which will solve for the interest rate, though it requires a little more setup than the functions we've used so far. The function, **@IRATE**, is defined as:

---

1. These are powerful techniques for solving these types of problems. The bisection method, briefly, involves choosing two initial guesses at the answer that are sure to bracket the true answer. Each successive guess is halfway between the two previous guesses that bracket the solution. The Newton-Raphson technique requires calculus and is beyond the scope of this book. For more information, consult any numerical methods textbook.

@I$RATE$(*TERM, P$AYMENT$, P$RESENT$-V$ALUE$, TYPE, F$UTURE$-V$ALUE$, G$UESS$*)

where the parameters are as defined earlier, and *GUESS* is your (optional) first guess at the correct answer. Ordinarily, the *GUESS* can be omitted.

> Suppose that you are approached with an offer to purchase an investment which will provide cash flows of $1,500 per year for ten years. The cost of purchasing this investment is $10,500. If you have alternative investment opportunity which will yield 8% per year, which should you accept?

There are actually several ways that a problem such as this could be solved. One method is to realize that 8% is your opportunity cost of funds, and should therefore be used as your discount rate. Using the worksheet created in Exhibit 7-3 we find that the present value (i.e., current worth to you) of the investment is only $10,065.12. Since the price ($10,500) is greater than the value, you should reject the investment and accept your alternative.[2]

Another method of solving this dilemma is to compare the yields (i.e., compound annual return) offered by the investments. All other things being equal, the investment with the highest yield should be accepted. We already know that your alternative investment offers an 8% yield, but what is the yield of your new opportunity? We will use the worksheet in Exhibit 7-7 to find out.

Into B6 place the equation: @I$RATE$(B5,B4,B2,0,B3,0.1). The result is 7.07% per year, so you should reject the new investment in favor of your alternative which offers 8% per year. This is the same result we obtained with the present value methodology, as we would hope. Later, we will see that this will always be the case when comparing mutually exclusive investment opportunities.[3]

---

2. Note that we are simply comparing the cost of the investment to its perceived benefit (present value). If the cost is greater than the benefit, the investment should be rejected. We will expand on this method in future chapters.

3. Mutually exclusive investment opportunities are those in which you may choose one investment or the other, but not both. That is, the choice of one precludes your also choosing the other.

EXHIBIT 7-7
YIELD ON AN ANNUITY

	A	B
1	Solving for i in an Annuity	
2	Present Value	(10,500)
3	Future Value	0
4	Annual Payment	$1,500
5	Number of Years	10.00
6	Annual Rate	

Deferred Annuities

Not all annuities begin their payments during the year following the analysis period. For example, if you are planning your retirement, you will probably start by figuring the amount of income that you will need each year during retirement. But, chances are if you are a student, you will probably not retire for many years. Your retirement income, then, is an annuity which won't begin until you retire. In other words it is a *deferred annuity*. How do we determine the value of a deferred annuity?

Assume that you own a time machine (made of a super-strong futuristic metal that can withstand the gravitational forces of a blackhole in space). This machine can transport you to any time period that you tell it. If we use this time machine to transport you to the year just prior to retirement, then valuing the stream of retirement income becomes a simple matter. Just use 1-2-3's **@PVAL** function. The year before retirement is now considered to be year 0, the first year of retirement is year 1, and so on. Figure 7-3 demonstrates this time-shifting technique.

FIGURE 7-3
TIME-SHIFTING AS A FIRST STEP IN SOLVING DEFERRED ANNUITY PROBLEMS

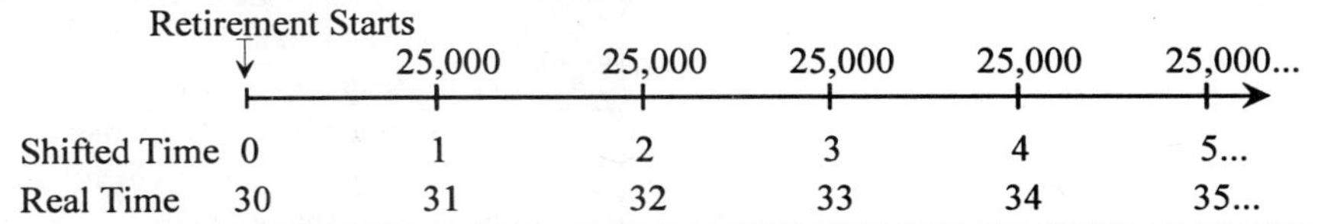

	Retirement Starts	25,000	25,000	25,000	25,000	25,000...
Shifted Time	0	1	2	3	4	5...
Real Time	30	31	32	33	34	35...

In constructing Figure 7-3, we have assumed that you will retire 30 years from now, and will require income of $25,000 per year during retirement. If we further assume that you will need your retirement income for 35 years (you come from very long-lived stock) and expect to earn 6% per year, you will need $362,456 at retirement (year 30) to provide this income. In other words, $362,456 is the present value, at year 30, of $25,000 per year for 35 years at 6%. You can use the worksheet created for Exhibit 7-3 to verify these numbers.

The problem in Figure 7-3 is that knowing the amount that we will need 30 years from now tells us nothing about how much we need to save today. The @PVAL function in 1-2-3, or the PV_A formula [(7-4)], must be thought of as a transformation function. That is, it transforms a series of payments into a lump sum. That lump sum ($362,456 in our example) is then placed *one period before the first payment occurs*. In our earlier examples, the annuities began payment at the end of period 1, so the present value was at time period 0 (one period earlier than period 1). In the current example, the present value is at time period 30, also one period before the first payment.

In order to determine the amount that we need to invest today, we must treat the required savings at retirement as a future value. This sum must then be discounted back to period 0. For example, if we assume that we can earn 8% per year before retirement, we would need to invest $36,019.93 today in order to meet our retirement goals.

Exhibit 7-8 presents a simple worksheet to determine the investment required today in order to provide a particular income during retirement. Open a new worksheet and enter the data and labels from Exhibit 7-8.

EXHIBIT 7-8
PLANNING FOR RETIREMENT

	A	B
1	**Retirement Worksheet**	
2	Annual Retirement Income Need	25,000
3	Years until Retirement	30
4	Years in Retirement	35
5	Rate of Return before Retirement	8%
6	Rate of Return during Retirement	6%
7	Savings Required at Retirement	
8	Investment Required Today	
9	Annual Investment Required	

To complete our retirement worksheet, we need to enter functions into cells B7..B9. Recall that the first step in our retirement income problem was to determine the present value of your retirement income at period 30. To do this in our worksheet, enter the **@PVAL** function into B7: `@PVAL(B2,B6,B4,0,0)`. The result, $362,456, tells us that you will need to have saved this amount in order to provide the income indicated in B2 for the number of years indicated in B4. To determine the amount that you would need to invest today (a lump sum), you need to determine the present value, at time period 0, of the amount in B7. To do this, in B8 enter the formula: `@PVAL(0,B5,B3,0,B7)`. As before, the amount required today is $36,019.93.

Another feature of the retirement planning worksheet is that it will calculate the annual savings required to reach your goal. To make 1-2-3 do this calculation, we need to use the **@PAYMT** function. In B9 enter: `@PAYMT(0,B5,B3,0,B7)`. The result is $3,199.56, which means that if you can save this amount each year for the next 30 years, and earn an average of 8% interest each year, you will reach your goal.

We have ignored the effect of inflation and taxes on your retirement planning for this worksheet. But if we assume that you save the amount in B9 in a tax-deferred account (say, a 401K), the results are a bit more realistic. Experiment with this worksheet. You may be surprised at the difficulty of saving for a comfortable retirement!

Uneven Cash Flow Streams

Annuities are very neat from a cash flow point of view. Most investments don't, however, have cash flows which are the same in each period. When the cash flows are different in each period we refer to them as *uneven cash flow streams*. Investments of this type are not as easy to deal with, though conceptually they are the same.

Recall our discussion of the principle of value additivity. This principle says that as long as cash flows occur in the same period, we can add them together to determine their combined value. This principle applies to any time period, not just to time period 0. So, to determine the present value of an uneven stream of cash flows, one option is to determine the present value of each cash flow separately, and then add them together. The same technique applies to the future value of an uneven stream.

Simply find the future value of each cash flow separately, and then add them together.

1-2-3's **@PVAL** and **@FVAL** functions cannot be used for uneven cash flow streams because they assume equal (annuity) payments or a lump sum. Set up the worksheet in Exhibit 7-9 and we'll see what needs to be done.

EXHIBIT 7-9
PV AND FV FOR UNEVEN CASH FLOWS

	A	B
1	Uneven Cash Flow Streams	
2	Year	Cash Flow
3	1	1000
4	2	2000
5	3	3000
6	4	4000
7	5	5000
8	Interest Rate	11.00%
9	Present Value	
10	Future Value	

First, we want to solve for the present value of the cash flows in B3..B7. To do this, we need to use the net present value, **@NPV**, function. This function will be especially valuable in capital budgeting in Chapter 10. The **@NPV** function is defined as:

$$@\text{NPV}(\textit{INTEREST}, \textit{RANGE}, \textit{TYPE})$$

where ***INTEREST*** is the per period rate of return (i.e., the discount rate), and ***RANGE*** is the set of cash flows to be discounted. *TYPE*, as always, indicates when the cash flows occur. To find the present value of the cash flows, enter: @NPV(B8,B3..B7) into B9. The result is $10,319.90. To verify this result, you can take the present value of each cash flow at 11% and add them together.

Finding the future value of an uneven stream is a bit more difficult because 1-2-3 has no built-in function to perform this calculation. Recall, however, the principle of value additivity. If we can get all of the cash flows into the same period, we can add them together and then move the result to the desired period. Figure 7-4 shows one possible solution.

FIGURE 7-4
FINDING THE FUTURE VALUE OF AN UNEVEN STREAM IN 1-2-3

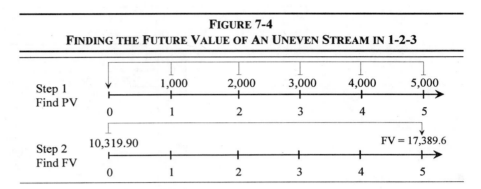

First, we find the present value of the uneven stream of cash flows, perhaps using the **@NPV** function, and then we find the future value of the present value of the cash flows. The easiest way to implement this method in 1-2-3 is to use the **@NPV** function nested within the **@FVAL** function. Remember, a nested function is one which is used inside another function. In B10 enter: @FVAL(0,B8,5,0,@NPV(B8, B3..B7)). The future value is found to be $17,389.63. We used the **@NPV** function inside the **@FVAL** function. As an alternative, we could have put B9 in for the present value parameter, but the result would be the same. Using nested functions can often simplify a worksheet by making use of fewer cells, though the formulas tend to be more complex.

Solving for the Yield in an Uneven Cash Flow Stream

Often in financial analysis, it is necessary to determine the yield of an investment given its price and cash flows. For example, we have already seen that one way to choose between alternative investments is to compare their yields, and we will see more examples in Chapter 10. This was easy when dealing with annuities and lump-sum investments. But, what about the case of uneven cash flow investments? We will use the worksheet in Exhibit 7-10 to find out.

To solve for the yield in problems such as this, we need to make use of the internal rate of return (**@IRR**) function. The IRR is defined as the rate of return which equates the present value of future cash flows with the cost of the investment ($10,319.90 in this problem). In 1-2-3, the **@IRR** function is defined as:

$$@IRR(GUESS, RANGE)$$

EXHIBIT 7-10
YIELD ON AN UNEVEN CASH FLOW STREAM

	A	B
1	Uneven Cash Flow Streams	
2	Year	Cash Flow
3	0	(10,319.90)
4	1	1000
5	2	2000
6	3	3000
7	4	4000
8	5	5000
9	Yield	

where *GUESS* is the first guess at the correct interest rate, and *RANGE* is a range of cash flows (including the cost). We will study the IRR in depth in Chapter 10, but for now we will just make use of it.

Before we find the solution, notice a couple of things about the worksheet. The cash flows are listed separately, so we cannot use the **@IRR** function like we did the **@FVAL**, **@PVAL**, and **@PAYMT** functions. Also, we must include the cost of the investment as one of the cash flows (it must be a negative number because it is a cash outflow). To find the yield on this investment, insert into B9: `@IRR(0.1,B3..B8)`. The result is 11%, which means that if you purchase this investment you will earn a compound annual rate of 11%.

Note that we used 10% as our *GUESS* in B9. Sometimes, however, 1-2-3 will not be able to converge on a solution with your initial *GUESS*, so you might have to try another value. Remember that this is essentially a trial and error process, and sometimes 1-2-3 needs a little help to go in the right direction.

There are few situations which may cause an error when using the **IRR** function. One that we've already discussed is that 1-2-3 may not converge to a solution. In this case, you can usually find the answer by supplying 1-2-3 with a different *GUESS*. Another occurs if you have no negative cash flows. As an example, change the purchase price to a positive `10,500`. 1-2-3 will return an ERR message indicating that there is a problem. In this case the problem is that your return is infinite (why?[4]). A third problem can result from more than one negative cash flow

---

4. Because you are receiving income, but have made no investment.

in the stream. In general, there will be one solution to the problem for each sign change in the cash flow stream. In our original example, there is only one sign change (from negative to positive after the initial purchase). When there is more than one solution, 1-2-3 will usually report the first that it finds. In other situations, it will report an error.

Non-annual Compounding Periods

There is no reason why we should restrict our analyses to investments which pay cash flows annually. Some investments make payments (e.g., interest) semiannually, monthly, daily, or even more frequently. Everything that we have learned to this point still applies, with only a minor change.

Recall our basic time value of money formula (7-1):

$$FV_N = PV(1 + i)^N$$

Originally, we defined i as the annual rate of interest, and N as the number of years. Actually, i is the periodic rate of interest and N is the total number of periods. As an example, i might be the weekly interest rate and N the number of weeks for which we will hold the investment.[5] Since rates are usually quoted in terms of simple (i.e., not compounded) annual rates, we can restate our basic formula as:

$$FV_N = PV\left(1 + \frac{i}{m}\right)^{Nm} \qquad (7\text{-}9)$$

where i is the annual rate, N is the number of years, and m is the number of periods per year.

1-2-3 can handle non-annual compounding just as easily as annual compounding. Just enter the rate and number of periods adjusted for the length of the compounding period. Let's look at an example.

---

5. Since there are 52 weeks in a year, we would normally calculate the weekly rate as the annual rate divided by 52. Similarly, the number of weeks would be calculated by multiplying the number of years (perhaps a fractional number of years) by 52.

Assume that you are shopping for a new bank to set up a savings account (a lousy investment, but play along anyway). As you start shopping, you notice that all of the banks offer the same stated interest rate, but different compounding periods. To help make your decision, you set up the worksheet in Exhibit 7-11.

(Hint: the easiest way to set up this worksheet is to enter the data for the First National Bank and then make two copies. Next, edit the bank names, change the appropriate data, and adjust the column widths to accommodate the labels.)

EXHIBIT 7-11
NON-ANNUAL COMPOUNDING PERIODS

	A	B
1	Non-Annual Compounding Worksheet	
2	First National Bank	
3	Investment	1000
4	Simple Rate	10.00%
5	Periods per Year	1
6	Term of Investment (Years)	1
7	Future Value	
8	Second National Bank	
9	Investment	1000
10	Simple Rate	10.00%
11	Periods per Year	2
12	Term of Investment (Years)	1
13	Future Value	
14	Third National Bank	
15	Investment	1000
16	Simple Rate	10.00%
17	Periods per Year	12
18	Term of Investment (Years)	1
19	Future Value	

Notice that all of the banks are advertising a 10% annual rate. The only difference is how often they credit the interest to your account (i.e., the frequency of compounding). Being a rational economic thinker, you will choose the bank that will provide the highest balance at the end of the year. To determine the end of year balances, enter the **@FVAL** formula in B7: `@FVAL(0,B4/B5, B6*B5,0,B3)`. Copy the formula from B7 to both B13 and B19. Note that we have again made use of nested functions. In this case, the rate is defined as the annual rate *divided* by the number of periods in a year, and the number of periods is the number of years *times* the number of periods in a year.

The choice is clear. You should choose the Third National Bank since it offers the highest end of year balance ($1,104.71). All other things being equal, the more frequent the compounding, the higher your future value will be. To see this more clearly, set up the worksheet in Exhibit 7-12.

EXHIBIT 7-12
COMPARING VARIOUS NON-ANNUAL COMPOUNDING PERIODS

	A	B	C
1	Non-Annual Compounding Periods		
2	Present Value	1000	
3	Annual Rate	10.00%	
4	**Frequency**	**Periods/Year**	**FV**
5	Annual	1	
6	Semiannual	2	
7	Quarterly	4	
8	Bi-monthly	6	
9	Monthly	12	
10	Bi-weekly	26	
11	Weekly	52	
12	Daily	365	

To complete the worksheet, enter the **Fv** formula in C5: `@FVAL(0,$B$3/B5, B5,0,$B$2)` and copy it down to the other cells. It is important that you insert the dollar signs as indicated so that the references to the present value and interest rate remain fixed when copying.

Notice that, as before, the more frequent the compounding, the higher the future value. Furthermore, the future value increases at a decreasing rate as the number of compounding periods increases. This can be seen more easily if we create a graph of the future values. To accomplish this, select the labels in A5..A13 and the numbers in C5..C13 (remember, you can select non-contiguous ranges by holding down the Ctrl key while dragging the mouse). Note that you are selecting one extra row because we will use this worksheet again later to add one more data point. Now, click on the Chart icon to create the chart. You should end up with a worksheet that resembles the one in Exhibit 7-13. (You will have to re-scale the Y-axis values. Right-click the Y-axis and choose Y-axis from the pop-up menu. Now, set the Upper limit to 1106 and the Lower limit to 1097.)

EXHIBIT 7-13
NON-ANNUAL COMPOUNDING RESULTS

	A	B	C	D	E	F	G	H
1	Non-Annual Compounding Periods							
2	Present Value	1000						
3	Annual Rate	10.00%						
4	Frequency	Periods/Year	FV					
5	Annual	1	$1,100.00					
6	Semiannual	2	$1,102.50					
7	Quarterly	4	$1,103.81					
8	Bi-monthly	6	$1,104.26					
9	Monthly	12	$1,104.71					
10	Bi-weekly	26	$1,104.96					
11	Weekly	52	$1,105.06					
12	Daily	365	$1,105.16					

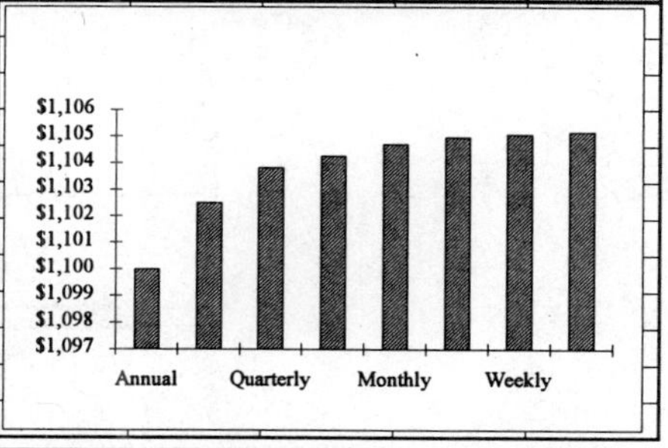

Continuous Compounding

We have seen that more frequent compounding leads to higher future values. However, our examples extended this idea only as far as daily compounding. There is no reason that we can't also compound every half-day, every hour, or even every minute. In fact, this concept can be extended to the smallest imaginable time period, the instant. This type of compounding is referred to as *continuous compounding*.

Continuous compounding is an extension of what we have seen already. To recap, recall that we changed the basic future value function (7-1) to (7-9):

$$FV_N = PV\left(1 + \frac{i}{m}\right)^{Nm}$$

The more frequently we compound, the larger m is going to be. For example, with semiannual compounding $m = 2$, but with daily compounding $m = 365$. What if we set m equal to infinity? Actually, we can't do that because i/∞ is effectively equal to zero. What we can do is to take the limit as m approaches infinity. When we do this, we get:

$$\lim_{m \to \infty} FV_N = PVe^{iN} \tag{7-10}$$

where e is the base of the natural logarithm, and is approximately equal to 2.718.

1-2-3 does not offer functions to solve for the present or future value when compounding is continuous. However, we can easily create the formulas. To do so requires that you know about the @**EXP** function which raises e to a specified power.[6] This function is defined as:

$$@\text{E\textsc{xp}}(\textsc{Number})$$

Using the worksheet in Exhibit 7-13, we can add, in cell C13: `+B2*@EXP(B3)`. Since we have assumed a one year period in this example, the power to which e is raised is simply the interest rate. Add the label: `Continuous` in A13 and the worksheet is complete.

We can also calculate the present value of a continuously compounded sum. All that needs to be done is to solve Equation (7-10) for PV:[7]

$$\lim_{m \to \infty} PV = FV_N e^{-iN}. \tag{7-11}$$

Summary

In this chapter we have discussed the concept of the time value of money. Present value represents the amount of money that needs to be invested today in order to purchase a future cash flow or stream of cash flows. Future value represents the amount of money that will be accumulated if we invest known cash flows at known interest rates. Further, we discussed various types of cash flows. Annuities are equal cash flows, equally spaced through time. Uneven cash flows are those in which the periodic cash flows are not equal.

---

6. e is the base of the natural logarithm, so $\exp(\cdot)$ is the inverse of $\ln(\cdot)$. In other words, $\exp(\ln(x)) = x$.

7. Many students find that the continuous compounding equations are easier to recall if we change the notation slightly. Specifically, let P be the present value, F be the future value, r is the annual rate of interest, and T is the number of years (which can be fractional). With this notation, Equation (7-10) becomes: $F = Pe^{rT}$, and Equation (7-11) becomes: $P = Fe^{-rT}$. This is easier because the formulas can be pronounced. For example, (7-10) is pronounced "Pert."

Before continuing with future chapters you should be comfortable with these concepts. Practice by changing the worksheets presented in this chapter until you develop a sense for the type of results that you will obtain.

TABLE 7-1
TIME-VALUE OF MONEY FORMULAS

Purpose	Formula
Future Value of a Single Sum	$FV = PV(1 + i)^N$
Present Value of a Single Sum	$PV = \dfrac{FV}{(1 + i)^N}$
Solve for N for a Single Sum	$N = \dfrac{\ln\left(\dfrac{FV}{PV}\right)}{\ln(1 + i)}$
Solve for i for a Single Sum	$i = \sqrt[N]{\dfrac{FV}{PV}} - 1$
Present Value of an Ordinary Annuity	$PV_A = Pmt\left[\dfrac{1 - 1/(1 + i)^N}{i}\right]$
Future Value of an Ordinary Annuity	$FV_A = Pmt\left[\dfrac{(1 + i)^N - 1}{i}\right]$
Present Value of an Annuity Due	$PV_{Ad} = Pmt\left[\dfrac{1 - 1/(1 + i)^{(N-1)}}{i}\right] + Pmt$
Future Value of an Annuity Due	$FV_{Ad} = Pmt\left[\dfrac{(1 + i)^N - 1}{i}\right](1 + i)$

TABLE 7-2
FINANCIAL FUNCTIONS USED IN THIS CHAPTER

Purpose	Function	Page
Find the future value	@FVAL(*PAYMENTS, INTEREST, TERM, TYPE, PRESENT-VALUE*)	127
Find the future value of a regular annuity	@FV(*PAYMENTS, INTEREST, TERM*)	134
Find the present value	@PVAL(*PAYMENTS, INTEREST, TERM, TYPE, FUTURE-VALUE*)	129
Find the present value of a regular annuity	@PV(*PAYMENTS, INTEREST, TERM*)	132
Payment of an annuity	@PAYMT(*PRINCIPAL, INTEREST, TERM, TYPE, FUTURE-VALUE*)	135
Number of periods	@NPER(*PAYMENTS, INTEREST, FUTURE-VALUE, TYPE, PRESENT-VALUE*)	136
Yield of an annuity	@IRATE(*TERM, PAYMENT, PRESENT-VALUE, TYPE, FUTURE-VALUE, GUESS*)	138
Present value of unequal cash flows	@NPV(*INTEREST, RANGE, TYPE*)	142
Find the yield of unequal cash flows	@IRR(*GUESS, RANGE*)	143
Raise *e* to a power	@EXP(*NUMBER*)	149

CHAPTER 8

Valuation and Rates of Return

After studying this chapter, you should be able to:

1. *Differentiate among the definitions of "value" and explain the importance of intrinsic value in making financial decisions.*

2. *Explain how intrinsic value is calculated by considering the size, timing, and perceived riskiness of the cash flows.*

3. *Explain the concept of "required rate of return" and calculate this rate using the Capital Asset Pricing Model (CAPM).*

4. *Show how any security (common or preferred stocks, bonds, etc.) can be valued in 1-2-3 and by hand.*

5. *Calculate the various bond return measures in 1-2-3.*

Determining the value of financial assets is important to both investors and corporate financial managers. The obvious reason is that nobody wants to pay more than an asset is worth, since such behavior would lead to lower returns. Less obvious, but equally important, is that we can draw some valuable conclusions from the observed prices of assets. In this chapter we will see how to calculate the intrinsic value of corporate securities, and in the next chapter we will use the value of these securities to determine the required rate of return on investments.

What is Value?

The term "value" has many different meanings depending on the context in which it is used. For our purposes, there are three important types of value: book value, intrinsic value, and market value.

Generally, value can be defined as the amount that a willing and able buyer agrees to pay for an asset to a willing and able seller. In order to establish the value of an asset, it is important that both the buyer and seller be willing and able. Otherwise, no transaction can take place, and value cannot be determined without an exchange.

Notice that we did not say that the value of an asset is always the same as its price. Price and value are distinct, though related, concepts. The price of an asset can be greater than its value (in which case we say that the asset is over-valued or over-priced), less than its value (under-valued), or equal to its value (fairly-valued).

Book value is the price of an asset minus its accumulated depreciation. Deprecation is a systematic method of accounting for the reduction in the value of an asset over its useful life. Because of the systematic nature of depreciation (i.e., it is determined in advance according to some well-defined formula) book value does not necessarily fairly represent the actual market value of the asset. Because of this, and other distortions of value, a school of investors (known as value investors) has arisen. These investors seek out the stocks of companies that they believe to be under-valued, in hopes that the market will eventually recognize the true value of the company.

Intrinsic value is the value of an asset to an individual investor. Intrinsic value can be determined by taking the present value of the future cash flows *at the investor's required rate of return.* Because we use the investor's required rate of return in the calculation, and because each investor has different preferences and perceptions, intrinsic value is unique to each individual. Without these differences in intrinsic values markets could not function.

Market value is the price of an asset as determined in a competitive marketplace. Because markets are composed of individuals and these individuals cannot be induced to buy or sell unless the price is different from their intrinsic value, the market value of an asset must be a weighted average of everybody's intrinsic value. Symbolically:

$$MV = \sum_{n=1}^{N} w_n V_n$$

where MV is the market value, V_n is the intrinsic value of the asset to the nth investor, w_n is the wealth of the nth investor as a proportion of the wealth of all investors, and N is the total number of investors. This definition assumes that investors will buy until the market value rises to their intrinsic value, and sell (short sell if necessary) until the market value falls to their intrinsic value.

Unless otherwise modified, or obvious from the context, all references to the term "value" from this point forward will refer to the individual's intrinsic value.

Fundamentals of Valuation

As noted above, the intrinsic value of an asset is the *present value of the expected future cash flows* provided by the asset. Mathematically, intrinsic value is given by:

$$V = \sum_{t=1}^{N} \frac{Cf_t}{(1+i)^t} \qquad \text{(8-1)}$$

where Cf_t is the expected cash flow in period t, and i is the required rate of return for the investor performing the calculation.[1]

The most important components of value are likely to be the size and timing of the expected cash flows. The larger the expected cash flows, the higher the value will be. The earlier the cash flows, the higher the value. In other words, there is a positive relationship between the size of the cash flows and value, and a negative relationship between the time until the cash flows are received and value.

The other component of value is the investor's required rate of return. The required return is affected by the rates of return offered by competing investment vehicles and the riskiness of the investment. For example, if bonds are offering higher

---

1. At this point we will assume that all future cash flows are known with certainty. In Chapter 11 we will examine what happens when future cash flows are uncertain.

returns than stocks, we would expect that the prices of stocks would drop (and the prices of bonds would rise) as investors moved their money out of stocks and into bonds. This would occur because investors would recognize that bonds are less risky than are stocks, and they would raise their required returns for stocks. Since an increase in the required return will decrease value, investors would sell stocks thereby driving down the prices.

To determine the value of a security, we must first answer three questions:

1. What are the expected cash flows?

2. When will the cash flows occur?

3. What is the required rate of return for this particular stream of cash flows?

As we discuss the methods of valuing securities, keep these ideas in mind as they are the fundamentals of all security valuation.

Determining the Required Rate of Return

As mentioned above, one of the determinants of the required return for any stream of cash flows is the perceived riskiness of those cash flows. We will leave an in-depth discussion of risk for Chapter 11, but for now we will assume that the risk of a security is known.

In general, each investor can be classified by risk preference into three basic categories:

1. **Risk Aversion** - The risk averter prefers less risk for a given rate of return. The risk averter can be encouraged to accept nearly any level of risk, but only if the rate of return is expected to compensate him fairly. In other words, he must be paid in order to accept risk.

2. **Risk Neutral** - The risk neutral investor is indifferent to the level of risk. His rate of return will not change, regardless of the risk involved.

3. **Risk Lover** - The risk loving investor will actually lower her required rate of return as the risk increases. In other words, she is willing to pay to take on extra risk.

Under ordinary circumstances we assume that all investors are risk averse, and must receive a higher rate of return in order to accept a higher risk. Realize, however, that even investors in the same category can have different risk preferences, so two risk averse investors will likely have different required returns for the same asset.

Figure 8-1 illustrates the *ex-ante* (expected) risk-return trade-off for two risk averse investors. We know they are risk averse because the lines have a positive slope. In this case security B is riskier than A and therefore has the higher expected return for both investors. Investor I_1 can be seen to be more risk averse than I_2 because the slope of the risk-return line is steeper. In other words, the risk premium grows at a faster rate for I_1 than it does for I_2.

FIGURE 8-1

THEORETICAL RISK-RETURN TRADE-OFF FOR TWO RISK AVERSE INVESTORS

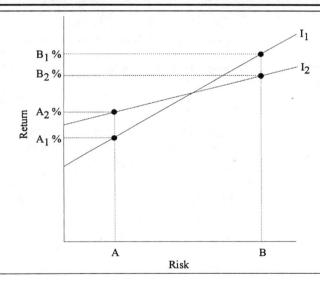

A Simple Risk Premium Model

An easy method of determining the rate of return for a security can be derived by assuming that the relationship pictured in Figure 8-1 is constant. If this is the case, then we can define the expected rate of return for an asset as a base rate (Y-axis intercept) plus a premium which is based on the riskiness of the security. In equation form:

$$E(R_i) = \text{Base Rate} + \text{Risk Premium}$$

where $E(R_i)$ is the expected rate of return for security i, the base rate is the rate of return on some benchmark security, and the risk premium is subjectively determined.

The problem with this model is that it is entirely subjective. Both the security chosen to provide the base rate and the risk premium are defined by the individual using the model. For example, one individual might choose as the base rate the rate of return on bonds issued by his company, while another might choose the average rate paid on AAA rated corporate bonds. Furthermore, because of individual differences in risk preferences, each individual is likely to assign a different value to the risk premium. Obviously, what is needed is a more objective approach.

CAPM: A More Scientific Model

The Capital Asset Pricing Model (CAPM) provides us with a more objective version of the simple risk premium model for determining expected returns. For our purposes, we can consider the CAPM to be a version of the simple risk premium model with its inputs more rigorously defined. The CAPM is given by:

$$E(R_i) = R_f + \beta_i[E(R_m) - R_f] \qquad \text{(8-2)}$$

where R_f is the risk-free rate of interest, β_i is a measure of the riskiness of security i relative to the riskiness of a large portfolio of assets, and $E(R_m)$ is the expected rate of return on the market portfolio.

In the CAPM, R_f serves as the base rate of interest. It is defined as the rate of return on a security with zero risk. Sometimes R_f is referred to as the "pure time value of money," or, in other words, the rate of return that is earned for delaying consumption but not accepting any risk. Ordinarily, R_f is assumed to be the rate of return on a U.S. Treasury security with time to maturity equal to the expected holding period of the security in question. Treasury securities are chosen because they are free of default risk, and are therefore the closest to being a true risk-free security that is known.

The second term in the CAPM is the risk premium and is more difficult to understand. The market portfolio is a portfolio of all risky assets, usually proxied by a stock index such as the S&P 500, which serves as a sort of benchmark against which other portfolios are measured. Subtracting the risk-free rate of return from the expected market return gives the expected market risk premium. Beta (β) is an index of systematic risk.[2] It measures the risk of a particular security relative to the market portfolio. If a stock has a beta of 2, then we could say that the stock is twice as risky as the market portfolio. If it is twice as risky, then common sense (and the CAPM) tells us that the risk premium for this stock should be twice that of the market. Likewise, a stock with a beta of 0.5 should carry half of the risk premium of the market.

So the CAPM is no more than a sophisticated version of the simple risk premium model. With this in mind, we can redraw the risk-return trade-off graph (known as the security market line) in Figure 8-2.

FIGURE 8-2
THE SECURITY MARKET LINE

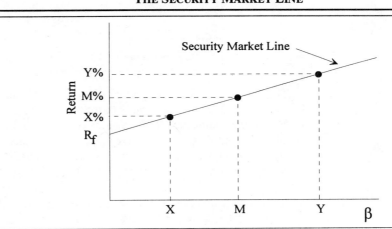

To see the CAPM in action, consider the following example:

> As a security analyst for Dewey, Cheatham, and Howe Securities you are preparing a report detailing your firm's expectations

---

2. In the world of CAPM there are two types of risk: systematic and unsystematic. Systematic risk is the market-related risk that affects all assets. An example would be changes in interest rates. Unsystematic risk is the company-specific risk such as the risk of a strike or of losing a major contract. As we will see in Chapter 11, through proper diversification, unsystematic risk can often be eliminated from a portfolio.

regarding two stocks for the year to come. Your report is to include the expected returns for these stocks and a graph illustrating the expected risk-return trade-off. Other analysts at DCH have informed you that the firm expects the S&P 500 to earn a return of 11% in the year ahead while the risk-free rate is 3%. According to *Value Line*, the betas for stocks X and Y are 0.5 and 1.5, respectively. What are the expected returns for X and Y?

To work this example, open a new worksheet and enter the data so that it resembles the worksheet in Exhibit 8-1.

EXHIBIT 8-1
CALCULATING EXPECTED RETURNS WITH THE CAPM

	A	B	C	D	E
1	The Security Market Line				
2		Risk-free	X	Market	Y
3	Beta	0.00	0.50	1.00	1.50
4	Expected Return	3.00%		11.00%	

Before continuing, it is important to understand some of these inputs. The example problem did not mention the betas of the risk-free asset or of the market portfolio. How did we know that the beta of the risk-free asset is 0? Recall that beta measures the riskiness of the asset relative to the market. Since the risk-free asset has no risk, by definition, any measure of its risk must be equal to zero. Similarly, by definition the market must have a beta of 1.00 (why?).

To complete this example, we need to enter the formula for the CAPM, equation (8-2), into C4 and E4. In C4 enter: +$B$4+C3*($D$4-$B$4) and then copy this cell to E4. You should see that security X has an expected return of 7% and Y has an expected return of 15%. Notice that the return of X is not 0.5 times that of the market, nor is the return of Y 1.5 times that of the market. Instead, it is the risk premium of these securities that is 0.5 (for X) or 1.5 times (for Y) the risk premium of the market.

Finally, we can create a graph of the SML with these data points. Select B3..E4 and create an XY-chart being sure that you make the first row the x-axis labels. You can experiment with the SML by changing the expected return for the market or the risk-free rate. You will notice that the slope of the SML changes as you change the market risk premium. At this point your worksheet should match the one in Exhibit 8-2.

EXHIBIT 8-2
EXPECTED RETURNS AND THE SECURITY MARKET LINE

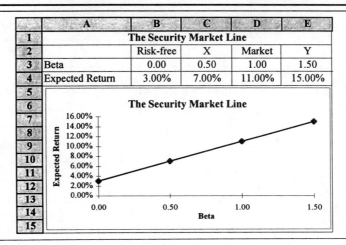

	A	B	C	D	E
1		The Security Market Line			
2		Risk-free	X	Market	Y
3	Beta	0.00	0.50	1.00	1.50
4	Expected Return	3.00%	7.00%	11.00%	15.00%

Valuing Common Stocks

The first question to ask when attempting to value any security is, "What are the expected cash flows?" In the case of common stocks there are two types of cash flows: dividends and the amount to be received at the time of the sale. Consider the following problem:

Suppose that you are interested in purchasing shares of the common stock of the XYZ Corporation. XYZ recently paid a dividend of $2.40, and you expect that this dividend will continue to be paid into the foreseeable future. Furthermore, you believe (for reasons that will become clear) that you will be able to sell this stock in three years for $20 per share. If your required return is 12% per year, what is the maximum amount that you should be willing to pay for a share of XYZ common stock?

To clarify the problem, it helps to examine it in terms of a timeline. Figure 8-3 presents the timeline.

FIGURE 8-3
TIMELINE FOR XYZ COMMON STOCK

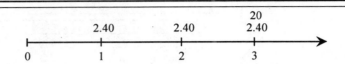

Calculating the value of this stock is a simple matter of calculating the present value of its cash flows. Given that your required return is 12%, the intrinsic value must be:

$$V = \frac{2.40}{1.12} + \frac{2.40}{(1.12)^2} + \frac{2.40 + 20}{(1.12)^3} = 20$$

If the stock is currently selling for $24 (the market value), would you purchase any shares? Obviously not, because the market value exceeds your intrinsic value by $4. If you did purchase the shares, and your cash flow expectations were realized, your average annual rate of return would be less than your required return.

Of course, the XYZ example problem is somewhat contrived, because there is no way to know, for sure, what the dividends and selling price are going to be in the future. With dividends this is not so much of a problem, because firms tend to have a somewhat stable (predictable) dividend policy. The advanced knowledge of the selling price is a different matter. It is impossible to know exactly what the market price will be tomorrow, and even more difficult to know the price three years hence.

The Constant-Growth Dividend Discount Model

To eliminate these problems, we can a make couple of assumptions. The first assumption is that dividends will grow at a constant rate.[3] With this assumption, knowing the most recent dividend is equivalent to knowing all future dividends. Also assume that we have an infinite holding period. In other words, we will never

---

3. Note that this is not an assumption that the dividend stream will always get larger. The growth rate could be negative, in which case the dividends would be shrinking over time. Furthermore, the growth rate could be zero, which means that the dividends are constant.

162

sell the stock, so we don't have to worry about forecasting the selling price. While this second assumption may sound ludicrous, we will see that it is little more than a mathematical trick which allows us to develop a model.

These assumptions lead to a model for the valuation of common stock which is known as the constant-growth dividend discount model, or the *Gordon Model*. Recall that we have defined the value of a common stock as the present value of future dividends plus the present value of the selling price. Since the stock will never be sold because of the infinite holding period, the model becomes:

$$V_{CS} = \frac{D_1}{(1 + k_{CS})} + \frac{D_2}{(1 + k_{CS})^2} + \frac{D_3}{(1 + k_{CS})^3} + \dots + \frac{D_\infty}{(1 + k_{CS})^\infty}$$

where V_{CS} is the value of the common stock, D is the dividend in a particular period, and k_{CS} is the required return.[4] Because the dividends are growing at a constant rate, they can be expressed as a function of the most recent dividend (D_0):

$$V_{CS} = \frac{D_0(1 + g)}{(1 + k_{CS})} + \frac{D_0(1 + g)^2}{(1 + k_{CS})^2} + \frac{D_0(1 + g)^3}{(1 + k_{CS})^3} + \dots + \frac{D_0(1 + g)^\infty}{(1 + k_{CS})^\infty}$$

This equation can be restated in closed-form as:

$$V_{CS} = \frac{D_0(1 + g)}{k_{CS} - g} = \frac{D_1}{k_{CS} - g} \tag{8-3}$$

Returning to the example, realize that XYZ's dividend growth rate is 0% (i.e., the dividend stream is not growing). Therefore, the value of a share is:

$$V_{CS} = \frac{2.40(1 + 0)}{0.12 - 0} = 20$$

which is exactly the same value as was found when assuming that you knew the value of the stock three years hence.

---

4. k_{CS} is the same as i, but is the more common notation for this model. As we will see later, this notation also helps to distinguish between the investor's required return for the different securities issued by the firm.

To see how you knew that the value of the stock would be $20 in three years, we can again use the time-shifting technique which was used for deferred annuities in Chapter 7. Let's look at another example.

> Suppose that you are interested in purchasing a share of the common stock of the ABC Corporation. ABC has not recently paid any dividends, nor is it expected to for the next three years. However, ABC is expected to begin paying a dividend of $1.50 per share four years from now. In the future, that dividend is expected to grow at a rate of 7% per year. If your required return is 15% per year, what is the maximum amount that you should be willing to pay for a share of ABC common stock?

FIGURE 8-4
VALUING ABC COMMON STOCK WITH TIME-SHIFTING

	?	0	0	0	1.50	1.61	1.72	1.84	1.97	2.10	2.25...
Real Time	0	1	2	3	4	5	6	7	8	9	10...
Shifted Time	-3	-2	-1	0	1	2	3	4	5	6	7...

In order to determine the value of ABC common stock as of today (period 0), we must first find the value as of some future time period. The constant growth dividend discount model can be used at any time period, and will always provide the value of the stock at the time period that is one period before the dividend which is used in the numerator. For this particular problem, the future time period we choose is somewhat arbitrary as long as it is period 3 or later (but period 3 is the easiest). In this case, let's find the value as of period 3 (using the period 4 dividend):

$$V_3 = \frac{1.50}{0.15 - 0.07} = 18.75$$

So we know that the stock will be worth $18.75 per share three years from today. Remembering that the value of a stock is the present value of its cash flows, and that the only relevant cash flow in this case is the value at year three (which encapsulates the value of all future dividends), the value as of today must be:

$$V_0 = \frac{18.75}{1.15^3} = 12.33$$

We could also begin the valuation process at period 5 (or any other period). In this case, the value at period 5 (using the period 6 dividend) is:

$$V_5 = \frac{1.72}{0.15 - 0.07} = 21.50$$

The next step is to take the present value of all future cash flows (in this case: D_4, D_5, and V_5):

$$V_0 = \frac{1.50}{1.15^4} + \frac{1.61 + 21.50}{1.15^5} = 12.35$$

The $0.02 difference in values is due to rounding. Incidentally, note that had we only discounted back to period 3, the value at that time would have been $18.75.

Earlier we said that the assumption of an infinite holding period was not as ludicrous as it sounds. Let's examine this assumption in more detail with a worksheet. Open a new worksheet and enter the labels in the first two rows so that it matches the fragment of a worksheet in Exhibit 8-3.

EXHIBIT 8-3
WORKSHEET TO TEST THE INFINITE HOLDING PERIOD ASSUMPTION

	A	B	C
1	Infinite Holding Period Assumption		
2	Period	Dividends	Present Value
3	1	0.00	
4	2	0.00	
5	3	0.00	
6	4	1.50	
7	5	1.61	
8	6	1.72	
9	7	1.84	
10	8	1.97	
11	9	2.10	
12	10	2.25	

Note that the series of numbers representing the periods extends from 1 to 120 in cells A3..A123. To easily input these numbers, enter a 1 in A3 and then highlight the cells in the range A3..A123. Use the **R**ange Fill by **E**xample command to fill in the numbers.

In this worksheet we want to calculate the value of the stock for various numbers of dividends included. From the example problem, we know that ABC will first pay a dividend of $1.50 in period 4 and that the dividend will grow at a 7% rate each year. Before continuing, enter the dividends into the worksheet as follows: First, enter a 0 for each of the first three dividends. For period 4, enter: 1.50 in B6. In B7 we want to calculate the period 5 dividend, so enter: +B6*1.07. Now copy this formula to each cell in the range B8..B123. To make sure that the copy was successful, note that the value in B123 should be 3842.46 (the power of compounding!).

Now, we want to find the present values of dividends in cells C3..C123. We will use the **@NPV** function to calculate the present values of the dividends. In C3 enter: @NPV(0.15,B$3..B3). The dollar sign will effectively freeze the first cell reference, so if we copy this formula down the range will expand. Copy the formula over the range C4..C123. Now, column C gives the value of the stock if we include only the dividends above the present value cell. For example, the value in C20 ($8.15) is the value of the stock if we consider only the first 18 dividends. Similarly, the value in C50 ($11.85) is the value of the stock if we consider only the first 48 dividends.

Notice how the present value of the dividends converges to the value of the stock ($12.33) as we include more and more dividends in the calculation. It is not necessary to include more than about 120 dividends because the present value of all dividends beyond that point is effectively zero. This is easier to see if we create a graph of the values versus the number of dividends. Highlight C3..C123 and create a line chart. Next, choose **C**hart **R**anges and make A3..A123 you X-axis labels. Your worksheet should now resemble the one in Exhibit 8-4, except that we have added a line to represent the known value of the stock ($12.33).

Other Common Stock Valuation Models

Assuming that the dividends will grow at a constant rate forever is convenient from a mathematical perspective, but it isn't very realistic. Other valuation models have been developed that are more realistic. For example, there is a two-stage growth model which allows for a several periods of supra-normal growth followed by constant growth. In addition, a three-stage model modifies the two-stage model to allow for a gradual decline into the constant-growth stage. Both of these models are more complex than the constant-growth model, but they are essentially unnecessary because all of these models reduce to the present value of future dividends.

EXHIBIT 8-4
THE INFINITE HOLDING PERIOD IS JUST FOR SIMPLICITY

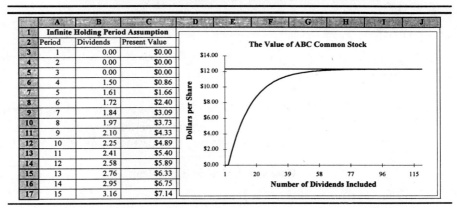

	A	B	C	D E F G H I J
1	Infinite Holding Period Assumption			
2	Period	Dividends	Present Value	
3	1	0.00	$0.00	
4	2	0.00	$0.00	
5	3	0.00	$0.00	
6	4	1.50	$0.86	
7	5	1.61	$1.66	
8	6	1.72	$2.40	
9	7	1.84	$3.09	
10	8	1.97	$3.73	
11	9	2.10	$4.33	
12	10	2.25	$4.89	
13	11	2.41	$5.40	
14	12	2.58	$5.89	
15	13	2.76	$6.33	
16	14	2.95	$6.75	
17	15	3.16	$7.14	

Bond Valuation

A bond is an interest-bearing, or discounted, security which obligates the issuer to pay the bondholder periodic interest payments and to repay the principal at maturity. Bonds are valued in the same manner as most other securities. That is, the value of a bond is the present value of its future cash flows.

For a bond the cash flows consist of periodic (usually semiannual) interest payments and the return of the principal at maturity. The cash flow at maturity will therefore consist of both the last interest payment and the principal (often $1,000). For a four-year, semiannual payment bond the timeline is pictured in Figure 8-5.

FIGURE 8-5
TIMELINE FOR A FOUR-YEAR BOND WITH SEMIANNUAL INTEREST PAYMENTS

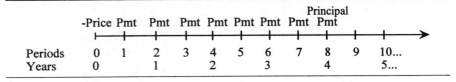

As Figure 8-5 makes clear, a bond consists of two types of cash flows: an annuity (the interest payments) and a lump sum (the principal). Recalling the principal of value additivity from Chapter 7, we know that this stream of cash flows can be valued by adding the present values of its components. For a bond, the value is given by:

$$V_B = Pmt \left[\frac{1 - \dfrac{1}{(1 + k_B)^N}}{k_B} \right] + \frac{FV}{(1 + k_B)^N} \qquad (8\text{-}4)$$

where Pmt is the periodic interest payment, k_B is the required rate of return for the bond, N is the number of periods, and FV is the face value. Recognize that this formula is valid only on a payment date.

Consider the example problem:

> Wrent-a-Wreck, Inc. has issued bonds with 20 years to maturity, an 8% coupon rate, and $1,000 face value. If your required rate of return is 9% and the bonds pay interest semiannually, what is the value of these bonds?

Before solving this problem, some definitions are required. Until fairly recently, bonds were printed on ornately decorated paper with small detachable coupons around the edges. These coupons were to be presented to the issuer in order to collect the periodic interest payments. Because of this practice, the interest payment has come to be known as the *coupon payment* and the rate of interest that the issuer has promised to pay is referred to as the *coupon rate*. The annual interest payment is determined by multiplying the *face value* (principal) by the coupon rate. For bonds which pay interest more frequently than annually, the annual interest payment is divided by the number of payments per year. Most often, interest is paid twice per year so the annual interest payment must be divided by two.

For the Wrent-a-Wreck bonds, the annual interest payment is $80 (= 0.08*1,000), but the semiannual payment is $40 (= 80/2). Furthermore, because the bond interest is paid twice per year, we must adjust the required return and number of periods to a semiannual basis. The required return is 9% per year which is 4.5% (= 9%/2) per six-month period. Since there are 20 years to maturity, there are 40 (= 20*2) six-month periods to maturity. Therefore, the value of the bonds is:

$$V_B = 40 \left[\frac{1 - \dfrac{1}{1.045^{40}}}{0.045} \right] + \frac{1,000}{1.045^{40}} = 907.99$$

1-2-3 has a number of built-in functions which can be used for bond valuation. Most of these functions are beyond the scope of this text, so we will examine only two. To find the value of a coupon bearing bond, 1-2-3 provides the @PRICE function which is defined as:

@PRICE(*SETTLEMENT*, *MATURITY*, *COUPON*, *YIELD*, *REDEMPTION*, *FREQUENCY*, *BASIS*).

SETTLEMENT is the date on which money and securities change hands, and *MATURITY* is the date on which the last coupon payment is made and the principal is returned. 1-2-3 uses the Windows date format to determine if what you have entered is a date. The Windows date format can be changed in the Control Panel if necessary, but most users will accept the default for their country. In the U.S. the default is the Month/Day/Year format so 1-2-3 will recognize, say, 2/4/97 as February 4, 1997 and treat it as a date. Other date formats are treated as text strings. Dates are converted to a number which represents the number of days since January 1, 1900. In the 1900 date system the serial number 1 corresponds to January 1, 1900. To see the actual serial number, you can use the General number format. Using serial numbers makes date math quite simple. For example, you can determine the number of days between two dates with simple subtraction. Also, note that the date serial number is independent of the date format applied.

COUPON is the annual coupon rate. *YIELD* is the annual required rate of return. In 1-2-3 functions, percentage rates are always entered in decimal form. If the coupon rate is 10%, you must enter it as 0.10, although 1-2-3 will convert a number followed by a percent sign (%) to this format. The effect of the percent sign is to cause 1-2-3 to divide the preceding number by 100.

REDEMPTION is the amount to be received per $100 of face value when the bond is redeemed. It is important to realize that the redemption price can be different than the face value of the bond. This would be the case, for example, if the bond was called by the issuer. Calling a bond issue is very similar to refinancing a mortgage in that the issuer usually wishes to reissue debt at a lower interest rate. There is often a premium that is paid to bondholders when bonds are called, and this premium plus the face value is the redemption price. If a bond issue has a 4% call premium, then *REDEMPTION* would be set to 104.

FREQUENCY is the number of coupons paid each year. Most commonly this will be 2, though other values are possible. 1-2-3 will return the ERR error if *FREQUENCY* is any value other than 1, 2, 4, or 12 (annual, semiannual, quarterly, or monthly).

BASIS describes the assumption regarding the number of days in a month and year. Historically, different financial markets have made different assumptions regarding the number of days in a month and a year. Corporate, agency, and municipal bonds are priced assuming that there are 30 days in a month and 360 days in a year. Treasury securities are priced assuming a 365-day year (366 days in a leap year) and the actual number of days in a month.[5] 1-2-3 allows for four possibilities [days per month/days per year (code)]: 30/360 (0 or omitted); actual/actual (1); actual/360 (2); actual/365 (3). Any number greater than 3 will result in an error. For our purposes, the basis is unlikely to make a difference in the calculated price. However, if you are trading in large numbers of bonds, the basis can make a significant difference.

EXHIBIT 8-5
BOND VALUATION WORKSHEET USING THE PRICE FUNCTION

	A	B
1	**Bond Valuation**	
2	Settlement Date	2/15/97
3	Maturity Date	2/10/17
4	Coupon Rate	8.00%
5	Required Return	9.00%
6	Redemption Value	100
7	Frequency	2
8	Basis	0
9	Value	

To see how the **@PRICE** function works, open a new worksheet and enter the data displayed in Exhibit 8-5 which is taken from the example. The settlement date should be entered by simply typing the date as it appears. As noted above, 1-2-3 will automatically recognize it as a date, though you may have to format it if the serial number (35476 for 2/15/97) appears. Recall that the Wrent-a-Wreck bonds mature in 20 years. We have assumed that the settlement date is 2/15/97. Your inclination is probably to enter 2/15/2017 for the maturity date, but that is actually

---

5. For more information on day count conventions, see "Standard Securities Calculation Methods," by John J. Lynch, Jr. and Jan H. Mayle, Securities Industry Association, 1986.

20 years and 5 days. To find the actual date that is exactly 20 years in the future, we have entered the formula: +B2+20*365 in B3. This formula takes the settlement date in B2 and adds 20 years to it. We do this to be consistent with the example calculations. In actual practice, the maturity date of the bond could be found in the indenture,[6] by simply asking a broker, or by consulting a bond guide.

The current value of the bond can now be found by entering the function: @PRICE(B2,B3,B4,B5,B6,B7,B8)*10 in B9. The value is $907.99, exactly as we found by hand. Since bond prices are normally quoted as a percentage of par value we have multiplied the @PRICE function's return value by 10. This will convert the output to an actual price. If the face value is something other than $1,000, you will have to use a different multiplier. Also notice that we have not made any adjustment to account for the fact that the bond pays interest semiannually. 1-2-3 automatically makes this adjustment for you based on the frequency.

In most textbooks, the homework problems don't provide dates for input to spreadsheet functions. There are two ways to attack these types of problems. The first method is illustrated above: simply assume the dates. The actual dates are not important, as long as the time between the dates is equal to the time specified in the problem.[7] The second method is to use other built-in time value functions. For example, we could have entered: @PVAL(B4*B6*10/2,B5/2,40,0,B6*10) in B9. Note that, because of the way that we set up the worksheet, we must adjust the required return and the interest payment to a semiannual basis. Note also that the result is exactly the same as the other methods that we have used, $907.99.

Bond Return Measures

Most often, investors do not decide to buy a bond because the price is below their arbitrarily determined intrinsic value. Instead, they examine the alternatives and

---

6. The indenture is the formal agreement which specifies all of the conditions of the bond issue.

7. In practice the actual dates might be important. For example, assume that you need a six-month period. If you were to choose 2/15/97 to 8/15/97, that would be 181 days. On the other hand, 8/15/97 to 2/15/98 is 184 days. The difference can be important if you are trading a large quantity of bonds.

compare bonds on the basis of the returns that they offer. There are several ways to calculate the returns offered by bonds. In this section we will cover three.

Current Yield

The *current yield* is defined as the annual coupon payment divided by the current price of the bond:

$$CY = \frac{Pmt}{V_B}. \tag{8-5}$$

The current yield is considered to be a rough measure of the return earned over the next year. We say that it is rough because it ignores compounding and the change in price which may occur.

1-2-3 has no built-in function to calculate the current yield, but it is a simple matter to write the formula yourself. On your worksheet, move to A11 and type: Current Yield. Now, in B11 enter: +(B4*B6*10)/B9. We must multiply the coupon rate (in B4) by 10 to convert to the annual interest payment.

Yield to Maturity

The *yield to maturity* is the compound annual rate of return that can be expected if the bond is held to maturity. The yield to maturity is not without its problems as a return measure, but it is superior to the current yield. Unfortunately, it is also much more complex to calculate.

Essentially, the yield to maturity is found by taking the bond price as given and solving the valuation equation for the required return (k_B).[8] No method exists, however, to solve directly for the yield to maturity. The yield can be found by using a trial and error approach, but it is a bit tedious. 1-2-3 makes the yield calculation simple with its built-in @**YIELD** function which is defined as:

---

8. It should be noted that for most purposes the terms "required return" and "yield to maturity" can be used interchangeably, and often are. However, there is a slight, but important difference between the terms. Specifically, the required return is specified by the investor, and can be different for different investors. The yield to maturity is not under the control of the investor. Instead it is merely a function of the current bond price and cash flows promised from the bond. As such, the yield to maturity will be the same regardless of who calculates it.

@Y<small>IELD</small>(S<small>ETTLEMENT</small>, M<small>ATURITY</small>, C<small>OUPON</small>, P<small>RICE</small>, R<small>EDEMPTION</small>, F<small>REQUENCY</small>,
B<small>ASIS</small>).

All of the variables are the same as previously defined with the exception of **PRICE**, which is the price of the bond as a percentage of the face value.

To make the calculation, first place the label: Yield to Maturity in A12 and then enter: @YIELD(B2,B3,B4,B9/10,B6,B7,B8) in B12. Note that the only difference from the **@PRICE** function is that we replaced *YIELD* with the current price of the bond as a percentage of par (i.e., face value). In this case, we had to convert the bond price (in B9) back to a percentage of par by dividing it by 10. The result, as should be expected, is 9%.

Yield to Call

One other common measure of return is the *yield to call*. As noted earlier, many issuers reserve the right to buy back the bonds that they sell if it serves their interests. In most cases, bonds will be called if interest rates drop substantially so that the firm will save money by refinancing at a lower rate. If we calculate the yield to maturity assuming that the bond will be called at the first opportunity, we will have calculated the yield to call. Since it is common to have a contractual obligation to pay a premium over par value if the bonds are called, this must be taken into account in our calculation.

In order to make this calculation we must add a couple of lines to our worksheet. First, insert a row above row 4. To do this highlight row 4, and choose **E**dit **I**nsert. Now, in A4 type: First Call Date to indicate that this is the first date at which the firm has the option of calling the bonds. In B4 enter: 2/15/2002. This date reflects the fact that the first call date is often five years after the issue date (which we are assuming is the same as the settlement date in this case). Next, insert a row above row 8 and label it in A8: Call Price. Cell B8 will be the price at which the bonds can be called, in this case 5% over par value, so enter: 105.

Finally, we will calculate the yield to call in B16 with the formula: @YIELD(B2,B4,B5,B11/10,B8,B9,B10). This is exactly the same formula as the yield to maturity, except that we have changed the maturity date to the call date, and the redemption value to the call price. Note that the call premium plus the earlier receipt of the face value has caused the yield to call to be 11.23%.

Your worksheet should now resemble the one in Exhibit 8-6.

EXHIBIT 8-6
BOND VALUATION WORKSHEET WITH YIELD TO CALL ADDED

	A	B
1	**Bond Valuation**	
2	Settlement Date	2/15/97
3	Maturity Date	2/10/17
4	First Call Date	2/15/02
5	Coupon Rate	8.00%
6	Required Return	9.00%
7	Redemption Value	100
8	Call Price	105
9	Frequency	2
10	Basis	0
11	Value	$ 907.99
12		
13	**Return Measures**	
14	Current Yield	8.81%
15	Yield to Maturity	9.00%
16	Yield to Call	11.23%

Preferred Stock Valuation

Preferred stock is a kind of hybrid security. It represents an ownership claim on the assets of the firm, like common stock, but holders of preferred stock do not benefit from increases in the firms earnings and they generally cannot vote in corporate elections, like bonds. Further, like a bond, preferred stock generally pays a fixed dividend payment each period. Also, like a common stock, there is no predefined maturity date, so the life of a share of preferred stock is effectively infinite.

With the complex nature of preferred stock, it would be natural to assume that it must be difficult to determine its value. As we will see, preferred stock is actually easier to value than either bonds or common stock. To see how we can derive the valuation formula for preferred stock, consider the following example.

> The XYZ Corporation has issued preferred stock which pays a 10% annual dividend on its $50 par value. If your required return

for investments of this type is 12%, what is the maximum amount that you should be willing to pay for a share of XYZ preferred?

As usual, the first step in valuing preferred stock is to determine the cash flows. In the case of XYZ preferred, we have an infinite stream of dividends which are 10% of the par value. That is, we have an infinite annuity, or perpetuity,[9] of $5 per year. Figure 8-6 illustrates the expected cash flows for XYZ preferred stock.

FIGURE 8-6
TIMELINE FOR XYZ PREFERRED STOCK

	5	5	5	5	5	5	5	5	5	5...
0	1	2	3	4	5	6	7	8	9	10...

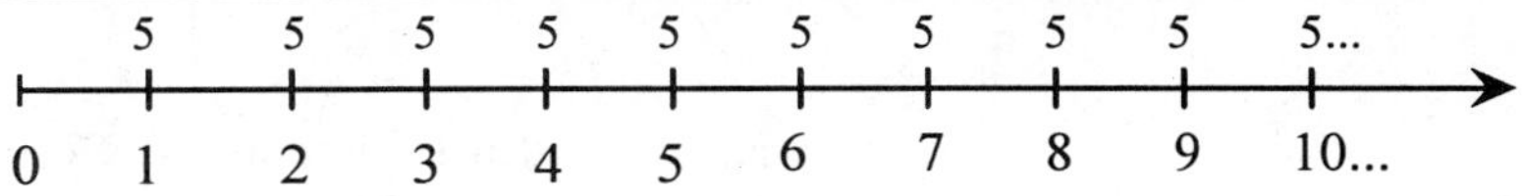

One way that we can arrive at a valuation formula for preferred stock is to realize that the cash flows resemble those of common stock. Preferred stock pays a dividend and never matures, just like common stock. The only difference, as far as the cash flows are concerned, is that the dividend never changes. In other words, the growth rate is zero. Therefore, we can say that the value of preferred stock is:

$$V_P = \frac{D_0(1+g)}{k_P - g}$$

but since the growth rate is 0 we can simplify this to:

$$V_P = \frac{D}{k_P} \tag{8-6}$$

Notice that the subscript has been dropped on the dividend because all dividends are equal.

As an alternative, we can value the perpetuity as if it were a bond with an infinite life. In this case, we have:

9. The term "perpetuity" derives from perpetual annuity. In other words, it is an annuity-type cash flow which pays forever.

$$V_P = D\left[\frac{1 - \dfrac{1}{(1+k_P)^\infty}}{k_P}\right] + \frac{FV}{(1+k_P)^\infty}$$

Realizing that any number greater than 1 raised to an infinite power is equal to infinity, we can rewrite this expression as:

$$V_P = D\left[\frac{1 - \dfrac{1}{\infty}}{k_P}\right] + \frac{FV}{\infty}$$

But any number divided by infinity is effectively equal to 0, so this equation reduces to:[10]

$$V_P = \frac{D}{k_P}$$

which is exactly the same as Equation (8-6). So, for valuation purposes, regardless of whether we treat preferred stock like common stock or bonds, we arrive at exactly the same valuation formula. To find the value of a share of preferred stock, we need to merely divide its dividend payment by our required rate of return. Therefore, the value of XYZ's preferred stock must be:

$$V_P = \frac{5}{0.12} = 41.66$$

You can prove this to yourself by recreating Exhibit 8-4 (page 167) with all of the dividends set to 5.

---

10. Actually, we can't divide by infinity. Instead, we should take the limit as N approaches infinity.

Summary

The valuation process is important to both financial managers and investors. As we will see in future chapters, understanding the valuation process is crucial to making sound financial decisions.

In this chapter we found that the value of a security depends on several factors:

- The size of the expected cash flows.
- The timing of the expected cash flows.
- The perceived riskiness of the expected cash flows.

Once the cash flows and required rate of return have been determined, we can value the security by finding the present value of its future cash flows.

The actual equations appear to be different, but they all reduce to the present value of future cash flows. The formulas are:

Common stock:
$$V_{CS} = \frac{D_0(1+g)}{k_{CS}-g} = \frac{D_1}{k_{CS}-g}$$

Bonds:
$$V_B = Pmt\left[\frac{1-\frac{1}{(1+k_B)^N}}{k_B}\right] + \frac{FV}{(1+k_B)^N}$$

Preferred stock:
$$V_P = \frac{D}{k_P}$$

TABLE 8-1
FUNCTIONS INTRODUCED IN THIS CHAPTER

Purpose	Function	Page
Find the value of a bond	@PRICE(*SETTLEMENT*, *MATURITY*, *COUPON*, *YIELD*, *REDEMPTION*, *FREQUENCY*, *BASIS*)	169
Find the yield to maturity of a bond	@YIELD(*SETTLEMENT*, *MATURITY*, *COUPON*, *PRICE*, *REDEMPTION*, *FREQUENCY*, *BASIS*)	173

CHAPTER 9 *The Cost of Capital*

After studying this chapter, you should be able to:

1. *Define "hurdle rate" and show how it relates to the firm's Weighted Average Cost of Capital (WACC).*

2. *Calculate the WACC using both book- and market-value rates.*

3. *Calculate component costs of capital with flotation costs and taxes.*

4. *Explain how and why a firm's WACC changes as total capital requirements change.*

5. *Use 1-2-3 to calculate the "break-points" in a firm's marginal WACC curve, and graph this curve in 1-2-3.*

Knowledge of a firm's cost of capital is vital if managers are to make appropriate decisions regarding the use of the firm's funds. Without this knowledge, poor investments may be made that actually reduce shareholder wealth. In this chapter we will examine what the cost of capital is and how to calculate it.

The Appropriate 'Hurdle' Rate

A firm's required rate of return on investments is often referred to as its *hurdle rate* because all projects must earn a rate of return high enough to clear this rate. Otherwise, a project will not cover its cost of financing, thereby reducing shareholder wealth. But what is the appropriate rate to use? Let's look at an example.

> The managers of the Rocky Mountain Motors are considering the purchase of a new tract of land which will be held for one year. The purchase price of the land is $10,000. RMM's capital structure is currently made up of 40% debt, 10% preferred stock and 50% common equity. Because this capital structure is considered to be optimal, any new financing will be raised in the same proportions. RMM must raise the new funds as indicated in Table 9-1.

TABLE 9-1
FUNDING FOR RMM'S LAND PURCHASE

Source of Funds	Amount	Dollar Cost	After-tax Cost
Debt	$ 4,000	$ 280	7%
Preferred Stock	1,000	100	10%
Common Stock	5,000	600	12%
Total	10,000	980	9.8%

> Before making the decision, RMM's managers must determine what required rate of return will simultaneously satisfy all of their stakeholders. What minimum rate of return will accomplish this goal?

Obviously, the land must generate at least $980 in excess of its cost in order to cover the financing costs. This represents a minimum required return of 9.8% on the investment of $10,000. Table 9-2 shows what would happen under three alternative rate of return scenarios.

TABLE 9-2
ALTERNATIVE SCENARIOS FOR RMM

Rate of Return	8%	9.8%	11%
Total Funds Available	$ 10,800	$ 10,980	$ 11,100
Less: Debt Costs	4,280	4,280	4,280
Less: Preferred Costs	1,100	1,100	1,100
Available to Common Shareholders	5,420	5,600	5,720

Recall that the common shareholders' required rate of return is 12% on the $5,000 that they provided. If RMM earns only 8%, the common shareholders will receive only $5,420 which is $180 (1.8%) less than required. Presumably, the common shareholders have alternative investment opportunities (with equal risk) which would return 12%. Therefore, if the project can return only 8%, the best decision that the managers could make would be to allow the common shareholders to hold on to their money. In other words, the project should be rejected.

On the other hand, if the project is expected to return 9.8% the common shareholders will receive exactly the amount that they require. If the project returns 11%, they will be more than satisfied. Under these latter two scenarios the project should be accepted because shareholder wealth will either be increased by the amount required (9.8%) or increased by more than required (11%).

The Weighted Average Cost of Capital

It still remains to determine, in a general way, what required rate of return will simultaneously satisfy all of the firm's stakeholders. Recall that 40% of RMM's funds were provided by the debtholders. Therefore, 40% of this minimum required rate of return must go to satisfy the debtholders. For the same reason, 10% of this minimum required rate of return must go to satisfy the preferred stockholders, and 50% will be required for the common stockholders. In general, the minimum required rate of return must be a weighted average of the capital providers' individual required rates of return.

We, therefore, refer to this minimum required rate of return as the *weighted average cost of capital* (*WACC*). The weighted average cost of capital can be found as follows:

$$WACC = w_d k_d + w_P k_P + w_{cs} k_{cs} \qquad \text{(9-1)}$$

where the w's are the weights of each source of capital, and the k's are the costs (required returns) for each source of capital. In the case of RMM, the *WACC* is:

$$WACC = 0.40(0.07) + 0.10(0.10) + 0.50(0.12) = 0.098 = 9.80\%$$

which is exactly the required return that we found above.

Determining the Weights

The weights that one uses in the calculation of the *WACC* will obviously affect the result. Therefore, an important question is, "where do the weights come from?" Actually, there are two possible answers to this question. Perhaps the most obvious answer is to find the weights on the balance sheet.

The balance sheet weights (usually referred to as the *book-value* weights) can be obtained by the following procedure. Find the total long-term debt, total preferred equity, and the total common equity. Add together each of these to arrive at the grand total of the long-term sources of capital. Finally, divide each component by the grand total to determine the percentage that each source is of total capital. Table 9-3 summarizes these calculations for RMM.

TABLE 9-3
CALCULATION OF BOOK-VALUE WEIGHTS FOR RMM

Source of Capital	Total Book Value	Percentage of Total
Long-term Debt	$400,000	40%
Preferred Equity	$100,000	10%
Common Stock	$500,000	50%
Grand Totals	$1,000,000	100%

The problem with book-value weights is that they represent the weights as they were when the securities were originally sold. That is, the book-value weights represent historical weights. The calculated *WACC* would better represent current reality if we used the present weights. Since the market constantly re-values the firm's securities, we can find the weights by using the current market values of the securities.

The procedure for determining the market-value weights is similar to that used to find the book-value weights. First, determine the total market value of each type of security. Total the results, and divide the market value of each source of capital by the total to determine the weights.

TABLE 9-4
CALCULATION OF MARKET-VALUE WEIGHTS FOR RMM

Source	Price Per Unit	Units	Total Market Value	Percentage of Total
Debt	$ 904.53	400	$ 362,000	31.15%
Preferred	100.00	1,000	100,000	8.61%
Common	70.00	10,000	700,000	60.24%
Totals			1,162,000	100.00%

Table 9-4 shows RMM's current capital structure in market-value terms. Using these weights we can see that their *WACC* is:

$$WACC = 0.3115(0.07) + 0.0861(0.10) + 0.6024(0.12) = 0.1027 = 10.27\%.$$

In this example, the book-value *WACC* and the market-value *WACC* are quite close together. This is not necessarily always so. Whenever possible, use the market values of the firm's securities to determine the *WACC*.

WACC Calculations in 1-2-3

We can easily set up a worksheet to do the calculations for the *WACC* as in Table 9-4. To do this, first copy the data from Table 9-4 into a new worksheet, starting with the headings in A1.

In column D, we want to calculate the total market value of the securities which is the price times the number of units outstanding. So, in D2 enter: +B2*C2 and copy the formula down to D3 and D4. Cell D5 should have the total market value of the securities, so enter: @Sum(D2..D4). In Column E we need the percentage that each security represents of the total market value. These are the weights that we will use to calculate the *WACC*. In E2 enter: `+D2/D$5` and copy down to E3 and E4. As a check, calculate the total in E5; it should equal 100%.

Next, we want a column for the after-tax costs of each source of capital, and the weighted-average cost of capital. In F1 enter the label: `After-tax Cost`. Now, in F2..F4 enter the after-tax cost of each component from Table 9-1. We will calculate the *WACC* in F5 with the formula: `+E2*F2+E3*F3+E4*F4`. The completed worksheet appears in Exhibit 9-1. Note that the *WACC* is exactly as we calculated earlier.[1] You are encouraged to experiment by changing the market prices of the securities to see how the weights, and subsequently the *WACC*, change.[2]

EXHIBIT 9-1
WORKSHEET TO CALCULATE RMM'S *WACC*

	A	B	C	D	E	F
1	Source	Price	Units	Total Market Value	Percentage of Total	After-tax Cost
2	Debt	905	400	$ 361,812	31.14%	7.00%
3	Preferred	100	1,000	$ 100,000	8.61%	10.00%
4	Common	70	10,000	$ 700,000	60.25%	12.00%
5	Totals			$ 1,161,812	100.00%	10.27%

Calculating the Component Costs

Up to this point, we have taken the component costs of capital as a given. In reality, these costs are anything but given, and, in fact, change continuously. How we calculate these costs is the subject of this section.

---

1. Note that this is a simplified example. In reality, most companies will have multiple debt issues outstanding, and many have more than one class of common and preferred stock outstanding as well. The calculations will work in exactly the same way, regardless of the number of issues outstanding.

2. It would be a fairly simple exercise to completely automate the calculation of the *WACC* for a firm. All that would be needed, in addition to 1-2-3, are a communications program and a subscription to an on-line service that provides prices for traded securities. Using Dynamic Data Exchange (DDE) or OLE a 1-2-3 programmer could have the communications program update the prices in the worksheet. The *WACC* would then be recalculated, all without further human intervention.

To begin, note that the obvious way of determining the required rate of returns is to simply ask each stakeholder what her required rate of return is for the particular security that she owns. For all but the most closely held of firms, this would be exceedingly impractical. However, there is a way by which we can accomplish the same end result.

Recall from Chapter 8 that the market value of a security is a weighted average of the intrinsic values of each individual shareholder. Further, if shareholders are rational, they will buy (sell) securities as the expected return rises above (falls below) their required return. Therefore, we can say that the common shareholders "vote with their dollars" on the issue of the firm's cost of equity. This force operates in all markets. So at any given moment, the price of a security will reflect the overall required rate of return for that security. All we need, then, is a method of converting the observed market prices of securities into required rates of return.

Since we have already discussed the valuation of securities (common stock, preferred stock, and bonds) you should recall that a major input was the investor's required rate of return. As we will see, we can simply invert the valuation equations to solve for the required rate of return.

The Cost of Common Equity

Because of complexities in the real world, finding a company's cost of common equity is not always straightforward. In this section we will look at two approaches to this problem, both of which we have seen previously in other guises.

Using the Dividend Discount Model

Recall that a share of common stock is a perpetual security which, we often assume, will periodically pay a cash flow which grows over time. We have previously demonstrated that the present value of such a stream of cash flows is given by Equation (8-3):

$$V_{CS} = \frac{D_0(1+g)}{k_{CS}-g} = \frac{D_1}{k_{CS}-g}$$

assuming an infinite holding period and a constant rate of growth for the cash flows.

If we know the current market price of the stock, we can use this knowledge to solve for the common shareholder's required rate of return. Simple algebraic manipulation will reveal that this rate of return is given by:

$$k_{CS} = \frac{D_0(1 + g)}{V_{CS}} + g = \frac{D_1}{V_{CS}} + g \tag{9-2}$$

Note that this equation says that the required rate of return on common equity is equal to the sum of the dividend yield and the growth rate of the dividend stream.

Using the CAPM

Not all common stocks will meet the assumptions of the Dividend Discount Model. In particular, many companies do not pay dividends, resulting in the ridiculous result that their cost of common equity appears to be 0% with this model. An alternative approach to determining the cost of equity is to use the Capital Asset Pricing Model (*CAPM*).

The *CAPM* gives the expected rate of return for a security if we know the risk-free rate of interest, the market risk premium, and the riskiness of the security relative to the market portfolio (i.e., the security's beta). The *CAPM*, you will recall, is the equation for the security market line:

$$E(R_i) = R_f + \beta_i(R_m - R_f)$$

Assuming that the stockholders are all price-takers, their expected return is the same as the firm's required rate of return.[3] Therefore, we can use the CAPM to determine the required rate of return on equity.

---

3. A price-taker cannot materially affect the price of an asset through individual buying or selling. This situation generally exists in the stock market because most investors are small when compared to the market value of the firm's common stock. In an earlier footnote, we distinguished between the expected and required rates of return for an *individual* investor. Note that we have not altered this distinction here. We are merely pointing out that the *investors'* expected return is the same as the *firm's* required return.

The Cost of Preferred Equity

Preferred stock, for valuation purposes, can be viewed as a special case of the common stock with the growth rate of dividends equal to zero. We can carry this idea to the process of solving for the preferred stockholders' required rate of return. First, recall that the value of a share of preferred stock was given by Equation (8-6):

$$V_P = \frac{D}{k_P}$$

As with common stock, we can algebraically manipulate this equation to solve for the required return if the market price is known:

$$k_P = \frac{D}{V_p} \qquad (9\text{-}3)$$

The Cost of Debt

Finding the cost of debt is more difficult than finding the cost of either preferred or common equity. The process is similar: determine the market price of the security, and then find the discount rate which makes the present value of the expected future cash flows equal to this price. However, we cannot directly solve for this discount rate. Instead, we must use an iterative trial and error process.

Recall that the value of a bond is given by Equation (8-4):

$$V_B = Pmt \left[\frac{1 - \frac{1}{(1 + k_d)^N}}{k_d} \right] + \frac{FV}{(1 + k_d)^N}$$

The problem is to find k_d such that the equality holds between the left and right sides of the equation. Suppose that, as in Exhibit 9-1, the current price of RMM's bonds is $904.53, the coupon rate is 10%, the face value of the bonds is $1,000 and the bonds will mature in 10 years. If the bonds pay interest annually, our equation looks as follows:

$$904.53 = 100\left[\dfrac{1 - \dfrac{1}{(1 + k_d)^{10}}}{k_d}\right] + \dfrac{1,000}{(1 + k_d)^{10}}$$

We must make an initial, but intelligent, guess as to the value of k_d. Since the bond is selling at a discount to its face value, we know that the yield to maturity (k_d) must be greater than the coupon rate. Therefore, our first guess should be something greater than 10%. If we choose 12% we will find that the price would be $886.99 which is lower than the actual price. Our first guess was incorrect, but we now know that the answer must lie between 10% and 12%. The next logical guess is 11%, which is the halfway point. Inserting this for k_d we get a price of $941.11 which is too high, but not by much. Further, we have narrowed the range of possible answers to those between 11% and 12%. Again, we choose the halfway point, 11.5%, as our next guess. This results in an answer of $913.48. Continuing this process we will eventually find the correct answer to be 11.67%.[4]

Making an Adjustment for Taxes

Notice that the answer that we found for the cost of debt, 11.67%, is not the same as that listed in Exhibit 9-1. Because interest is a tax-deductible expense, interest payments actually cost less than the full amount of the payment. In this case, if RMM were to make an interest payment of $116.70, and the marginal tax rate is 40%, it would only cost them $70.02 ($= 116.70 \times (1 - 0.40)$). Notice that $70.02 / 1,000 \approx 0.07$, or 7% which is the after-tax cost of debt listed in Exhibit 9-1.

In general, we need to adjust the cost of debt to account for the deductibility of the interest expense by multiplying the before-tax cost of debt (i.e., the yield to maturity) by 1 - t, where t is the marginal tax rate. Note that we do not make the same adjustment for the cost of common or preferred equity because dividends are not tax deductible.[5]

---

4. The method presented here is known as the bisection method. Briefly, the idea is to quickly bracket the solution and to then choose as the next approximation the answer that is exactly halfway between the previous possibilities. This method can lead to very rapid convergence on the solution if a good beginning guess is used.

5. This is just a close approximation. In actuality, it is more accurate to use the after-tax cash flows in the equation. This will result in the after-tax cost of debt with no additional adjustment required, and will differ slightly from that given above.

Using 1-2-3 to Calculate the Component Costs

A general principle that we have relied on in constructing our worksheet models is that we should make 1-2-3 do the calculations whenever possible. We will now make changes to our worksheet in Exhibit 9-1 to allow 1-2-3 to calculate the component costs of capital.

The After-tax Cost of Debt

We cannot calculate any of the component costs on our worksheet without adding some additional information. We will first add information which will be used to calculate the after-tax cost of debt. Beginning in A7 with the label: `Additional Bond Data`, add the information from Table 9-5 into your worksheet.

TABLE 9-5
ADDITIONAL DATA FOR CALCULATING THE COST OF DEBT FOR RMM

Additional Bond Data	
Tax Rate	40%
Coupon Rate	10%
Face Value	$1,000
Maturity	10

With this information entered, we now need a function to find the cost of debt. 1-2-3 provides two built-in functions that will do the job: **@IRATE** and **@YIELD**. We have already seen both of these functions. Since **@YIELD** (defined on page 173) requires more information than we have supplied, we will use **@IRATE** (see page 138). Recall that **@IRATE** will solve for the yield for an annuity-type stream of cash flows and allows for a different present value and future value. Specifically, **@IRATE** is defined as:

@IRATE(*TERM*, *PAYMENT*, *PRESENT-VALUE*, *TYPE*, *FUTURE-VALUE*, *GUESS*)

The only unusual aspect of our usage of this function is that we will be supplying both a *PRESENT-VALUE* and an *FUTURE-VALUE*. Specifically, *PRESENT-VALUE* will be the current bond price and *FUTURE-VALUE* is the face value of the bond. In F2 enter the **@IRATE** function as: `@IRATE(B11,B9*B10,B2,0,-B10,0.1)`. The result is 11.67% which we found to be the pre-tax cost of debt. Remember that we must also make an adjustment for taxes, so we need to multiply by 1 - t. The final form of the formula in F2 then is: `@IRATE(B11,B9*B10,B2,0,-B10, 0.1)*(1-B8)`, and the result is 7.00%. Note that in order to make this equation work properly, we must make the *FUTURE-VALUE* negative.

With the new bond information, your worksheet should resemble Exhibit 9-2.

EXHIBIT 9-2
RMM WORKSHEET WITH BOND DATA

	A	B	C	D	E	F
1	Source	Price	Units	Total Market Value	Percentage of Total	After-tax Cost
2	Debt	905	400	$ 361,812	31.14%	7.00%
3	Preferred	100	1,000	$ 100,000	8.61%	10.00%
4	Common	70	10,000	$ 700,000	60.25%	12.00%
5	Totals			$ 1,161,812	100.00%	10.27%
6						
7	Additional Bond Data					
8	Tax Rate	40%				
9	Coupon Rate	10%				
10	Face Value	$ 1,000				
11	Maturity	10				

The Cost of Preferred Stock

Compared to calculating the after-tax cost of debt, finding the cost of preferred stock is easy. We need only add one piece of information: the preferred dividend. In C7 type: `Additional Preferred Data`. In C8 type: `Dividend` and in D8 enter: `10`.

We know from Equation (9-3) that we need to divide the preferred dividend by the current price of the stock. Therefore, the equation in F3 is: `+D8/B3`.

The Cost of Common Stock

To calculate the cost of common stock, we need to know the most recent dividend and the dividend growth rate in addition to the current market price of the stock. In E7 type: `Additional Common Data`. In E8 type: `Dividend 0` and in F8 enter: `3.96`. In E9 enter the label: `Growth Rate` and in F9 enter: `6%`.

Finally, we will use Equation (9-2) to calculate the cost of common stock in F4. Since we know the most recent dividend (D_0) we need to multiply that by $1 + g$. The formula in F4 is: `+(F8*(1+F9))/B4+F9`, and the result is 12% as we found earlier.

As you will see, we have not yet completed the calculation of the WACC for RMM. We have left out one crucial component which we will discuss in the next section. At this point, your worksheet should resemble that in Exhibit 9-3.

EXHIBIT 9-3
RMM COST OF CAPITAL WORKSHEET

	A	B	C	D	E	F
1	Source	Price	Units	Total Market Value	Percentage of Total	After-tax Cost
2	Debt	905	400	$ 361,812	31.14%	7.00%
3	Preferred	100	1,000	$ 100,000	8.61%	10.00%
4	Common	70	10,000	$ 700,000	60.25%	12.00%
5	Totals			$ 1,161,812	100.00%	10.27%
6						
7	Additional Bond Data		Additional Preferred Data		Additional Common Data	
8	Tax Rate	40%	Dividend	$ 10.00	Dividend 0	$ 3.96
9	Coupon Rate	10%			Growth Rate	6%
10	Face Value	$ 1,000				
11	Maturity	10				

The Role of Flotation Costs

Any action that a corporation takes has costs associated with it. Up to this point we have implicitly assumed that securities can be issued without cost, but this is not the case. Selling securities directly to the public is a complicated procedure, generally requiring a lot of management time as well as the services of an *investment banker*. An investment banker is a firm which serves as an intermediary between the issuing firm and the public. In addition to forming the underwriting syndicate to sell the securities, the investment banker also functions as a consultant to the firm. As a consultant, the investment banker usually advises the firm on the pricing of the issue, and is responsible for preparing the registration statement for the Securities and Exchange Commission (SEC).

The cost of the investment banker's services, and other costs of issuance, are referred to as *flotation costs*. (The term derives from the fact that the process of selling a new issue is generally referred to as floating a new issue.) These flotation costs add to the total cost of the new securities to the firm, and we must increase the component cost of capital to account for them.

There are two methods of accounting for flotation costs.[6] The most popular method is the cost of capital adjustment. Under this method the market price of new securities is *decreased* by the per unit flotation costs. This results in the net amount that the company receives from the sale of the securities. The component costs are then calculated in the usual way.

The second, less common, method is the investment cost adjustment. Under this methodology we increase the initial outlay for the project under consideration to account for the total flotation costs. Component costs are then calculated as we did above. The primary disadvantage of this technique is that, because it assigns all flotation costs to one project, it implicitly assumes that the securities used to finance a project will be retired when the project is completed.

Because it is more common, and its assumptions are more realistic, we will use the cost of capital adjustment technique. When flotation costs are included in the analysis, the equations for the component costs are given in Table 9-6.

TABLE 9-6
COST OF CAPITAL EQUATIONS WITH FLOTATION COST ADJUSTMENT

Component	Equation[a]
Cost of new common equity	$k_{CS} = \dfrac{D_0(1+g)}{V_{CS}-f} + g = \dfrac{D_1}{V_{CS}-f} + g$
Cost of preferred equity	$k_P = \dfrac{D}{V_p-f}$
Pre-tax cost of debt (solve for k_d)	$V_B - f = Pmt\left[\dfrac{1 - \dfrac{1}{(1+k_d)^N}}{k_d}\right] + \dfrac{FV}{(1+k_d)^N}$

a. In these equations the flotation costs (*f*) are a dollar amount per unit. It is also common for flotation costs to be stated as a percentage of the unit price.

6. For more information on both methods, see Brigham and Gapenski, "Flotation Cost Adjustments," *Financial Practice and Education* (Fall/Winter 1991): 29-34.

Adding Flotation Costs to our Worksheet

We can easily incorporate the adjustment for flotation costs into our worksheet. All we need to do is change the references to the current price in each of our formulas to the current price minus the per unit flotation costs. These costs are given in Table 9-7.

TABLE 9-7
FLOTATION COSTS AS A PERCENTAGE OF SELLING PRICE FOR RMM

Security	Flotation Cost
Bonds	1%
Preferred Stock	2%
Common Stock	5%

Enter the information from Table 9-7 into your worksheet. For each security, we have added the information at the end of the "Additional information" section. For example, in A12 enter: Flotation Cost and in B12 enter: 1% which is the flotation cost for bonds.

To account for flotation costs, change your formulas to the following:

F2   @IRATE(B11,B9*B10,B2*(1-B12),0,-B10, 0.1)*(1-B8)

F3   +D8/(B3*(1-D9))

F4   +(F8*(1+F9))/(B4*(1-F10))+F9

Once these changes have been made, you will notice that the cost of each component has risen. Your worksheet should now resemble the one pictured in Exhibit 9-4.

The Cost of Retained Earnings

We have shown how to calculate the required returns for purchasers of new common equity, preferred stock, and bonds, but firms also have another source of long-term capital — retained earnings. Is there a cost to such internally generated funds, or are they free?

EXHIBIT 9-4
COST OF CAPITAL WORKSHEET WITH FLOTATION COSTS

	A	B	C	D	E	F
1	Source	Price	Units	Total Market Value	Percentage of Total	After-tax Cost
2	Debt	905	400	$ 361,812	31.14%	7.10%
3	Preferred	100	1,000	$ 100,000	8.61%	10.20%
4	Common	70	10,000	$ 700,000	60.25%	12.31%
5	Totals			$ 1,161,812	100.00%	10.51%
6						
7	dditional Bond Dat		Additional Preferred Data		Additional Common Data	
8	Tax Rate	40%	Dividend	$ 10.00	Dividend 0	$ 3.96
9	Coupon Rate	10%	Flotation	2%	Growth Rate	6%
10	Face Value	$ 1,000			Flotation	5%
11	Maturity	10				
12	Flotation	1%				

Consider that managers generally have two options as to what they do with the firm's internally generated funds. They can either reinvest them in profitable projects or return them to the shareholders in the form of dividends. Since these funds belong to the common shareholders alone, the definition of a "profitable project" is one that earns at least the common shareholder's required rate of return. If these funds will not be invested to earn at least this return, they should be returned to the common shareholders (in the form of extra dividends, share buybacks, etc.). So there is a cost (an opportunity cost) to internally generated funds, the cost of common equity.

Note that the only difference between retained earnings (old common equity) and new common equity is that the firm must pay flotation costs on the new common equity. Since no flotation costs are paid for retained earnings, we can find the cost of retained earnings in the same way we did before learning about flotation costs. In other words,

$$k_{RE} = \frac{D_0(1+g)}{V_{CS}} + g = \frac{D_1}{V_{CS}} + g. \tag{9-4}$$

This notion of an opportunity cost for retained earnings is important for a couple of reasons. Most importantly, managers should be disabused of the notion that the funds on hand are "free." As you now know, there is a cost to these funds and it should be accounted for when making decisions. In addition, there may be times when a project that otherwise appears to be unprofitable is really profitable when the cost of retained earnings is correctly accounted for. Rejecting such a project is contrary to the principle of shareholder wealth maximization.

The Marginal WACC Curve

A firm's weighted average cost of capital is not constant. Changes can occur in the *WACC* for a number of reasons. As firms raise more and more new capital, their *WACC* will likely increase due to an increase in supply relative to demand for the firm's securities. Furthermore, total flotation costs may increase as more capital is raised.

We will see in the next chapter that these increases in the *WACC* play an important role in determining the firm's optimal capital budget. For the remainder of this chapter we will concentrate on determining the *WACC* at varying levels of total capital.

Finding the Break-points

We can model a firm's marginal *WACC* curve with a *step function*. This type of function resembles a staircase when plotted. They are commonly used as a linear (though discontinuous) approximation to non-linear functions. The accuracy of the approximation improves as the number of steps increases.

Estimating the marginal *WACC* curve is a two step process:

1. Determine the levels of total capital at which the marginal WACC increases. These points are referred to as *break-points*.
2. Determine the marginal WACC at each break-point.

Figure 9-1 illustrates what a marginal WACC curve might look like for Rocky Mountain Motors. Notice that the break-points are measured in terms of dollars of total capital. In this section we will estimate where these break-points are likely to occur and the WACC at the break-points.

FIGURE 9-1
THE MARGINAL *WACC* CURVE AS A STEP FUNCTION

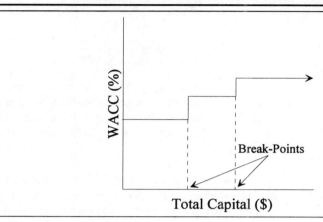

After consulting with their investment bankers, the managers of RMM have determined that they can raise new money at the costs indicated in Table 9-8. Open a new worksheet and enter the data from Table 9-8 beginning in cell A1.

TABLE 9-8
ROCKY MOUNTAIN MOTORS INFORMATION

Source	% of Total	Amounts which can be sold	Marginal After-tax Cost
Common	60.25%	Up to 100,000	12.31%
		100,001 to 500,000	15.00%
		More than 500,000	17.00%
Preferred	8.61%	Up to 50,000	10.20%
		More than 50,000	13.00%
Debt	31.14%	Up to 250,000	7.10%
		More than 250,000	8.00%

Note that you should enter just the numbers from the "Amounts which can be sold" column.

RMM feels that its current capital structure is optimal, so any new money will be raised in the same percentages. For example, if the firm decides to raise $200,000 in total capital, then $120,500 (60.25% of $200,000) will come from common equity, $62,280 (31.14%) will be debt, and $17,220 (8.61%) will be preferred equity.

Using the information in Table 9-8, we can determine the break-points in RMM's marginal WACC curve. To do this, first realize that a break will occur wherever the cost of an individual source of capital changes (why?). There will be a break-point associated with the issuance of $100,000 in common stock, for example. But recall that break-points are measured in dollars of total capital. So the question is, "How do we convert this $100,000 in common stock into the amount of total capital?"

Since all of the capital will be raised in constant proportion, we can use the following equation:

$$\text{\$ Total Capital} = \frac{\text{\$ Common Stock}}{\text{\% Common Stock}} \qquad (9\text{-}5)$$

In this case, we can see that if RMM raised $100,000 in new common stock, then it must have raised $165,973 in total capital. Using equation (9-5):

$$\$165{,}973 \approx \frac{\$100{,}000}{0.6025}.$$

We can use this information to see that if RMM issued $100,000 in new common stock, then it must also have raised $51,684 (= $165,973 \times 0.3114$) in new debt, and $14,290 (= $165,973 \times 0.0861$) in new preferred.

To locate all of the break-points, all we need to do is find the points at which the cost of each source changes, and then convert those into dollars of total capital. Table 9-9, using the information from Table 9-8, shows how to find these break-points.

TABLE 9-9
FINDING THE BREAK-POINTS IN RMM'S MARGINAL WACC CURVE

Source	Calculation	Break-point
Common Stock	100,000/0.6025	$ 165,973
Common Stock	500,000/0.6025	$ 829,866
Preferred Stock	50,000/0.0861	$ 580,906
Debt	250,000/0.3114	$ 802,773

In your worksheet enter `Break-points` in cell E1. The first break-point is associated with the $100,000 level of new common stock. In E2, enter the formula `+C2/B$2`. The result is $165,973, exactly as we found in Table 9-9. Copy this formula to E3, E5, and E7 to find the remaining break-points.

The next step is to determine the WACC at each of the break-points. To find the WACC we must convert each break-point into its components, and then determine the cost of each component. There are a number of ways we might approach this problem in the worksheet. Because we would ultimately like to generate a chart of the marginal WACC, we will set up a table which shows the amount of total capital, the cost of each component, and the WACC at that level of total capital.

Begin by entering the labels in A10..E10. In A10 enter: `Total Capital`. In B10: `Cost of Equity`. In C10: `Cost of Preferred`. In D10: `Cost of Debt`. In E10: `WACC`. Now, in A11..A36, enter a series from 0 to 2,500,000 in steps of 100,000. Use the **R**ange Fill by **E**xample menu choices to enter the series.

Next, we will determine the cost of each source for each level of total capital. In B11, we need to find the cost of equity at $0 of total capital. To facilitate later copying, we will set up a nested **@IF** statement to do this. In this case, the formula is: `@IF(A11*B$2<=C$2,D$2,@IF(A11*B$2<=C$3,D$3,D$4))`. In words, this formula says: "If the amount of total capital (A11) times the percentage of common stock (B2) is less than or equal to $100,000 (C2) then the cost is 12.31% (D2). Otherwise, if the amount is less than or equal to $500,000 then the cost is 15% (D3). Otherwise, the cost is 17% (D4)."

We use similar, but less complicated, formulas to determine the cost of preferred stock and debt at each level of total capital. For preferred stock, enter the formula:

`@IF(A11*B$5<=C$5,D$5,D$6)` into C11. In D11 enter the formula: `@IF(A11*B$7<=C$7,D$7,D$8)` to determine the appropriate cost of debt.

Finally, we can calculate the marginal weighted average cost of capital in E11 with the formula: `+$B$2*B11+$B$5*C11+$B$7*D11`. This formula calculates a weighted average of the costs which were previously calculated. Make sure that you have entered the formulas exactly as given, and then copy them down through each row to row 36.

We can create the chart of the marginal WACC by selecting A10..A36 and E10..E36 and then creating an XY scatter chart. Your worksheet should appear like that in Exhibit 9-5.

Note that in Exhibit 9-5 we have placed the chart on top of the data to save space. Also, your chart may not depict a perfect step function, as depicted in Figure 9-1. This can be accomplished, though the method is not intuitive.[7]

Summary

We began this chapter with a discussion of the appropriate required rate of return to use in the evaluation of a company's scarce capital resources. We demonstrated that a weighted average of the cost of each source of capital would be sufficient to simultaneously satisfy the providers of capital. In addition, we showed that the costs of the sources of capital can be found by simply inverting the valuation equations from Chapter 8 and including flotation costs. Finally, we saw that the firm's marginal weighted average cost of capital changes as the amount of total capital changes. We showed how to determine the location of the break-points and how to plot the marginal WACC curve.

---

7. Essentially, we need to have two entries for each break-point. Set the WACC for the first to the lower WACC and the second to the higher WACC. This will cause the transition between levels to be perfectly vertical rather than sloped.

EXHIBIT 9-5
MARGINAL WACC WORKSHEET FOR RMM

	A	B	C	D	E
1	Source	% of Total	Max Level	After-tax Cost	Break-points
2	Common	60.25%	100,000	12.31%	165,973
3			500,000	15.00%	829,866
4			500,000	17.00%	
5	Preferred	8.61%	50,000	10.20%	580,906
6			50,000	13.00%	
7	Debt	31.14%	250,000	7.21%	802,773
8			250,000	8.00%	
9					
10	Total Capital	Cost of Equity	Cost of Preferred	Cost of Debt	WACC
11	0	12.31%	10.20%	7.21%	10.54%
12	100,000	12.31%	10.20%	7.21%	10.54%
13	165,973	12.31%	10.20%	7.21%	10.54%
14	165,973	15.00%	10.20%	7.21%	12.16%

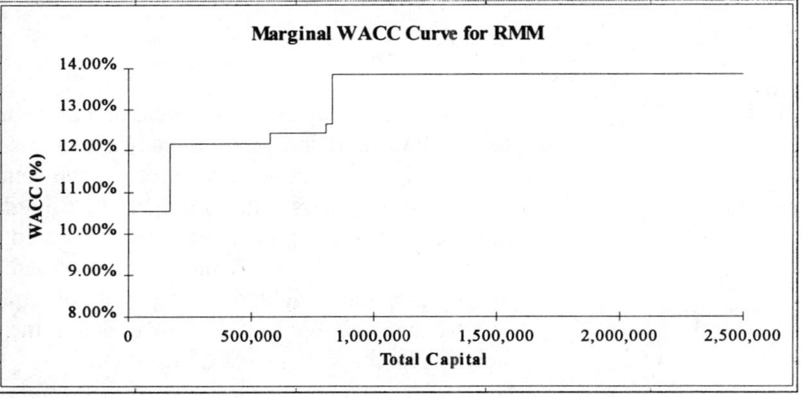

Marginal WACC Curve for RMM

TABLE 9-10
COST OF CAPITAL EQUATIONS

Purpose	Formula[a]
Cost of retained earnings (Dividend Discount Model)	$k_{RE} = \dfrac{D_0(1 + g)}{V_{CS}} + g = \dfrac{D_1}{V_{CS}} + g$
Cost of retained earnings (CAPM)	$E(R_i) = R_f + \beta_i(R_M - R_f)$
Cost of new common equity with flotation cost adjustment	$k_{CS} = \dfrac{D_0(1 + g)}{V_{CS} - f} + g = \dfrac{D_1}{V_{CS} - f} + g$
Cost of preferred equity with flotation cost adjustment	$k_P = \dfrac{D}{V_p - f}$
Pre-tax cost of debt (solve for k_d)	$V_B - f = Pmt\left[\dfrac{1 - \dfrac{1}{(1 + k_d)^N}}{k_d}\right] + \dfrac{FV}{(1 + k_d)^N}$

a. In these equations the flotation costs (f) are a dollar amount per unit. It is also common for flotation costs to be stated as a percentage of the unit price.

201

CHAPTER 10   *Capital Budgeting*

After studying this chapter, you should be able to:

1. *Identify the relevant cash flows in capital budgeting.*

2. *Demonstrate the use of 1-2-3 in calculating the after-tax cash flows used as inputs to the various decision making techniques.*

3. *Compare and contrast the five major capital budgeting decision techniques (payback period, NPV, PI, IRR, and MIRR).*

4. *Explain "scenario analysis," and show how it can be performed in 1-2-3.*

5. *Use 1-2-3's "Solver" to determine the firm's optimal capital budget under capital rationing.*

Capital budgeting is the term used to describe the process of determining how a firm should allocate its capital resources to available long-term investment opportunities. Some of these opportunities are expected to be profitable, while others are not. Inasmuch as the goal of the firm is to maximize shareholder's wealth, the financial manager is responsible for selecting only those investments that are expected to increase shareholder wealth.

The techniques that you will learn in this chapter have wide applicability beyond corporate asset management. Lease analysis, bond refunding decisions, mergers and acquisition analysis, corporate restructuring, and new product decisions are all examples where these techniques are used. On a more personal level, decisions regarding mortgage refinancing, renting versus buying, and choosing a credit card are but a few examples where these techniques are useful.

On the surface, capital budgeting decisions are simple. If the benefits exceed the costs the project should be accepted, otherwise it will be rejected. Unfortunately, quantifying costs and benefits is not always straightforward. We will examine this process in this chapter and extend it to decision making under conditions of uncertainty in the next.

Estimating the Cash Flows

Before we can determine whether or not an investment will increase shareholder wealth, we need to estimate the cash flows that it will generate. While this is usually easier said than done, there are some general guidelines to keep in mind. There are two important conditions that a cash flow must meet in order to be included in our analysis.

The cash flows must be:

1. **Incremental** – The cash flows must be in addition to those that the firm already has. For example, a firm may be considering an addition to an existing product line. But the new product may cause some current customers to switch from another of the firm's products. We must in this case consider both the cash flow increase from the new product and the cash flow decrease from the existing product. In other words, only the net new cash flows are considered.

2. **After-tax** – The cash flows must be considered on an after-tax basis. The shareholders are not concerned with before-tax cash flows because they can't be spent.

But we should disregard cash flows which are:

1. **Sunk costs** – These are cash flows which have occurred in the past and cannot be recovered. Since value is defined as the present value of *future* cash flows, we are only concerned with the expected future cash flows. Therefore, sunk costs are irrelevant for capital budgeting purposes.

2. **Financing costs** – The cost of financing is obviously important in the analysis, but it will be implicitly included in the discount rate used to evaluate the profitability of the project. Explicitly including the dollar amount of financing costs (e.g., extra interest expense) would amount to double counting. For example, suppose that you discovered an investment which promised a sure 15% return. If you could borrow money at 10% to finance the purchase of this investment, it obviously makes sense because you will earn 5% over your cost. Notice that the dollar interest cost is implicitly included, because you must earn at least 10% to cover your financing costs.

With these points in mind we can move on to discuss the estimation of the relevant cash flows. We will classify all cash flows as a part of one of the three groups illustrated in Figure 10-1.

FIGURE 10-1
TIMELINE ILLUSTRATING PROJECT CASH FLOWS

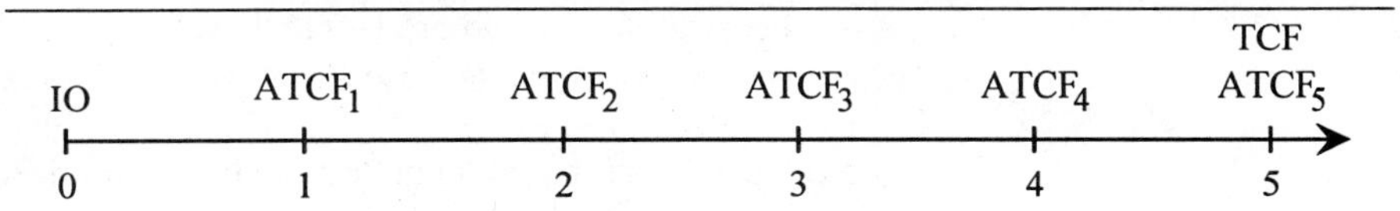

IO	$ATCF_1$	$ATCF_2$	$ATCF_3$	$ATCF_4$	TCF $ATCF_5$
0	1	2	3	4	5

The Initial Outlay

The *initial outlay* (usually abbreviated IO, as in Figure 10-1) represents the net cost of the project. Though we will presume that the initial outlay occurs at time period 0 (today), there are many cases, perhaps most, in which the cost of a project is spread out over several periods. For example, the contractor in large construction projects is usually paid some percentage up-front, with additional monies being paid as the project reaches various stages of completion. Furthermore, there is usually some delay between the analysis phase of a project and its implementation. So to be technically correct, the initial outlay actually occurs over some near-term future time period.

The initial outlay is comprised of several cash flows. It is impossible to enumerate all of the components for all possible projects, but we will provide some basic principles. The most obvious is the cash outlay required to purchase the project. The price of a piece of machinery or of a building are obvious examples. There are other components however. Any shipping expenses, labor costs to install machinery, or employee training costs should be included. Together, the costs to get a project up and running are referred to as the *depreciable base* for the project because this is the amount which we will depreciate over the life of the project.

There may also be cash flows which serve to reduce the initial outlay. For example, in a replacement decision (e.g., replacing an existing machine with a newer model) there is often some salvage value for the old machine. This amount will be deducted from the initial outlay. However, there may be taxes associated with the sale. Whenever an asset is sold for an amount that differs from its book value there are tax consequences. If an asset is sold for more than its book value, tax is owed on the difference. If it is sold for less than book value, the difference is used to offset the firm's taxable income thus resulting in a tax savings. These extra taxes (tax savings) will increase (decrease) the initial outlay.

Finally, there may be costs which are not at all obvious. For example, suppose that a company is considering an investment in a new machine which is substantially faster than the older model currently being used. Because of the extra speed, the company may find that it needs a permanent increase in its raw materials inventory. The cost of these extra raw materials should be included as an increase in the initial outlay because they would not be purchased unless the project is undertaken. This cost is referred to as the increase in net working capital.

The calculation of the initial outlay can be summarized by the following equation:

IO = Price of Project + Shipping + Installation + Training - (Salvage - Additional Taxes) + Increase in net working capital.

The Annual After-tax Cash Flows

Calculating the initial outlay, as complicated as it may appear, is relatively easy compared with accurately calculating the annual after-tax cash flows (ATCF). The reason is that we really can't be sure of the cash flows in the future. For the time being, we will assume that we do know exactly what the future cash flows will be, and in the next chapter we will consider the complications of uncertainty.

Generally, the annual after-tax cash flows are made up of four components, but not necessarily all four:

1. **Additional Revenue** – new products, and sometimes production processes, can lead to net new revenue. Remember that we must consider only the incremental revenues.

2. **Cost savings** – there may be some savings which will accompany the acceptance of a project. For example, the firm may decide to replace a manually operated machine with a fully automated version. Part of the savings would be the salary and benefits of the operators of the old machine. Another savings might come from lower maintenance costs of the new machine relative to the old one.

3. **Additional expenses** – instead of purchasing a fully automated machine, the firm might opt for a process which is more labor intensive. This would allow the company more flexibility to adjust to changes in the market, but the extra labor costs must be considered when determining the cash flows.

4. **Additional depreciation benefits** – whenever the asset mix of the firm changes, there is likely to be a change in the amount of depreciation expense. Since depreciation expense is a non-cash expense that serves to reduce taxes, we need to consider the tax savings, or extra taxes, due to depreciation.

We must be careful to remember that the only relevant cash flows are those that are after-tax and incremental. Keeping this in mind, we can summarize the calculation of the after-tax cash flows as follows:

ATCF = (Revenues + Savings - Additional Expenses) × (1 - marginal tax rate) + (Change in Depreciation × marginal tax rate)

The Terminal Cash Flow

The terminal cash flow (TCF) consists of those cash flow events which occur only in the final time period of the project. Normally, there will also be other cash flows that occur in this period, but we have categorized those as the final period after-tax cash flows. The terminal cash flow will consist of things such as the expected salvage value of the new machine, any tax effects associated with the sale of the machine, recovery of any investment in net working capital, and perhaps some shut-down costs.

TCF = (Recovery of NWC - Shut-down Expenses) × (1 - marginal tax rate) + Salvage - Salvage Taxes

Estimating the Cash Flows: an Example

Throughout this chapter we will demonstrate the concepts with the following example.

> The Supreme Shoe Company is considering purchasing a new, fully automated machine to replace a manually operated one. The machine being replaced, now 5 years old, originally had an expected life of 10 years, is being depreciated using the straight line method from $40,000 down to $0, and can now be sold for $22,000. It takes one person to operate the machine and he earns $29,000 per year in salary and benefits. The annual costs of maintenance and defects on the old machine are $6,000 and $4,000, respectively. The replacement machine being considered has a purchase price of $75,000 and an expected salvage value of $15,000 at the end of its 5 year life. There will also be shipping and installation expenses of $6,000. Because the new machine would work faster, investment in raw materials would increase by a total of $3,000. The company expects that annual maintenance costs on the new machine will be $5,000 while defects will cost $2,000. Before considering this project the company undertook an engineering analysis of current facilities to determine if other changes would be necessitated by the purchase of this machine. The study cost the company $5,000 and determined that existing facilities could support this new machine with no other changes. In order to purchase the new machine, the company would have to take on new debt of $30,000 at 10% interest, resulting in increased interest expense of $3,000 per year. The required rate of return for this project is 15% and the company's marginal tax rate is 34%. Furthermore, management has determined that the maximum allowable time to recover its investment is 3 years. Is this project acceptable?

For this type of problem, it is generally easiest to separate the important data from the text. This is true regardless of whether you are doing problems by hand or with a spreadsheet program. Of course, a spreadsheet offers many advantages that we will examine later. For now, open a new worksheet and enter the data displayed in Exhibit 10-1.

Notice that in creating Exhibit 10-1 we have simply listed all of the relevant data from the Supreme Shoe problem. There are also some minor calculations entered.

Remember, it is important that you set up your worksheets so that 1-2-3 does all of the possible calculations for you. This will allow us to more easily experiment with different values (i.e., perform a "what-if" analysis) later.

EXHIBIT 10-1
RELEVANT CASH FLOWS FOR SUPREME SHOE

	A	B	C	D
1	The Supreme Shoe Company			
2	Replacement Analysis			
3		Old Machine	New Machine	Difference
4	Price	40,000	75,000	
5	Shipping and Install	0	6,000	
6	Original Life	10	5	
7	Current Life	5	5	
8	Original Salvage Value	0	15,000	
9	Current Salvage Value	22,000	0	
10	Book Value	20,000	81,000	
11	Increase in Raw Materials	0	3,000	
12	Depreciation	4,000	13,200	(9,200)
13	Salaries	29,000		29,000
14	Maintenance	6,000	5,000	1,000
15	Defects	4,000	2,000	2,000
16	Marginal Tax Rate	34.00%		
17	Required Return	15.00%		

We have left the cost of the engineering study out of our model. Because the $5,000 was spent before our analysis it is considered to be a sunk cost. That is, there is no way to recover that money, even if we reject the project, so it is irrelevant to any future decisions. Adding this to the cost of the project would unnecessarily penalize the project. Furthermore, we haven't considered the $3,000 in extra interest expense that will be incurred each year. The money spent to finance a project must be ignored because we will account for it in the required return. In addition, Supreme Shoe has decided to take on the debt for 10 years, which is longer than the expected life of the new machine. Therefore it wouldn't be correct to apply all of the interest expense to this one project.

With this in mind, the first calculation is depreciation. Supreme Shoe uses the straight-line method for analysis purposes. Straight-line depreciation applies depreciation equally throughout the expected useful life of the project, and is calculated as follows:

$$\frac{\text{Depreciable Base} - \text{Salvage Value}}{\text{Useful Life}}$$

1-2-3 has built-in functions for calculating depreciation in five different ways: straight-line (**@SLN**), double-declining balance (**@DDB**), fixed-declining balance (**@DB**), sum of the years' digits (**@SYD**), and variably-declining balance (**@VDB**). The **@VDB** function is interesting because it allows you to specify the rate at which the asset value declines, and whether to switch to straight-line when that method leads to higher depreciation. Since Supreme Shoe uses the straight-line method, we will use the **@SLN** function which is defined as:

@SLN(*COST*, *SALVAGE*, *LIFE*)

where *COST* is the depreciable base of the asset, *SALVAGE* is the estimated salvage value, and *LIFE* is the number of years over which the asset is to be depreciated.

Recall that the depreciable base includes the price of the asset plus the shipping and installation costs. For the old machine then, in cell B12 insert: `@SLN(B4+B5,B8,B6)`. Because the annual depreciation will be calculated the same way for the new machine, simply copy the formula in B12 to C12.

We calculate the book value of the current machine in B10 because the book value and the salvage value together will determine the tax liability from the sale of this machine. Book value is calculated as the difference between the depreciable base and the accumulated depreciation. In this instance, the depreciable base is found by adding B4 and B5. The accumulated depreciation is the annual depreciation expense times the number of years of the original life that have passed. In our worksheet this is B12*(B6-B7). So the formula in B10 is: `+B4+B5-B12*(B6-B7)`. Just for informational purposes copy the formula to C10.

The difference column presents the savings that the new machine will provide (negative numbers indicate additional costs). The formulas are simply the difference between the expenses of the current machine and those of the proposed machine. In D12 place the formula: `+B12-C12` and then copy it to cells D13..D15. To avoid confusion, we only calculate differences for the relevant cells. Your worksheet should now resemble the one in Exhibit 10-1 (page 209).

Now that the data are more clearly presented we can calculate the relevant cash flows. The initial outlay consists of the price of the new machine, the shipping and installation costs, the salvage value of the old machine and any taxes that might be due from that sale. We will calculate the initial outlay in B19 as:

$-(C4+C5-B9+(B9-B10)*B16+C11)$. The formula is less complex than it looks. The first three terms simply represent the total cost of the new machine minus the salvage value of the old machine. The next part of the formula calculates the tax that is due on the sale of the old machine. Notice that if the book value were less than the salvage value this formula will add a negative value thus reducing the initial outlay. Again, it is important that you construct the worksheet formulas so that any changes are automatically reflected in the calculated values. Finally, we add the increased investment in raw materials because this investment would not be necessary unless the new machine were purchased.

Next we need to calculate the annual after-tax cash flows for this project. We will separate the calculation of the depreciation tax benefit from the other cash flows because it is informative to see the savings generated by the increased depreciation (also because, as we will see in the next chapter, the depreciation tax benefit is a less risky cash flow than the others). In B20 we calculate the annual after-tax savings as: @SUM(D13..D15)*(1-B16). We have used the **@SUM** function because it is more compact than simply adding the three cell addresses individually. Also, if we later discover any other savings (or extra costs) we can insert them into the range and the formula will automatically reflect the change.

The depreciation tax benefit represents the savings in taxes that we will have because of the extra depreciation expense. Remember that depreciation is a non-cash expense so that the only result of increasing depreciation is to reduce taxes and thereby increase cash flow. To calculate the depreciation tax benefit in cell B21 enter the formula: -D12*B16. We make the depreciation amount negative because the change in depreciation in D12 is negative (indicating extra expense). In B22 we total the annual after-tax savings and the depreciation tax benefit with the formula: @SUM(B20..B21).

Finally, the terminal cash flow consists of the annual after-tax cash flow for the last year and any other cash flows which occur only in the final period. For the Supreme Shoe project, the additional cash flows are the after-tax salvage value and the recovery of the investment in raw materials. In this case, there is no tax consequence of salvaging the machine for $15,000 because that is the same as the book value. The formula in B23 is: +B22+C11+C8.

At this point, your worksheet should resemble the one pictured in Exhibit 10-2.

EXHIBIT 10-2
CASH FLOWS FOR SUPREME SHOE

	A	B	C	D
1	The Supreme Shoe Company			
2	Replacement Analysis			
3		Old Machine	New Machine	Difference
4	Price	40,000	75,000	
5	Shipping and Install	0	6,000	
6	Original Life	10	5	
7	Current Life	5	5	
8	Original Salvage Value	0	15,000	
9	Current Salvage Value	22,000	0	
10	Book Value	20,000	81,000	
11	Increase in Raw Materials	0	3,000	
12	Depreciation	4,000	13,200	(9,200)
13	Salaries	29,000		29,000
14	Maintenance	6,000	5,000	1,000
15	Defects	4,000	2,000	2,000
16	Marginal Tax Rate	34.00%		
17	Required Return	15.00%		
18	Cash Flows			
19	Initial Outlay	(62,680)		
20	Annual After-Tax Savings	21,120		
21	Depreciation Tax Benefit	3,128		
22	Total ATCF	24,248		
23	Terminal Cash Flow	42,248		

Making the Decision

We are now ready to make a decision as to the profitability of this project. Financial managers have a number of tools at their disposal to evaluate profitability. We will examine six of these. Before beginning the analysis, examine the time line presented in Figure 10-2 which summarizes the cash flows for the Supreme Shoe replacement decision.

FIGURE 10-2
TIME LINE FOR THE SUPREME SHOE REPLACEMENT DECISION

-62,680	24,248	24,248	24,248	24,248	42,248
0	1	2	3	4	5

The Payback Method

The payback method answers the question, "How long will it take to recoup our initial investment?" If the answer is less than or equal to the maximum allowable period, the project is considered to be acceptable. If the payback period is longer than acceptable, then the project is rejected. Note that the payback period serves as a kind of break-even period, and thus provides some information regarding the liquidity of the project under analysis.

There are two ways to calculate the payback period. The easiest method, which we can use for the Supreme Shoe problem, is used when the cash flows are an annuity. To calculate the payback for these types of cash flows, simply divide the initial outlay by the annuity payment:

$$\text{Payback Period} = \frac{\text{Initial Outlay}}{\text{Annuity Payment}}$$

For Supreme Shoe, the cash flows are not strictly an annuity, except for the first four years. If the payback period is less than four years then we can use this method. For this project the payback period is calculated as:

$$\text{Payback Period} = \frac{62,680}{24,248} = 2.58 \text{ years}$$

Because Supreme Shoe requires that projects have a maximum payback period of three years, the replacement machine is acceptable by this criteria.

An alternative way to calculate the payback period subtracts the cash flows from the initial outlay until the outlay is recovered. This method is much easier to demonstrate than to describe. So let's look at the Supreme Shoe problem using this method. Table 10-1 illustrates this procedure.

TABLE 10-1
CALCULATING THE PAYBACK PERIOD

	Calculation	Comments	Cumulative Payback
	62,680	Initial outlay	
-	24,248	minus first cash flow	1 year
=	38,432	left to be recovered	
-	24,248	minus second cash flow	2 years
=	14,184	left to be recovered	2 years < payback < 3 years

At this point we know that the payback period must be between two and three years, and that the remainder will be recovered during the third year. Assuming that the cash flow in year 3 is evenly spread out through the year, we can simply divide the amount yet to be recovered by the cash flow in year 3 to arrive at the fraction of the year required to recover this amount. In this case, it will take 0.58 years ($= 14,184 \div 24,248$) to recover the remainder. Add this to the two years that we have already counted, and we arrive at 2.58 years, exactly as before.

While the payback period makes a great deal of sense intuitively, it is not without its problems. Specifically, the principal problem is that the payback method ignores the time value of money. You know from the discussion of time value in Chapter 7, that we cannot simply add cash flows which occur in different time periods. We will address this problem shortly. A second difficulty with the payback period is that it does not take all of the cash flows into account. Because it ignores all cash flows beyond the payback period, it can lead to less than optimal decisions. Suppose that Supreme Shoe was considering a similar machine which was expected to have higher cash flows in years 4 and 5, but also had a slightly higher cost. It might be the case that these higher cash flows outweigh the extra cost, but the payback period would ignore those cash flows.

The Discounted Payback Period

We can remedy the time value problem with the discounted payback period. This method is identical to the regular payback period, except that we use the present value of the cash flows instead of the nominal values. Because present values are always less than nominal values, the discounted payback period will always be longer than the regular payback period.

For Supreme Shoe, the discounted payback period is 3.53 years. In this case, calculating this number is slightly more difficult than calculating the regular payback period because the present values of the cash flows are different in each period. For this reason we will use the method shown in Table 10-1 to calculate the discounted payback period.

EXHIBIT 10-3
CASH FLOWS FOR CALCULATING THE DISCOUNTED PAYBACK PERIOD

	C	D	E
18	Period	Cash Flows	PV of CF
19	0	(62,680)	(62,680)
20	1	24,248	21,085
21	2	24,248	18,335
22	3	24,248	15,943
23	4	24,248	13,864
24	5	42,248	21,005

In order to set up the table in Exhibit 10-3 very little data input is required since most of the data already exists or can be calculated. Start by typing the column labels in cells C18, D18 and E18. To enter the period numbers, in cell C19 type a zero and then select the range C19..C24. From the **R**ange menu select Fill by **E**xample. This command will enter a series of numbers starting with the first number in the selected range. It can be very helpful in situations where you need a list of consecutive numbers or dates.

The cash flows are most easily entered by using references to the cells where the original calculations exist. Entering the numbers in this way, rather than retyping them, will later allow us to experiment with various scenarios. In cell D19 enter: +B19 to capture the initial outlay. In cell D20 we need the first cash flow, so enter: +B$22. Note that the dollar sign will freeze the cell reference so that it will remain at row 22 when we copy it. Copy the formula from D20 to the range D21..D23, and note that the value is the same in each cell as it was in D20. Finally, to get the last year's cash flow in D24 enter: +B23.

To calculate the present values of these cash flows, it is easiest to simply enter the present value equation. In cell E19 enter the formula: +D19/(1+B$17)^C19. This formula will divide the number in D19 by 1 plus the discount rate (in B17) raised to the power indicated by the period number. (You could use the **@NPV** function to accomplish the same result.) Copying this formula down to the other cells in the range will calculate the present values of each of the cash flows.

Now that the table of cash flows is set up, calculating the discounted payback period by hand is a simple matter of following the instructions presented in Table 10-1. The discounted payback period is 3.53 years which is longer than the maximum acceptable payback.

As an alternative, since the nominal cash flows are an annuity (except for the last year), we can find the discounted payback period using the **@NPER** function. With the discounted payback period we are trying to find out how many periods it will take for the present values of the cash flows to add up to the initial outlay. In other words, we want to solve for N in an annuity. (See "Solving for the Number of Periods in an Annuity" on page 136.). In B26, enter: @NPER(B22,B17,0,0, B19). The result is 3.51 years. The slight difference is insignificant.

Using the three-year benchmark in this case would be incorrect, since it was presumably determined under the assumptions of the regular payback period. Some allowance must be made for the fact that the discounted payback period will always be greater than the regular payback period (why?). Suppose then that management decides that the discounted payback must be 3.75 years or less to be acceptable. With the new criteria, the project is acceptable under both payback methods. However, the value of the discounted payback period is that the acceptability of a project will change as required returns change. If the required return should rise to 18%, the discounted payback period will rise to 3.80 years and the project would be rejected. Since the regular payback period ignores the time value of money it would still suggest that the project is acceptable, regardless of the required return.

Note that the discounted payback period still ignores cash flows beyond the period where payback is achieved. All of the remaining techniques that we will introduce are considered to be superior because they recognize the time value of money and they consider all of the cash flows in the analysis.

Net Present Value

Neither the regular payback period nor the discounted payback period are economically correct decision criteria. Even with the discounted payback method we are ignoring cash flows beyond the payback period. How then can the financial analyst make the correct decision? In this section we will cover the net present value technique as one solution.

Most people would agree that purchasing an asset for less than its value is a good deal. Further, purchasing an asset for exactly its value isn't bad. What most people try to avoid is purchasing an asset for more than its value.[1] If we define value as the present value of future cash flows (see Chapter 8), then net present value represents the excess value captured by purchasing an asset. More specifically:

$$NPV = PVCF - IO = Value - Cost$$

or more mathematically:

$$NPV = \sum_{t=1}^{N} \frac{ATCF_t}{(1+i)^t} - IO \qquad \text{(10-1)}$$

There are a couple of important things to note about the *NPV*. Most importantly, since value can be greater than, equal to, or less than cost, the *NPV* can be greater than, equal to, or less than zero. If the value is less than the cost, the *NPV* will be less than zero, and the project will be rejected. Otherwise, the project will be accepted because the value is greater than (or equal to) the cost. In the latter case, the wealth of the shareholders will be increased (or at least unchanged) by the acceptance of the project. So *NPV* really represents the change in shareholder wealth that accompanies the acceptance of an investment. Since the goal of the firm is to maximize shareholder wealth, it must accept all projects where the *NPV* is greater than or equal to zero.

Why does *NPV* represent a change in shareholder wealth? To see this important point, remember that any cash flows in excess of expenses accrue to the common stockholders of the firm. Therefore, any project which generates cash flows sufficient to cover its expenses will result in an increase in shareholder wealth. Consider the following example:

> Huey and Louie are considering the purchase of a lemonade stand which will operate during the summer months. It will cost them $100 to build and operate the stand. Since they only have $50 of their own (common equity) they will need to raise the additional capital elsewhere. Huey's father agrees to loan the pair $30 (debt), with the understanding that they will repay him a total of $33 at the end of the summer. The other $20 can be raised in a preferred stock offering to several of the other kids in

---

1. Theoretically, nobody would ever purchase an asset for more than it is worth to them. Purchasing an asset proves, *ipso facto*, that the cost is, at most, equal to the value to that individual.

the neighborhood. The preferred stock is sold with the promise to pay a five dollar dividend, if possible, at the end of the summer. Huey and Louie would have to earn at least $10 in order to compensate them for their time and effort. Assuming that the stand will be demolished at the end of the summer, should they undertake this project?

The answer to this question depends on the cash flows that Huey and Louie expect the lemonade stand to generate. The three scenarios in Table 10-2 will demonstrate the possibilities:

TABLE 10-2
POSSIBLE SCENARIOS FOR THE LEMONADE STAND

	Scenario 1	Scenario 2	Scenario 3
Total cash inflow after operating expenses	$118	$130	$110
less cost of debt	(33)	(33)	(33)
less cost of preferred stock	(25)	(25)	(25)
less cost of common equity	(60)	(60)	(60)
Remainder (to common stockholders)	0	12	-8

For this example, we have purposely ignored taxes to concentrate on the definition of net present value. Notice that the required returns of each of the stakeholders is unchanged in each scenario. The only variable is the cash inflow after operating expenses. In the first scenario all of the stakeholders are exactly satisfied, even Huey and Louie get the $10 return that they have demanded. Therefore, the project is acceptable, and it has a net present value of zero (as indicated by the remainder). Under the second scenario, everybody is satisfied and there is an extra $12 which goes directly to Huey and Louie. This is an example of a positive *NPV*. Finally, under scenario 3, the debtholder and the preferred stockholders are satisfied, but there is a shortfall of $8 which will reduce Huey and Louie's return to only $2. Notice that in the last case, the return to the common stockholders is positive (i.e., they do make money), but less than required. This is an example of a negative *NPV* and will cause Huey and Louie to reject the project.

Returning now to our Supreme Shoe example, the *NPV* of this project can be determined by taking the present value of the after-tax cash flows and subtracting the initial outlay. In this case, performing the calculations by hand poses no great difficulty. However, 1-2-3 can calculate the *NPV* just as easily and allow us to experiment. You have already made use of the built-in **@NPV** function in Chapter 7. At that point, we did not make clear the misleading nature of this function. It does not really calculate the *NPV* as we defined it. Instead, it simply calculates the sum of present values of the cash flows as of one period before the first cash flow. It is vitally important that you understand this point before using this function.

To use the **@NPV** function for this problem, insert: `@NPV(B17, D20..D24)+B19` into B27. Note that we do *not* include the initial outlay in the range used in the **@NPV** function. Instead, we use the **@NPV** function to determine the present value of the cash flows and then add the (negative) initial outlay to this result. The net present value is shown to be $27,552.24, so the project is acceptable (*NPV* >= 0). An alternative method is to include the initial outlay and then adjust the result. In this case, the present value would be as of time period -1, so multiplying by $(1 + i)$ will bring it to time period 0. The alternative, then, is to place the formula: `@NPV(B17,D19..D24)*(1+B17)` into B27. This will give exactly the same result.

The Profitability Index

The beauty of the net present value is that it reports the dollar increase in shareholder wealth that would result from acceptance of a project. Most of the time this is desirable, but there is one problem. Comparing projects of differing sizes can be misleading when a firm is operating with a fixed amount of investment capital. Assuming that both projects are acceptable and mutually exclusive, the larger project will likely have a higher *NPV*. The profitability index (*PI*) provides a measure of the dollar benefit per dollar of cost ("bang for the buck"). *PI* is calculated by:

$$PI = \frac{\$ \text{ Benefit}}{\$ \text{ Cost}} = \frac{\sum_{t=1}^{N} \dfrac{ATCF_t}{(1+i)^t}}{IO} = \frac{PVCF}{IO} \tag{10-2}$$

As indicated in the equation, the benefit is calculated as the present value of the after-tax cash flows and the cost is the initial outlay. Obviously, then, if the *PI* is greater than or equal to 1, the project is acceptable because the benefit exceeds the cost. Otherwise, the benefit is less than the cost and the project would be rejected.

There are two ways that we can calculate the *PI* in 1-2-3. The most apparent is to use the **@NPV** function and to divide that result by the initial outlay. In other words, in B28 type: `@NPV(B17,D20..D24)/(-B19)`. This will give 1.4396 as the result, indicating that the project is acceptable. The alternative is to make use of the following relationship:

$$NPV = PVCF - IO$$

or, by rearranging we get:

$$PVCF = NPV + IO$$

Therefore, since we have already calculated the NPV in B27, we can calculate the PI with: `+(B27-B19)/(-B19)`. This method will be slightly faster because 1-2-3 doesn't have to recalculate the present values. In all but the largest problems, the increase in speed probably won't be noticeable on a PC, but the technique is especially helpful when doing problems by hand.

The Internal Rate of Return

The internal rate of return (*IRR*) provides a measure of the average annual rate of return that a project will provide. If the *IRR* exceeds the required return for a project, the project will be accepted. Because it is a measure of the percentage return, many analysts prefer it to the other methods that we have discussed, but, as we will see, there are many problems with the *IRR*.

The *IRR* is the discount rate which makes the net present value equal to zero. An alternative, but equivalent, definition is that the *IRR* is the discount rate which equates the present value of the cash flows to the initial outlay. In other words, the *IRR* is the discount rate which makes the following equality true:

$$IO = \sum_{t=1}^{N} \frac{ATCF_t}{(1 + IRR)^t} \tag{10-3}$$

Unfortunately, in most cases there is no closed-form method for solving for the *IRR*. The primary method of solving this equation is an iterative trial-and-error approach. While this may sound tedious, generally a solution can be found within three or four iterations if some intelligence is used. However, there is little need for this procedure since 1-2-3 has a built-in function that performs this operation.

The built-in **@IRATE** function in 1-2-3 will find the *IRR* for an annuity-type of cash flow stream, but it cannot accept an uneven series of cash flows. To deal with uneven cash flows, 1-2-3 provides the **@IRR** function which is defined as:

$$@\text{IRR}(\textit{GUESS}, \textit{RANGE})$$

where *GUESS* is the initial guess at the true *IRR, and RANGE* is the contiguous range of cash flows. Note that your cash flow stream must include at least one negative cash flow (payment) or else the *IRR* would be infinite (why?). Since solving for the *IRR* is an iterative process, it is possible that 1-2-3 will not converge to a solution. 1-2-3 will indicate this situation by displaying ERR in the cell rather than an answer. If this error occurs, one possible solution is to change your *GUESS* until 1-2-3 can converge to a solution. Normally, the cost of capital serves as a good *GUESS*.

To calculate the *IRR* for the Supreme Shoe example, enter: @IRR(B17,D19..D24) into cell B29. The result is 30.95% which is greater than the required return of 15%. So the project is acceptable. At this point, let's try an experiment to prove our definition of the *IRR*. Recall that the *IRR* was defined as the discount rate which makes the *NPV* equal zero. To prove this, temporarily change B17 to: +0.30945. Notice that the net present value in B27 changes to $0.29 which is essentially zero, except for a rounding error. Note also that the profitability index changes to 1.0000 (why?). Before continuing, change the required return back to its original value of 15%.

Problems with the IRR

The internal rate of return is a popular profitability measure because, as a percentage, it is easy to understand and easy to compare to the required return. However, the *IRR* suffers from several problems that could lead to less-than-optimal decisions. In this section we will discuss these difficulties, and solutions where they exist.

Earlier, we mentioned that the *NPV* will almost always lead you to the economically correct decision. Unfortunately, the *IRR* and *NPV* will not always lead to the same decision when projects are mutually exclusive. *Mutually exclusive* projects are those for which the selection of one project precludes the acceptance of another. When projects that are being compared are mutually exclusive, a ranking conflict may arise between the *NPV* and *IRR*.[2] In other words, the *NPV* method may suggest that Project A be accepted while the *IRR* may suggest Project B. If you can't select both, which profitability measure do you believe?

---

2. This is not a problem with independent projects because all independent projects with a positive *NPV* (*IRR* > required) will be accepted. In other words, ranking is not required.

There are two causes of this type of problem: 1) the projects are of greatly different sizes; or 2) the timing of the cash flows are different. To see the size problem more clearly, consider the following question. "Would you rather earn a 100% return on a $10 investment (Project A), or a 10% return on a $1,000 investment (Project B)?" Obviously, most of us would be more concerned with the dollar amounts and would choose the 10% return because that would provide $100 versus only $10 in the other case. The solution to this problem is actually quite simple. If you can raise $1,000 for the Project B, then the correct comparison is not between A and B, but between B and A plus whatever you could do with the other $990 (call it Project C) that is available if you choose Project A. If Project C would return 10%, then you could earn $109 by investing in both A and C, which is preferable to investing in B.

The timing problem is more difficult to deal with. Suppose that you are given the task of evaluating the two mutually exclusive projects in Table 10-3, with a 10% required return. Project A generates larger cash flows in the last few years, while Project B generates larger cash flows in the early years.

TABLE 10-3
THE TIMING OF CASH FLOWS CAN LEAD TO A CONFLICT

Period	Project A	Project B	Project C (= A - B)
0	(1000)	(1000)	0
1	0	400	(400)
2	200	400	(200)
3	300	300	0
4	500	300	200
5	900	200	700
NPV	$291.02	$248.70	$42.32
IRR	17.32%	20.49%	12.48%

Which would you choose? Obviously there is a conflict because Project A would be selected under the *NPV* criteria, but Project B would be selected by the *IRR* criteria. We can use logic similar to that used for the size problem to see that *NPV* is the correct criteria. If Project B is accepted, we must reject Project A and the differential cash flows (Project C). If the differential cash flows provide a positive *NPV*, then they should not be rejected. In effect, what we are arguing is that Project A is equivalent to Project B plus the differential cash flows. So choosing between these projects is effectively deciding whether the differential cash flows are profitable or not. Conveniently, all that we really need to do is to accept the project with the highest *NPV*.

Yet another problem with the *IRR* is one that there may be more than one *IRR*. Specifically, because the general equation for the *IRR* is an *N*th degree polynomial, it will have *N* solutions. In the usual case, where there is one cash outflow followed by several inflows, there will be only one real number solution. However, when there are net cash outflows in the outlying periods, we will be able to find more than one real solution. In particular, there can be one real solution per sign change in the cash flow stream.

FIGURE 10-3
CASH FLOWS FOR MULTIPLE *IRR*s

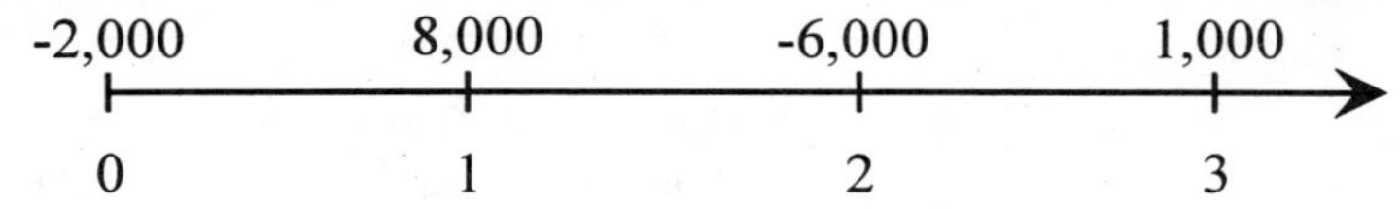

-2,000	8,000	-6,000	1,000
0	1	2	3

Consider, as an example, the cash flows depicted in Figure 10-3. Solving for the *IRR* in this example will lead you to three solutions (because there are three sign changes): 207.82%, -31.54%, and -76.27%. The answer that you get from 1-2-3 will depend on the initial *GUESS* that you supply. A *GUESS* of 80% or less will give -31.54% as the answer. Any *GUESS* between 84% and 93% will get an answer of -76.27%. A *GUESS* greater than 122% will return 207.82% as the IRR. Other choices will return ERR. It is impossible to say which of these answers is correct since all will return an *NPV* of zero if used as the discount rate (try it!).

The Modified Internal Rate of Return

An easy solution to the problems of the *IRR* as a profitability measure is to simply use the *NPV* instead. This is not likely to please everyone, however. Despite its problems, executives continue to prefer the *IRR* to the *NPV*. To understand how we can use the *IRR* and still arrive at correct answers requires that you understand the root cause of the problems with the *IRR*.

Implicit in the calculation of the *IRR* is the assumption that the cash flows are reinvested at the *IRR*. In other words, the *IRR* method assumes that as each cash flow is received, it is reinvested for the remaining life of the project at a rate which is the same as the *IRR*. For projects with a very high or very low *IRR*, this assumption is likely to be violated. If the cash flows are reinvested at some other rate, the actual average annual rate of return will be different than the *IRR*. To see this assumption at work, consider again our Supreme Shoe project. The timeline is pictured in Figure 10-4 with the explicit reinvestment of the cash flows at the *IRR* of 30.945%.

FIGURE 10-4
SUPREME SHOE CASH FLOWS WITH EXPLICIT REINVESTMENT AT THE *IRR*

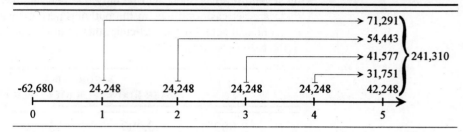

Assuming that the cash flows are reinvested at 30.945% per year, at the end of year 5 Supreme Shoe will have accumulated \$241,310 from their original investment of \$62,680. The compound average annual return, then, must be:

$$\sqrt[5]{\frac{241,310}{62,680}} - 1 \approx 30.945\%$$

which is exactly the same as the *IRR*. Note that we have used the geometric mean, equation (1-1) from Chapter 1, in this example.

It seems unlikely that Supreme Shoe can earn a rate this high over a five-year period. If we change the reinvestment rate to a more reasonable 15% (the required rate of return), then we have the timeline in Figure 10-5.

FIGURE 10-5
SUPREME SHOE CASH FLOWS WITH EXPLICIT REINVESTMENT AT 15%

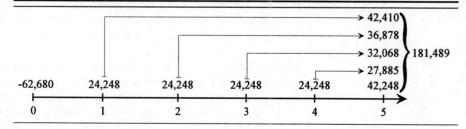

In this case, Supreme Shoe will have accumulated only $181,489 by the end of the fifth year. Their average annual rate of return with a 15% reinvestment rate will be:

$$\sqrt[5]{\frac{181,489}{62,680}} - 1 \approx 23.69\%$$

which is substantially lower than the 30.95% *IRR*. When we calculate the average annual return with a reinvestment rate that is different than the *IRR* we refer to it as the *modified internal rate of return*, or *MIRR*. For Supreme Shoe, the *MIRR* is 23.69% which is greater than the required return of 15%, so the project should be accepted.

1-2-3 has a built-in function to calculate the *MIRR*. The function is defined as:

@MIRR(*RANGE*, *FINANCE_RATE*, *REINVEST_RATE*, *TYPE*)

where ***RANGE*** is the range of cash flows, ***FINANCE_RATE*** is the required rate of return, and ***REINVEST_RATE*** is the rate at which the cash flows are to be reinvested. *TYPE* tells 1-2-3 whether the cash flows occur at the beginning or end of the period. To calculate the *MIRR* in your Supreme Shoe worksheet, enter: @MIRR(D19..D24,B17,B17,1) into B30. Note that 1-2-3 is inconsistent in its use of the *TYPE* parameter in this function. The cash flows actually occur at the end of each period, but we must specify *TYPE* = 1 (beginning) to get the correct answer of 23.69%. In this example we have used the same rate for the required return and the reinvestment rate. This is normally the appropriate assumption to make (it is the same assumption that is implicit within the *NPV* calculation). But if you have other information which suggests a different rate, then that different rate should be used.

Sensitivity Analysis

Probably the most important benefit of using a spreadsheet program is that it allows us to play "what-if" games with the data. That is, we can experiment with different values to determine how sensitive the results are to changes in the assumptions.

NPV Profile Charts

One useful technique that we can use is referred to as the *NPV profile*. This is simply a chart of the *NPV* at various discount rates. The analyst can determine, at a glance, how sensitive the *NPV* is to the assumed discount rate. To create an *NPV* profile chart, we merely set up a range of discount rates and *NPV* calculations and then create a chart.

To create an *NPV* profile chart for Supreme Shoe, let's create a range of discount rates from 0% to 35% in 5% increments. Move to cell A36 and enter: 0. In A37 enter 0.05. To create the range of discount rates, select A36..A43 and then choose **R**ange Fill by **E**xample from the menus. You should now have a range of discount rates from 0% to 35%. We will use these rates in our *NPV* calculations.

To calculate the *NPV* at each discount rate, enter: @NPV(A36,D$20..D$24)+ D$19 in B35. Notice that this is exactly the same formula as in B27, except that we have added a few dollar signs to freeze the references and we changed the discount rate to reference A36. Copying this formula to B37..B43 will calculate the *NPV* for each discount rate. Note that the *NPV* becomes negative at a discount rate just over 30% because the *IRR* was 30.95%.

Finally, select A36..B43 and create an XY chart. This section of your worksheet should resemble the one in Exhibit 10-4. Notice that the chart clearly shows the *IRR* is about 30%. This is the point where the *NPV* line crosses the x-axis of the *NPV* profile chart. Furthermore, it is obvious that for any discount rate below 30% the project has a positive *NPV*, thus it is acceptable.

If there was more than one IRR for the project, we would clearly see the NPV profile line crossing the X-axis at each IRR. To see this, create an NPV profile chart for the project in Figure 10-3.

EXHIBIT 10-4
NPV PROFILE FOR SUPREME SHOE

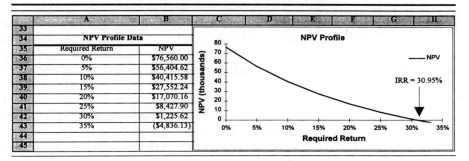

Scenario Analysis

One of the major benefits of spreadsheets is that they make sensitivity analysis easy. *Sensitivity analysis*, also called "what-if" analysis, is a technique in which one variable is changed to see the effect it has on the profitability of a project. A more powerful technique is *scenario analysis*. With this technique, we change multiple variables at one time and evaluate the effect on the profitability of a project.

1-2-3 contains a very powerful tool called the *Version Manager* which helps in analyzing the effects of different assumptions. Version Manager can be used to toggle your worksheet between various views, or it can create a summary of the effects of changing the assumptions.

As an example we will create three scenarios in which the estimates of maintenance and defect costs are different than expected. The three scenarios are listed in Table 10-4.

TABLE 10-4
THREE POSSIBLE SCENARIOS FOR SUPREME SHOE

	Best Case	Expected Case	Worst Case
Maintenance	$2,000	$5,000	$8,000
Defects	$1,000	$2,000	$5,000

227

In the Best Case scenario both maintenance and defects are lower than in the Expected Case (which represents the original estimates). In the Worst Case, both are higher than expected.

Creating scenarios is quite simple. First, we must name the cells that will be used in the scenarios. Select C14 and then choose **R**ange **N**ame from the menus. In the **N**ame edit box, type: Maint then click the **A**dd button. Next, type: Defects in the **N**ame edit box, set the **R**ange to C15, and click the **A**dd button.. Now close the dialog box.

The next step is to define the versions (Expected, Best, and Worst) for each cell. With C14 selected in the worksheet, choose **R**ange **V**ersion to open the Version Manager. Click the **C**reate button in the lower-left corner of the dialog box. Notice that the **R**ange name is set to MAINT, and change the **V**ersion name to: Expected, and click the OK button. You have just created the first version for the maintenance expense.

EXHIBIT 10-5
VERSION MANAGER

Now we will create the Best version for maintenance expense. To switch from the Version Manager to the worksheet, press Alt-T on the keyboard. Change C14 to 2000. Press Alt-T to return to the Version Manager. Click the **C**reate button and name the version: Best.

To create the Worst case version for maintenance expense, switch to the worksheet (Alt-T) and change C14 to 8000. Now, switch back to the Version Manager and click the **C**reate button. Name the version: Worst, and click the OK button.

You now have three versions of the maintenance expense. You can easily show the different versions by selecting them from the "With **v**ersion(s)" drop-down list. For example, to return the worksheet to its original values (the Expected case) select Expected from the list. Note that the value in C14 changes to 2,000 and the worksheet recalculates with the new value.

The next step is to create the same three versions for the defects expense. Follow the same steps as outlined for the maintenance expense versions, and use the numbers for defects from Table 10-4.

Once you have created the three versions for each cell, you can create scenarios (combinations of the versions). Click the To Index button which will display the Version Manager Index (Exhibit 10-6). This index shows all of the versions and scenarios that you have created, and allows you to display them simply by selecting the one you want to see.

EXHIBIT 10-6
THE VERSION MANAGER INDEX

To create a scenario, click the Scenario... button which will launch the Create Scenario dialog box (see Exhibit 10-7). First, enter Expected for the Scenario name. Next, we need to tell 1-2-3 which versions to include in this scenario. In the lower-right corner the Available versions list shows the versions that you have defined. For this scenario, we want to select the Expected version for both DEFECTS and MAINT. Click on Expected under DEFECTS, and then click the << button to include it in the scenario. Repeat this process for MAINT Expected and then click OK.

You have now created the Expected scenario. Repeat the same steps to create Best and Worst scenarios. When you have finished, the Version Manager Index should look similar to Exhibit 10-6. To show a particular scenario in the worksheet, simply highlight the scenario name and then click on the Show button on the Index toolbar. For example, select the Best scenario and show it. Notice that the worksheet now shows that maintenance expense is 2,000 and defects are 1,000.

EXHIBIT 10-7
CREATE SCENARIO DIALOG BOX

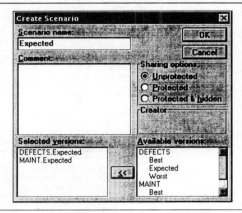

Further, the NPV for this scenario is 36,401.93. If you show the Worst scenario, the NPV is 14,277.70 (still acceptable). This type of flexibility is one of the promised results of proper worksheet design. Scenario analysis will not work properly unless you are diligent about using formulas, rather than retyping values, whenever possible.

A summary of the different versions (not scenarios, unfortunately) can be easily created if you press the Report... button. First we need to change the display so that it is sorted by versions, rather than scenarios. Click on Scenario name S<u>o</u>rt, and choose Version name from this list. Now click the Re<u>p</u>ort... button.

EXHIBIT 10-8
VERSION REPORT DIALOG BOX

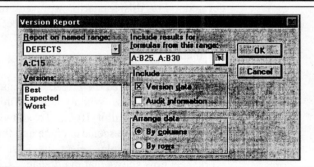

When the Version Report dialog box appears (Exhibit 10-8), choose DEFECTS in the **R**eport on named range list, and then click on each of the versions to select them for the report. Now choose the range B25..B30 (our profitability measures) as the result formulas. Click OK, and 1-2-3 will create a new workbook containing the report which should look like the one in Exhibit 10-9.

EXHIBIT 10-9
DEFECTS VERSION REPORT FOR SUPREME SHOE

File	D:\WORKSHTS\CH10.WK4		
Named range	DEFECTS (A:C15)		
Version name	Best	Expected	Worst
Version cells			
A:C15	1000	2000	5000
Formula results			
Payback Period	2.52	2.58	2.81
Discounted Payback	3.39	3.51	3.92
Net Present Value (NPV)	29,764.66	27,552.24	20,914.97
Profitability Index (PI)	1.47	1.44	1.33
Internal Rate of Return (IRR)	32.18%	30.95%	27.21%
MIRR	24.29%	23.69%	21.82%

The Optimal Capital Budget

How large a firm's capital budget should be is a serious problem that confronts financial managers. One solution that is often chosen is capital rationing. *Capital rationing* is the arbitrary limiting of the amount of capital available for investment purposes. This solution is, however, economically irrational and contrary to the goal of the firm. In order to maximize shareholder wealth, the firm must accept all positive *NPV* projects. Remember that a positive *NPV* project is one which will cover the cost of financing (the weighted average cost of capital). In effect, a positive *NPV* project is self-liquidating, so there should be no problem raising the required funds to make the investment.

No matter how much must be raised, as long as positive *NPV* projects exist, a firm should continue to invest until the cost of investing exceeds the benefits to be gained.[3]

Optimal Capital Budget Without Capital Rationing

We have seen in the previous chapter that a firm's weighted average cost of capital will increase as the amount of capital to be raised increases. We can make use of this fact to determine exactly what a firm's optimal capital budget should be in the absence of capital rationing. Briefly, we rank all projects by their IRR and compare this ranking to the marginal weighted average cost of capital schedule.

Recall from the previous chapter the Rocky Mountain Motors example. Assume that RMM has found 10 potential new projects, each of which would be profitable at its current *WACC* of 10.54% (i.e., all have *IRR*s > 10.54%). The projects are listed in Table 10-5.

TABLE 10-5
ROCKY MOUNTAIN MOTORS PROJECTS

Cost	Cumulative Cost	IRR
$445,529	$445,529	15.02%
439,207	884,736	15.87%
407,769	1,292,505	16.51%
396,209	1,688,714	16.16%
271,477	1,960,191	15.38%
201,843	2,162,034	11.69%
189,921	2,351,955	13.82%
146,661	2,498,616	12.19%
138,298	2,636,914	11.48%
74,950	2,711,864	13.00%

---

3. From your economics classes, recall that to maximize profits a firm should continue to produce until the marginal cost equals the marginal revenue. This is the same idea, but in a different context. Furthermore, we are evaluating costs and benefits in present value terms and, as we will see in the next chapter, we are taking risk into account.

Enter the data from Table 10-5 into a new worksheet beginning with the labels in A1. The cumulative cost can be calculated by entering: @SUM($A$2..A2) into B2 and then copying the formula to the other cells. The first step in determining the optimal capital budget is to sort all independent projects by their *IRR*. Select the data in A2..C11. To sort the data choose **R**ange **S**ort... from the menus, and enter C2 in the "**S**ort by" list. Since we want to select the projects with the highest *IRR*s, choose to sort in **D**escending order. This sorted list of *IRR*s is known as the Investment Opportunity Schedule (IOS).

Next, we want to create a chart showing the marginal weighted-average cost of capital curve and the investment opportunity schedule. To do this we need to copy the Total Capital (A10..A48) and WACC (E10..E48) data from your RMM worksheet (Exhibit 9-5). Paste these areas into the new worksheet in A15..B15. Now, and this is a bit tedious, enter the *IRR*s in column C. Since the first project will use $407,769 of the capital raised, enter 16.51% in C16..C23. The second-best project will cost an additional $306,209, so enter 16.16% C24..C33. Continue adding the *IRR*s in this manner until all 10 projects have been entered.

Finally, select the data in all three columns (A15:C70), and create an XY chart. Your worksheet should now resemble that in Exhibit 10-10.

EXHIBIT 10-10
MARGINAL WACC AND THE IOS FOR RMM

	A	B	C	D	E	F	G	H
15	Total Capital	WACC	IRR					
16	0	10.54%	16.51%					
17	100,000	10.54%	16.51%					
18	165,973	10.54%	16.51%					
19	165,973	12.16%	16.51%					
20	200,000	12.16%	16.51%					
21	300,000	12.16%	16.51%					
22	400,000	12.16%	16.51%					
23	407,769	12.16%	16.51%					
24	407,769	12.16%	16.16%					
25	500,000	12.16%	16.16%					
26	580,906	12.16%	16.16%					
27	580,906	12.40%	16.16%					
28	600,000	12.40%	16.16%					
29	700,000	12.40%	16.16%					
30	800,000	12.40%	16.16%					
31	802,773	12.40%	16.16%					
32	802,773	12.65%	16.16%					
33	803,978	12.65%	16.16%					
34	803,978	12.65%	15.87%					

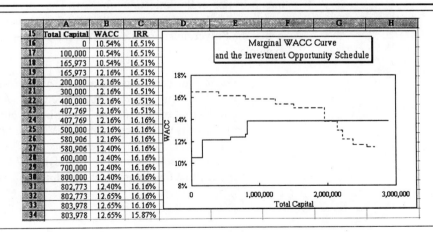

The optimal capital budget without capital rationing is the level of total capital at which the marginal *WACC* schedule and the Investment Opportunity Schedule cross. In this case that would be $1,960,191.

Optimal Capital Budget Under Capital Rationing

Though irrational, capital rationing is common. How then, can we determine the optimal capital budget in the presence of restricted capital? In this situation we need to find that combination of projects which maximizes the total net present value, subject to a capital constraint.

This can be a tedious exercise when there are a large number of positive *NPV* projects to choose among. For example, assume that we have four positive *NPV* projects to choose among. At a minimum we must select one project, but we can select up to four. If we must look at every possible combination of these four projects, then we must examine 16 possible combinations. As the number of projects grows, the number of combinations grows even faster. In general there are 2^N possible combinations, where N is the number of positive *NPV* projects. Note that negative *NPV* projects are excluded from this calculation and further consideration because we cannot increase the total *NPV* by adding a negative *NPV* project.[4]

1-2-3 provides a tool called the *Solver* which can be used in any type of constrained maximization or minimization problem. The Solver provides a dialog box in which you describe the problem, the cells that may be changed, and the constraints under which the Solver must operate. It then finds the optimal solution. Let's look at an example.

> Because of declining demand for high-pressure frammis valves, the Frammis Valve Corporation of America (FVCA) is considering expanding into a number of other businesses. After discussions with its consultants, FVCA has determined that it has thirteen potential new investments (see Table 10-6). The total cost of these investments would be $7,611,990, but they are limited to a maximum total investment of only $3,000,000. You

---

4. Strictly speaking, this is not always true. Under a multi-period capital budgeting scenario with multi-period cash flow constraints, it is possible that adding negative *NPV* projects could increase the total *NPV*.

have been asked to determine which combination of the projects the company should choose.

Since there are thirteen acceptable projects, you will have to examine each of the 8,192 $(= 2^{13})$ possible combinations and determine which provides the highest total *NPV*. This problem is obviously going to be time consuming unless you have access to a computer. Enter the data from the problem into a new worksheet beginning in cell A4.

TABLE 10-6
FVCA'S AVAILABLE PROJECTS UNDER CAPITAL RATIONING

Project	Cost	NPV
A	$237,005	$84,334
B	766,496	26,881
C	304,049	23,162
D	565,178	82,598
E	108,990	20,590
F	89,135	90,404
G	795,664	18,163
H	814,493	97,682
I	480,321	52,063
J	826,610	53,911
K	734,830	56,323
L	910,598	88,349
M	978,621	69,352

To solve this problem, we need some way to determine the sum of the costs and *NPV*s for only those projects which are to be selected. Since each project will either be selected or not, this is a perfect use for a binary variable. A binary variable can take on one of two values; most commonly 0 or 1. In this case, we will set up a column with 0's and 1's where 1 indicates that a project is selected, and 0 indicates rejection. Your worksheet should resemble that in Exhibit 10-11.

Note that we have initially set each cell in D4..D16 to 1 (all are selected). Also, due to the nature of the problem, we can not use an ordinary @Sum function to total columns B and C. Recall that we only want the sum of the costs and NPVs of the projects which are to be selected.

We will use the @SUMPRODUCT function which first multiplies the cells in corresponding ranges and then adds them together. It is defined as:

$$\text{@S{\small UM}P{\small RODUCT}}(\textit{RANGE1}, \textit{RANGE2})$$

where **RANGE1** and **RANGE2** are the data. Note that any project which has a 0 in the Include column will not add to the total.

EXHIBIT 10-11
FVCA'S CAPITAL BUDGETING PROBLEM

	A	B	C	D
1	The Optimal Capital Budget			
2	Under Capital Rationing			
3	Project	Cost	NPV	Include
4	A	237,005	84,334	1
5	B	766,496	26,881	1
6	C	304,049	23,162	1
7	D	565,178	82,598	1
8	E	108,990	20,590	1
9	F	89,135	90,404	1
10	G	795,664	18,163	1
11	H	814,493	97,682	1
12	I	480,321	52,063	1
13	J	826,610	53,911	1
14	K	734,830	56,323	1
15	L	910,598	88,349	1
16	M	978,621	69,352	1
17	Total	7,611,990	763,812	13
18	Constraint	3,000,000		

Since we want to find the total cost of the accepted projects, we could write a formula such as: +B4*D4+B5*D5+B6*D6.... However, this would be a long formula to enter. Instead, enter: @SUMPRODUCT(B4..B16,$D$4..$D$16) into B17. This is much shorter and easier to understand. To find the total *NPV*, copy the formula to C17, and your totals should be the same as those in Exhibit 10-11.

To restate the problem, we want to maximize the total *NPV* in C17 by changing the cells in D4..D16 subject to several constraints. The first constraint is that the total cost, in B17, must be less than or equal to 3,000,000. Next we must constrain the values in D4..D16 to be either 0 or 1, but they cannot take on any non-integer values.

In 1-2-3, a constraint cell must be a formula which evaluates to either true (1) or false (0). In B19, we'll set up our cost constraint with the formula: +B17<=B18. At this point, you should see a 0 in B19 since the total cost is greater than $3,000,000. If you change the values in D11..D17 to zeros, the total cost will change to $2,866,517 and B19 will show a 1.

Setting up the constraints for the "Include" cells (D4..D17) is a bit more complicated. Recall that we need to constrain these cells to be either 0 or 1. This requires three constraints. In E4 enter: +D4>=0 to make sure that D4 is greater than or equal to zero. In F4 enter: +D4<=1 to make sure that D4 is less than or equal to one. For the third constraint, we need to make sure that D4 is *not* between 0 and 1. It must be an integer value, so in G4 enter: +D4-@INT(D4)=0 to make sure that the fractional value is zero. Note that we have used the **@INT** function which returns just the integer portion of a value. For example: @Int(1.58) would return 1. Copy these constraints down through row 16 so that they will apply to each project.

You are now ready to run the Solver. Choose **R**ange **A**nalyze **S**olver from the menus to launch the Solver (Exhibit 10-12). The **A**djustable cells are those that the Solver is allowed to change while solving the problem. For our example, enter D4..D16 which is the "Include" cells. The **C**onstraint cells are the location of the constraints, so enter: E4..G16, B19. The **O**ptimal cell is the one that contains the formula to optimize, in this case C17. Finally, make sure that Ma**x** is selected since we want to maximize the total *NPV*.

EXHIBIT 10-12
THE SOLVER DIALOG BOX

EXHIBIT 10-13
THE OPTIMAL SOLUTION FOR THE FVCA CAPITAL BUDGET

	A	B	C	D
1	The Optimal Capital Budget			
2	Under Capital Rationing			
3	Project	Cost	NPV	Include
4	A	237,005	84,334	1
5	B	766,496	26,881	0
6	C	304,049	23,162	1
7	D	565,178	82,598	1
8	E	108,990	20,590	0
9	F	89,135	90,404	1
10	G	795,664	18,163	0
11	H	814,493	97,682	1
12	I	480,321	52,063	0
13	J	826,610	53,911	0
14	K	734,830	56,323	0
15	L	910,598	88,349	1
16	M	978,621	69,352	0
17	Total	2,920,458	466,529	6
18	Constraint	3,000,000		

To start the Solver working on the problem, click the Solve button. In a few seconds, the Solver will finish and show the best answer that it could find in the worksheet.[5] Exhibit 10-13 shows the optimal solution: FVCA should accept A, C, D, F, H and L for a total NPV of $466,529 and a total cost of $2,920,458.

As a final point about the Solver, you can easily change the constraint of $3,000,000 to any other value and then run the Solver again. Since the Solver settings are saved, you do not need to re-enter the data every time.

---

5. For reasons that neither the authors, nor Lotus technicians can understand, the Solver in 1-2-3 Release 5 does not find the correct solution (which is shown in Exhibit 10-13). However, we are including this section because this may be fixed in future releases of the program.

Other Techniques

Because of the time required to maximize the total *NPV*, other techniques can be used to approximate the optimal capital budget. The first is to select the projects with the highest profitability indices. You may have to discard some high *PI* projects, and you will likely not achieve the maximum *NPV*, but the solution can often be found with less work than maximizing *NPV*. As an alternative, we could choose the projects with the highest *IRR*s. However, this could be misleading if the projects are of greatly different sizes (as in the RMM example).

Summary

Capital budgeting is one of the most important functions of the corporate financial manager. In this chapter we have seen how to calculate the relevant cash flows and how to evaluate those cash flows to determine the profitability of accepting the project.

We demonstrated six profitability measures which are summarized in Table 10-7.

TABLE 10-7
SUMMARY OF PROFITABILITY MEASURES

Profitability Measure	Acceptance Criteria
Payback Period	<= Maximum allowable period
Discounted Payback	<= Maximum allowable period
Net Present Value	>= 0
Profitability Index	>= 1
Internal Rate of Return	>= *WACC*
Modified IRR	>= *WACC*

In addition, we introduced the Version Manager and Solver tools which are provided by 1-2-3. The Version Manager tool allows us to easily compare the outcomes based on various inputs. The Solver allows us to find optimal values for a cell in a model.

TABLE 10-8
FUNCTIONS INTRODUCED IN THIS CHAPTER

Purpose	Function	Page
Calculates straight-line depreciation	@SLN(*COST, SALVAGE, LIFE*)	210
Calculates the *IRR*	@IRR(*GUESS, RANGE*)	221
Calculates the *MIRR*	@MIRR(*RANGE, FINANCE_RATE, REINVEST_RATE*)	225
Calculates the sum of the products of corresponding ranges	@SUMPRODUCT(*RANGE1, RANGE2*)	236
Returns only the integer portion of the argument	@INT(*X*)	237

CHAPTER 11

Risk, Capital Budgeting, and Diversification

After studying this chapter, you should be able to:

1. *Define the five major statistical measures used in finance and calculate these manually and in 1-2-3.*

2. *Incorporate risk into capital budgeting decisions and show how to calculate the "risk-adjusted discount rate" (RADR) in 1-2-3.*

3. *Explain three alternative techniques for incorporating risk into the analysis.*

4. *Explain diversification, and give an example using 1-2-3.*

5. *Calculate portfolio risk measures with 1-2-3.*

Risk is a difficult concept to define, but most people recognize such obvious risks as swimming in shark-infested waters. If you consider risky situations for a moment, you will realize that the thing that they all have in common is the possibility of a loss. Many times the loss is of life or money. In this chapter we are concerned with the possibility of a financial loss. Specifically, we will say that the larger the possibility of loss, the larger the risk.

We will begin by attempting to measure the riskiness of an investment, and then we will consider how we can adjust our decision making process to account for the risk that we have measured. Finally, we will consider how we can reduce risk through diversification.

Review of Some Useful Statistical Concepts

Any situation that has an uncertain outcome can be said to have a probability distribution associated with the possible outcomes. A *probability distribution* is simply a listing of the probabilities associated with potential outcomes. A probability distribution is said to be *discrete* if there is a limited number of potential outcomes, and *continuous* if there is an infinite number of possible outcomes. Figure 11-1 illustrates both continuous and discrete probability distributions. Continuous probability distributions can be approximated by discrete distributions if we have enough possible outcomes. To keep things simple in this chapter we will use only discrete distributions.

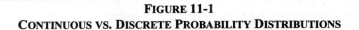

FIGURE 11-1
CONTINUOUS VS. DISCRETE PROBABILITY DISTRIBUTIONS

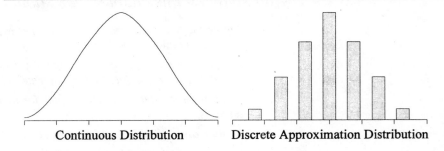

Continuous Distribution   Discrete Approximation Distribution

One type of probability distribution has numerous properties that makes it attractive for our use, the *normal distribution*. In particular, the normal distribution can be completely described by its mean and variance, which will prove useful in our efforts to understand risk.

The Expected Value

The *expected value* of a distribution is a weighted average of all possible outcomes where the weights are the probabilities of occurrence. The expected value can be thought of as the most likely outcome, or the average outcome if we could run an experiment thousands of times. For any discrete probability distribution, the expected value is given by:

$$E(X) = \sum_{t=1}^{N} \rho_t X_t \qquad (11\text{-}1)$$

where $E(X)$ is the expected or most likely X, X_t is the tth possible outcome, and ρ_t is the probability that X_t will occur. For the normal distribution the expected value is the same as the more familiar arithmetic mean.

To illustrate the calculation of the expected value, suppose that you have been offered an opportunity to participate in a game of chance. The rules of this particular game are such that you must pay $200 to play, and Table 11-1 describes the possible payoffs.

TABLE 11-1
PROBABILITY DISTRIBUTION FOR A GAME OF CHANCE

Probability	Cash Flow
0.25	100
0.50	200
0.25	300

To determine whether or not you should play this game, it is necessary to compare the expected payoff to the cost of playing. If the expected cash flow is equal to or exceeds your cost, it makes sense to play. The expected value of this game is:

$$E(Cf) = 0.25(100) + 0.50(200) + 0.25(300) = 200$$

so that you expect to break-even. Note that in actuality, if the game is played only once you could lose as much as $100 or win as much as $100 net of your cost of entry. However, the most likely outcome is a net gain of $0.00. Comparing this to the arithmetic mean:

$$\overline{Cf} = \frac{100 + 200 + 300}{3} = 200$$

and subtracting your cost, you can see that they are the same. Again, this is because the outcomes of this game are symmetrically distributed.

It is important to understand that many times the assumption of a symmetrical distribution is not correct, and in this case the arithmetic mean and the expected value will not be the same. Whenever possible, it is better to use the expected value as an estimate instead of the arithmetic mean.

Measures of Dispersion

Whenever an expected value is used, it is useful to know how much, on average, the actual outcome might deviate from the expected outcome. The larger these potential deviations are, the less confidence we will have that the expected outcome will actually occur. Another way of saying this is that the larger the potential deviations, the higher the probability of an outcome far away from the expected outcome.

Recall that we earlier said that high probabilities of loss indicated a high risk situation. Therefore, when comparing distributions we can say that the distribution with the larger potential deviations has a higher probability of loss, and therefore has higher risk.

The Variance and Standard Deviation

To measure risk, we need a way to measure the size of the potential deviations from the mean. One measure we could use is the average deviation. The average deviation is calculated as:

$$\bar{D} = \sum_{t=1}^{N} \rho_t(X_t - \bar{X}) \tag{11-2}$$

But in the case of the normal distribution the average deviation will always be zero (why?). So we need another measure of dispersion which doesn't suffer from this flaw. One possibility is the *variance*. The variance is the average of the squared deviations from the mean and is calculated as:[1]

---

1. Note that in your beginning statistics class you probably defined the population variance as:

$$\sigma_X^2 = \frac{1}{N} \sum_{t=1}^{N} (X_t - \bar{X})^2$$

Our definition is equivalent if we assume that all outcomes are equally likely.

$$\sigma_X^2 = \sum_{t=1}^{N} \rho_t (X_t - \bar{X})^2 \qquad \text{(11-3)}$$

Because we are squaring the deviations from the mean, and the result of squaring a number is always positive, the variance must be positive.[2] The larger the variance, the less likely it is that the actual outcome will be near the expected outcome, and the riskier it is considered to be. Figure 11-2 illustrates this by comparing two distributions.

FIGURE 11-2
COMPARISON OF THE RISKINESS OF TWO DISTRIBUTIONS

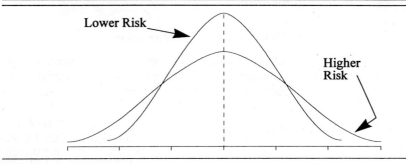

Returning to the example in Table 11-1, we can calculate the variance of possible outcomes as follows:

$$\sigma^2 = 0.25(100 - 200)^2 + 0.50(200 - 200)^2 + 0.25(300 - 200)^2 = 5,000$$

So the variance of possible outcomes is 5,000. But 5,000 in what units? In this case the units are squared dollars, an unusual unit of measurement to be sure. In order to make this measurement more understandable, it is common to take the square root of the variance which gives us the standard deviation:[3]

---

2. It is possible that the variance could be zero, but only if there is just one possible outcome.

3. Mathematically inclined students will instantly grasp the fact that $\sqrt{\$^2} = \$$

$$\sigma_X = \sqrt{\sum_{t=1}^{N} p_t(X_t - \bar{X})^2} \qquad \text{(11-4)}$$

The standard deviation of potential outcomes in our game example is:

$$\sigma = \sqrt{5,000} = 70.71$$

which means that about 68% of all outcomes will be within one standard deviation of the mean (200 ± 70.71), and about 95.5% will be within two standard deviations (200 ± 141.42). Furthermore, it is exceedingly unlikely ($< 0.1\%$), but not impossible, that the actual outcome will fall beyond three standard deviations from the mean.

The Coefficient of Variation

Suppose that after playing our original game, you are offered a chance to play the game again, but this time the game is ten times larger as is your cost to play. The possible outcomes are presented in Table 11-2.

TABLE 11-2
SAME GAME, BUT TEN TIMES LARGER

Probability	Cash Flow
0.25	1000
0.50	2000
0.25	3000

Is this game riskier than the old game? Let's look at the standard deviation to see:

$$\sigma = \sqrt{0.25(1000 - 2000)^2 + 0.50(2,000 - 2,000)^2 + 0.25(3,000 - 2,000)^2}$$
$$\sigma = 707.106$$

Since the standard deviation is ten times larger, it appears that the new game is much riskier. Recall, however, that we said that high risk was associated with a high probability of loss. In the new game your probability of loss is unchanged (25%). Since the probability of loss is unchanged, the risk should be the same.

Apparently the standard deviation has a scale problem. That is, larger numbers cause larger standard deviations even if the relative dispersion is unchanged. The coefficient of variation handles the scale problem by dividing the standard deviation by the mean:

$$\gamma_X = \frac{\sigma_X}{X} \tag{11-5}$$

where γ_X is the coefficient of variation. If the new game is truly riskier than the old game, it will have a higher coefficient of variation. Let's compare the coefficients of variation for both games:

$$\gamma_1 = \frac{70.7106}{200} = 0.3535$$

$$\gamma_2 = \frac{707.106}{2,000} = 0.3535$$

Since $\gamma_1 = \gamma_2$ both games must be equally risky.

Using 1-2-3 to Measure Risk

Now that we understand how risk can be evaluated, let's look at how 1-2-3 might be used to simplify the calculations. In this section we will introduce several of 1-2-3's built-in functions. Before continuing open a new workbook.

A Short Example

Suppose that you are involved in analyzing a potential new product for the Freshly Frozen Fish Company. As an expert in the catfish market, you have been asked to develop cash flow forecasts for a new frozen catfish product the company is considering. As an approximation you have developed the following projections for the first year's cash flows from the product.

TABLE 11-3
FIRST YEAR PROJECTIONS FOR FRESHLY FROZEN

Probability	Cash Flow
0.05	-500,000
0.20	100,000
0.50	700,000
0.20	1,300,000
0.05	1,900,000

Enter your probabilities and cash flow projections into your worksheet beginning with the title "Freshly Frozen Risk Analysis" in cell A1.

Finding Expected Values in 1-2-3

There are several ways that we might calculate the expected cash flow in 1-2-3. The easiest is to realize that the distribution of possible cash flows is normally distributed, so the expected value and arithmetic mean are the same. Therefore, we can use 1-2-3's built-in **@AVG** function:

$$@\text{AVG}(\textit{LIST})$$

where **LIST** is the range of numbers to be averaged. In our example, we want to average the possible cash flows, so in B8 type: `@AVG(B3..B7)`. Note that the answer is $700,000.

One problem with using the **@AVG** function is that it will give incorrect results if we change the probability distribution so that it is asymmetrical. The expected value calculation that we looked at earlier will always give the correct result regardless of the distribution. But, 1-2-3 has no built-in expected value function. We could use a formula such as: `+A3*B3+A4*B4+A5*B5+A6*B6+A7*B7`, but this is tedious and error-prone. Furthermore, if we later decide to insert more possible cash flows and probabilities, this formula will not automatically accommodate them.

Still another solution, which deals with these problems, is to use the **@WEIGHTAVG** function. As its name implies, this function calculates a weighted average. It is defined as:

$$@\textbf{WEIGHTAVG}(\textit{DATA-RANGE}, \textit{WEIGHTS-RANGE}, \textit{TYPE})$$

where **DATA-RANGE** is the data that you wish to average, **WEIGHTS-RANGE** is the range of weights, and *TYPE* is an optional argument which tells 1-2-3 whether the divisor should be based on the number of cells in **DATA-RANGE** or **WEIGHTS-RANGE**. Generally, *TYPE* should be omitted.

In this case we want to calculate a weighted average of the cash flows in B3..B7, with the weights being the probabilities in A3..A7. To do this, enter: `@WEIGHTAVG(B3..B7,A3..A7)` in B8.[4] Again, the result is $700,000, but now we could change the distribution without worry that our answer will be incorrect.

Calculating the Measures of Dispersion with 1-2-3

Again, in order to judge the riskiness of a project it is important to calculate at least one of the measures of dispersion that were mentioned above. As with the arithmetic average, 1-2-3 provides built-in functions to calculate the variance and standard deviation. We will see, however, that these functions cannot handle any situation where the probability distribution is known.

The Variance

1-2-3 provides two functions for calculating the variance when the probability distribution is unknown (or assumed to be uniform): **@VAR** and **@VARS**. The functions are defined in exactly the same way, but **@VAR** calculates the population variance while **@VARS** calculates the sample variance.[5] These functions are defined as:

$$@\textbf{VAR}(\textit{LIST})$$

and

---

4. We could also use the **@SumProduct** function.

5. The difference between a sample statistic and a population parameter is that the sample statistic includes an adjustment to account for the bias introduced because we aren't dealing with the full population. In the case of the sample standard deviation, the adjustment is to divide by N-1 instead of N.

$$@\text{VARS}(\textit{LIST}).$$

For our purposes we should use the population version of the variance because we know the entire set of possible outcomes. In B9, insert: `@VAR(B3..B7)` and note that the answer is 720,000,000,000 (or, you might see 7.20E+11). Remember, this function is not taking account of the fact that we know the probability distribution of the possible cash flows, so it is incorrect.

We can correct this problem by writing our own formula to implement equation (11-3). In B9, enter: `+A3*(B3-B8)^2+A4*(B4-B8)^2+A5*(B5-B8)^2+ A6*(B6-B8)^2+A7*(B7-B8)^2`. This formula says to take each cash flow minus the expected cash flow, square the result, and multiply it by the appropriate probability. Finally, each of these is added. The result should be 288,000,000,000 (or, 2.88E+11) which is substantially different from the result calculated by the built-in function. The moral is that you must understand what the built-in functions are really calculating or you can get into trouble.

Just for informational purposes, let's see what would happen if each possible outcome were equally likely (i.e., each cash flow will occur with probability 0.2). In each cell in A3..A7 enter: `0.2`. The result is 720,000,000,000 which is the same result as 1-2-3's built-in **@VAR** function.

The Standard Deviation

The standard deviation provides us with the same information as the variance, but is in the same units as the raw data. The easiest way to calculate the standard deviation at this point is to simply take the square root of the variance. Since the variance was calculated in B9, we can enter: `@Sqrt(B9)` in cell B10. This will provide the correct standard deviation because we have correctly calculated the variance. But, most of the time, we are not really interested in the variance so we will look at the different ways in which we might calculate the standard deviation directly.

As with the variance, 1-2-3 provides two built-in functions for calculating the standard deviation: **@STD** (population) and **@STDS** (sample). These functions are defined as:

$$@\text{STD}(\textit{LIST})$$

and

$$@\text{STDS}(\textit{LIST}).$$

Because we know the entire population of potential outcomes, we will use the population version of this function. In B10 enter: @STD(B3..B7). The result is a standard deviation of 848,528, and, just like the variance, it is incorrect because it ignores the probability distribution.

To take account of the information provided by the probability distribution, we could use a formula such as: @SQRT(A3*(B3-B8)^2+A4*(B4-B8)^2+A5*(B5-B8)^2+A6*(B6-B8)^2+A7*(B7-B8)^2) which will give the correct result of 536,656. Note that this is exactly the same formula that we used for the variance, except that we are taking the square root.

The interpretation of the standard deviation is that there is about a 68% probability that the actual first year cash flow will be within $536,656 of the expected cash flow. This means that there is a 68% probability that the actual cash flow will fall into the range $163,344 to $1,236,656. In other words, it is quite likely that the first year cash flow will be positive, but this seems to be a highly risky project because of the large range of possible outcomes.

The Coefficient of Variation

1-2-3 does not have a built-in function to calculate the coefficient of variation. However, as you have seen, this is an easy statistic to calculate. Since we have already calculated the expected cash flow and the standard deviation, we need only enter: +B10/B8 into cell B11. The result is 0.7667 which confirms our statement that this project is fairly risky. Remember that the coefficient of variation adjusts for the size of the cash flows so it can safely be used to compare the riskiness of alternative projects.

Charting the Probability Distribution

It is often helpful to create a histogram of the probability distribution to help visualize the possibilities. Select the range of probabilities in A3..A7 and create a chart (the default is a bar chart which is exactly what we want). Now, choose Chart Ranges and set the X-Axis labels to B3..B7. Your completed worksheet should now resemble the one pictured in Exhibit 11-1.

EXHIBIT 11-1
THE FRESHLY FROZEN FISH WORKSHEET

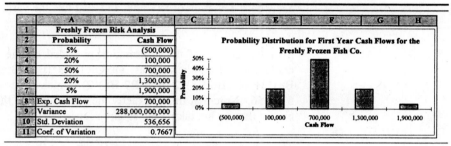

	A	B	C	D	E	F	G	H
1	Freshly Frozen Risk Analysis							
2	Probability	Cash Flow						
3	5%	(500,000)						
4	20%	100,000						
5	50%	700,000						
6	20%	1,300,000						
7	5%	1,900,000						
8	Exp. Cash Flow	700,000						
9	Variance	288,000,000,000						
10	Std. Deviation	536,656						
11	Coef. of Variation	0.7667						

Incorporating Risk into Capital Budgeting Decisions

In Chapter 10 we ignored the riskiness of the cash flows in evaluating capital investments. However, we have seen that risk is an important variable in determining a firm's weighted average cost of capital. Recall that the *WACC* is the discount rate that should be applied to projects which have an average level of risk for the firm. What, then, are we to do with projects that exhibit a higher or lower level of risk than the firm's average project?

There are actually several methods for incorporating risk into our decision making. Before we discuss these methods, let's expand the Freshly Frozen Fish example:

> Management at the Freshly Frozen Fish Company has decided, based on your first-year projections, that they are interested in considering the catfish project further. As a result they have asked you to expand your study to cover the next five years, and to determine whether the project is acceptable or not. Further, they have informed you that the firm's *WACC* is 12% and that they believe that the project would have a net initial outlay of $2,100,000. Freshly Frozen Fish uses all of the usual discounted cash flow techniques to evaluate projects. As a first approximation, and subject to later refinement, you decide that the cash flow projections apply to each of the five years of the project's life. Is the project acceptable?

The Risk-Adjusted Discount Rate

In our discussion of the determination of interest rates we mentioned a model referred to as a "simple risk premium model" (page 157). The risk-adjusted discount rate (*RADR*) is an example of this model. Recall that the simple risk premium model was defined as:

$$\text{Required Return} = \text{Base Rate} + \text{Risk Premium}$$

and that the base rate and risk premium are subjectively determined. In using the *RADR* technique, we will modify this model so that it becomes:

$$RADR = WACC + \text{Risk Premium}.$$

Note that the risk premium is still subjectively determined, but the base rate is the *WACC*.

Normally, the risk premium will be determined according to a schedule that has been approved by the firm's upper management. This schedule may assign risk premiums according to some calculated risk measure, by the type of project, or perhaps by some other method. Suppose that management at Freshly Frozen Fish has given you the following schedule of risk premiums which is based on the coefficient of variation:

TABLE 11-4
COEFFICIENT OF VARIATION AND RISK PREMIUM

Coefficient of Variation	Risk Premium	RADR
$CV \le 0.20$	-0.03	$0.12 - 0.03 = 0.09$
$0.20 \ge CV < 0.30$	0.00	$0.12 + 0.00 = 0.12$
$0.30 \ge CV < 0.40$	0.03	$0.12 + 0.03 = 0.15$
$0.40 \ge CV < 0.50$	0.05	$0.12 + 0.05 = 0.17$
$CV \ge 0.50$	0.07	$0.12 + 0.07 = 0.19$

Note that the coefficient of variation for the company's average project is between 0.20 and 0.30, so they do not assign a risk premium to these projects. For projects with less than average risk, they assign a negative risk premium. For those with greater than average risk they assign a progressively higher risk premium.

In this case we have assumed that each of the next five years' cash flows has the same probability distribution, and therefore the same expected value and standard deviation. The timeline in Figure 11-3 depicts this situation.

FIGURE 11-3
TIMELINE FOR THE FRESHLY FROZEN FISH PROJECT

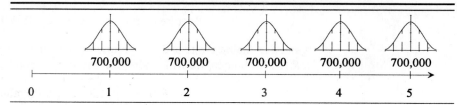

The cash flow forecast for each year is the expected value of the probability distribution which describes the possible outcomes. Since the expected value is the most likely value, we use it as our forecast. You should realize that we have purposely simplified this example by using the same distribution for each year. In actuality, your distribution would likely be different in each period thereby necessitating a different *RADR* for each period.

Let's use the Freshly Frozen Fish worksheet to evaluate this project. In cells A14..B21 enter the data (including the titles) from Table 11-5:

TABLE 11-5
PROJECT CASH FLOWS

Year	Cash Flow
0	(2,100,000)
1	700,000
2	700,000
3	700,000
4	700,000
5	700,000

Note that the cash flows in years 1 through 5 can be entered by referencing the expected cash flow calculation, so in B16..B20 enter: +B$8. We also need to enter the *WACC* in cell B13: 0.12.

To determine whether Freshly Frozen Fish should accept this project, we need to calculate the *NPV*, *IRR* and *MIRR*. For the *NPV* calculation, we will use the information in Table 11-4 to determine the appropriate risk-adjusted discount rate. Since the coefficient of variation is greater than 0.50, we will add 7% to the *WACC* to arrive at the discount rate. The formula in B22 is: `@NPV(B13+0.07,B17..B21)+B16`. Note that we use B13 + 0.07 to calculate the discount rate, rather than just inserting 0.19. This will allow changes in the *WACC* to be instantly incorporated into our result. We will refine this to account for changes in the schedule of risk premiums shortly. The *NPV* is $40,344.42, so the project is acceptable. You can calculate the profitability index in B23 with the formula: `+(B22-B16)/(-B16)`. Note that we are subtracting the (negative) initial outlay to arrive at the present value of the cash flows. The *PI* is 1.0192.

Since we have calculated the *NPV*, there is little need for the *IRR* and *MIRR* calculations, but we may find them useful later. We will calculate the *IRR* in B24 with the formula: `@IRR(B13,B16..B21)`. (The WACC is a good choice as the **GUESS** in this formula.) The *MIRR* will be calculated with: `@MIRR(B16..B21,B13+0.07,B13+0.07)` in B25. Notice that, just like the *NPV*, we calculate the *MIRR* with the risk-adjusted discount rate. Your results should show that the *IRR* is 19.86% and the *MIRR* is 19.38%. Since both are greater than the *RADR*, Freshly Frozen Fish should accept this project.

Take a moment to re-examine the results that you have obtained. Since this project is quite risky, does it really make sense to accept it given the narrow margin by which it is acceptable? The answer, of course, is yes! Remember that we have made an adjustment to account for the risk. So, if the project is still acceptable even after penalizing it for having high risk, this must be a good project.

What if Freshly Frozen Fish revised their schedule of risk premiums (i.e., the management became more, or less, risk averse)? You would have to manually revise your NPV and MIRR formulas to take account of the change. We can actually automate the calculation of the risk premium by making use of a *lookup table*. Lookup tables are simply tables of information in which 1-2-3 will search for values based on information in the first column. In cells E14..F20 enter the data from Table 11-6.

TABLE 11-6
SCHEDULE OF RISK PREMIUMS

CV	Risk Premium
0.00	-3.00%
0.20	0.00%
0.30	3.00%
0.40	5.00%
0.50	7.00%

We will use the lookup table to have 1-2-3 automatically determine the appropriate risk premium for the project. The function that we will use is **@VLOOKUP**, which looks vertically in a table. We will not discuss **@HLOOKUP**, which is similar but looks horizontally in the table. **@VLOOKUP** is defined as:

$$\text{@VLOOKUP}(X, \textit{RANGE}, \textit{COLUMN-OFFSET})$$

where X is the number that you want to find in the first column of the table, *RANGE* is the location of the table, and *COLUMN-OFFSET* is the number of the column from which the data should be retrieved (the first column is numbered 0, the second is 1, etc.).

In this case, we want 1-2-3 to do a search for the coefficient of variation, and return the value that it finds in the second column of the table. The formula that will do this is: @VLOOKUP(B11,E16..F20,1). Note that the value that we want to find, 0.7667 in B11, is not in the table. In this case, 1-2-3 will go to the last row in the table and return 7% as the risk premium. If we had specified 0.25 as the search value, the return value would have been 0%. Of course, the beauty of this approach is two-fold: it allows us to change the risk premium associated with different levels of risk, and it allows us to change our cash flow distribution and still use the appropriate *RADR*. All without modifying our formulas.

We now need to change our *NPV* formula to take advantage of the lookup table. Recall that the discount rate was given as B13+0.07. We want to change that portion of the formula to: B13+@VLOOKUP(B11,E16..F20,1). The NPV that you see in B22 should still be $40,344.42. Your worksheet should now look like the one in Exhibit 11-2.

EXHIBIT 11-2
THE FRESHLY FROZEN FISH WORKSHEET WITH PROFITABILITY MEASURES

	A	B	C	D	E	F	G	H
1	Freshly Frozen Risk Analysis							
2	Probability	Cash Flow		Probability Distribution for First Year Cash Flows for the Freshly Frozen Fish Co.				
3	5%	(500,000)						
4	20%	100,000						
5	50%	700,000						
6	20%	1,300,000						
7	5%	1,900,000						
8	Exp. Cash Flow	700,000						
9	Variance	288,000,000,000						
10	Std. Deviation	536,656		(500,000)	100,000	700,000	1,300,000	1,900,000
11	Coef. of Variation	0.7667				Cash Flow		
12								
13	WACC	12%						
14	Project Cash Flows				Schedule of Risk Premiums			
15	Year	Cash Flow			CV	Risk Premium		
16	0	(2,100,000)			0.0	-3.00%		
17	1	700,000			0.2	0.00%		
18	2	700,000			0.3	3.00%		
19	3	700,000			0.4	5.00%		
20	4	700,000			0.5	7.00%		
21	5	700,000						
22	NPV	$40,344.42						
23	PI	1.0192						
24	IRR	19.86%						
25	MIRR	16.19%						

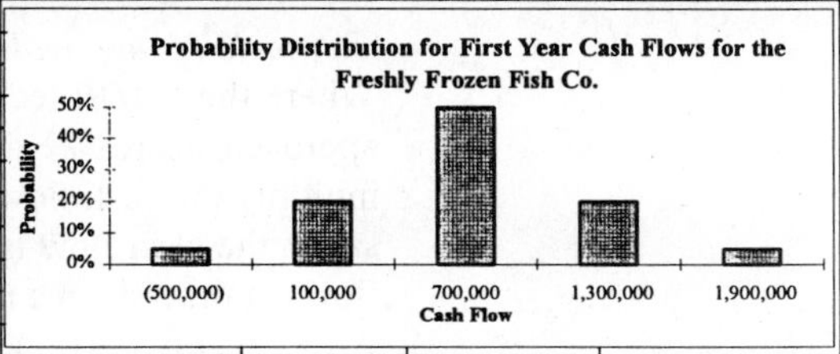

In addition, we need to make the same change the MIRR formula, so the formula in B25 should be: `@MIRR(B16..B21,B13+@VLOOKUP(B11,E16..F20,1), B13+@VLOOKUP(B11,E16..F20,1))`.

Alternatives to the RADR

While the risk-adjusted discount rate technique is the most popular method of incorporating risk into capital budgeting, it is not the only technique, nor is it the most theoretically correct. Several other techniques are available, and we will discuss them in this section.

The Certainty Equivalent Approach

The problem with the *RADR* approach to adjusting for risk is that it combines two adjustments: one for risk and another for time. This approach implicitly assumes that risk is an increasing function of time. In many cases this may be true. Cash flow forecasts for a period five years from now are generally less certain than are forecasts for next year. However, this is not necessarily the case. For example, suppose that a firm has a maintenance contract which calls for a major overhaul of a machine in three years. If the cost of this overhaul is specified in the contract, this is a zero-risk cost, even though it occurs in three years.

The *certainty-equivalent* (*CE*) approach separates the adjustments for time and risk. Where the *RADR* technique increases the discount rate to adjust for risk, the *CE* approach decreases the cash flow. To adjust for risk with the *CE* approach, we multiply the cash flow by the certainty equivalent coefficient. The net result is the same: the cash flow is penalized for risk. To adjust for time, we discount the cash flows at the risk-free rate of interest.

Certainty equivalent coefficients are determined as follows: the decision maker is asked what *certain* cash flow she would be willing to accept in exchange for the risky cash flow. The ratio of these cash flows determines the CE coefficient (α). As an example, assume that you are willing to accept $95 dollars for sure in place of a risky $100 one year from now. Your CE coefficient for this cash flow would be:

$$\alpha = \frac{\text{Riskless cash flow}}{\text{Risky cash flow}} = \frac{95}{100} = 0.95$$

Note that the *CE* coefficient will always be between 0 and 1, and will generally decrease with time because of increased risk. To use the certainty equivalent approach, each cash flow is multiplied by the appropriate coefficient, α_n, and then the net present value is found using the risk-free rate of interest as the discount rate. The risk-free rate is used to discount the cash flows because the risk has been removed by the adjustment. Effectively, the *CE* technique converts a risky stream of cash flows into a risk-free stream of cash flows.

To continue with the Freshly Frozen Fish example, assume that the risk-free rate of interest is 9% and that management has provided you with the schedule of certainty equivalent coefficients presented in Table 11-7.

Enter the risk-free rate in D13 and the certainty equivalents in C16..C21. In D16..D21 we want to enter the adjusted cash flows. To calculate these adjusted cash flows, each of the forecasted cash flows needs to be multiplied by the *CE* coefficient. In D16 enter: +B16*C16 and copy it down to D21. Now, to calculate the risk-adjusted *NPV*, in D22 enter the formula: @NPV(D13,D17..D21)+D16. The *PI* can be calculated as before. Note that the *NPV* is $41,528.50, which is very close to our previous result.

TABLE 11-7
FRESHLY FROZEN FISH *CE*s

Year	CE Coefficient (α)
0	1.00
1	0.90
2	0.81
3	0.76
4	0.72
5	0.70

If the certainty equivalents and the *RADR* are correctly determined, the results from both methods will be the same. However, the *CE* technique suffers from the need to understand the utility function of the decision maker, and thus is very difficult to correctly implement in practice.

The Decision Tree Approach

A decision tree is a graphical depiction of the potential cash flows and associated probabilities for a project. A simple decision tree is shown in Figure 11-4.

In this example there are two possible outcomes in the first period, each with a 50% probability of occurrence. Similarly, in the second period there are four possible outcomes, each with an associated *conditional probability*. We say that the probabilities in the second period (and any succeeding periods) are conditional because they depend on which event occurs in the first period. For example, there is a 60% probability that the cash flow in period 2 will be $600 if the period 1 cash flow was $500. Note that if the period 1 cash flow was $400, then there would be a 0% probability of a cash flow of $600.

Once the conditional probability distributions have been defined for each period, we next determine the *joint probability* of following each potential path. The joint probability is the probability of following each branch along a given path. This probability is determined by taking the product of the conditional probabilities along the path.

FIGURE 11-4
A SIMPLE DECISION TREE[6]

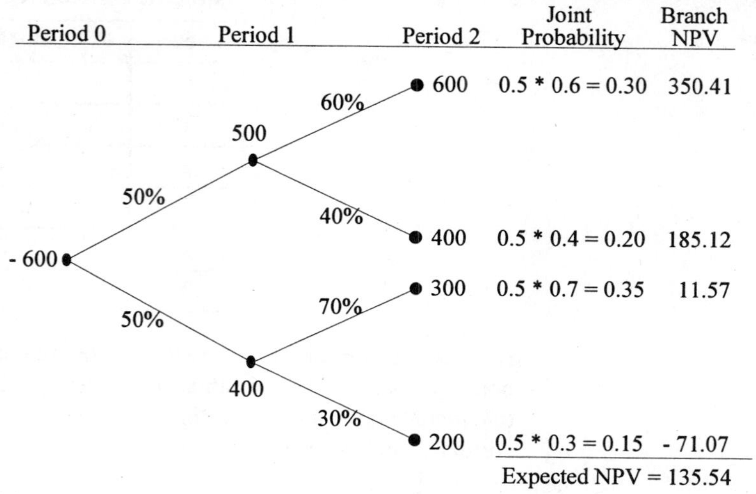

			Joint Probability	Branch NPV

			Joint Probability	Branch NPV
Period 0	Period 1	Period 2		
	500 (60%)	600	0.5 * 0.6 = 0.30	350.41
-600 (50%)		400 (40%)	0.5 * 0.4 = 0.20	185.12
(50%)	400	300 (70%)	0.5 * 0.7 = 0.35	11.57
		200 (30%)	0.5 * 0.3 = 0.15	- 71.07
			Expected NPV =	135.54

For the third step in the analysis, we calculate the *NPV* for each branch of the tree. This "branch *NPV*" has a probability of occurrence equal to the joint probability for the branch. Note that the risk-free rate of return should be used as the discount rate because we are using the full probability distribution. Finally, we calculate the expected *NPV* from the branch *NPVs* and the joint probabilities. In this case, the expected *NPV* is:

$$E(NPV) = 0.3(350.41) + 0.2(185.12) + 0.35(11.57) + 0.15(-71.07)$$
$$E(NPV) = 135.54$$

To recap, there are four steps in a decision tree analysis:

1. Estimate the conditional probability distributions for each period.
2. Calculate the joint probability for each potential path.
3. Calculate the *NPV* for each path.
4. Calculate the expected *NPV* using the joint probabilities and branch *NPVs*.

---

6. We have used a 10% risk-free rate of return as the discount rate.

The decision tree methodology is an extremely useful method of dealing with risk because it forces the decision maker to quantify all of the potential outcomes and their probabilities. Unfortunately, this methodology is not well-suited to spreadsheets because of its inherently graphical nature.

Monte-Carlo Simulation

Still another method for dealing with risk is *Monte-Carlo simulation.* Simulation analysis involves specifying a probability distribution for each uncertain input in a model and then inserting random numbers drawn from that distribution into the model. This process is repeated hundreds of times with the model outputs collected for each run. We can then calculate summary statistics for the outputs to gain a better understanding of the likely outcomes.

1-2-3 does not have any built-in simulation tools, however there are commercial add-on products that perform simulations.

Portfolio Diversification Effects

So far, we have examined investment risk in isolation. However, from the stockholder's point of view, a corporation is nothing more than a collection of investments managed by a professional management team. Therefore, it will be helpful to examine the effect that the addition of risky projects has on the overall risk of the firm. Let's look at an example, using stock selection rather than a capital investment project.

> Suppose that you have $10,000 available for investment purposes. Your stockbroker has suggested that you invest in either Stock A or Stock B, but you are concerned about the riskiness of these stocks. During your investigation, you have gathered the historical returns for these stocks, which is presented in Table 11-8.

To quantify your concerns about the riskiness of these stocks, you open a new worksheet and enter the data from Table 11-8.

TABLE 11-8
HISTORICAL ANNUAL RETURNS FOR A AND B

Year	Stock A Returns	Stock B Returns
1993	10.30%	10.71%
1994	-0.10%	25.00%
1995	23.30%	0.38%
1996	2.20%	26.20%
1997	14.00%	11.52%

Since both firms have had their ups and downs, you want to calculate the average annual return for the last five years. Further, to get a feeling for their riskiness, you want to calculate the standard deviation of these returns. Assuming that you have entered the data from Table 11-8 starting in A1, you can calculate the average return for Stock A in B7 with: @AVG(B2..B6). Copying this to C7 will calculate the average return for Stock B. The results show that Stock A has earned an average of 9.94% per year over the last five years, while Stock B has earned 14.76% per year.[7]

Obviously, if the average historical return reflects the expected future average return, Stock B is to be preferred. Recall, however, that higher returns are generally accompanied by higher risk. We can measure the riskiness of these returns with the standard deviation. To calculate the standard deviation of Stock A's returns enter: @STDS(B2..B6) in B8 and copy it to C8. We can use 1-2-3's built-in formula for the sample standard deviation because we do not have information regarding the probability distribution of returns. The results show that the standard deviation of returns is 9.43% for Stock A and 10.83% for Stock B.

Now you have a problem. If the risk of Stock B was less than Stock A, you would obviously prefer B with a higher return for less risk. In this case, though, you do not have enough information to know if the extra 4.82% return per year from Stock B is enough to offset the extra risk. Suppose that, in your confusion, you decided to purchase both stocks. You will put 50% of your funds in Stock A, and 50% in Stock B. You can determine the returns that you would have earned in each year,

---

7. We are ignoring compounding for simplicity. To find the compound average annual rate of return use the **@GEOMEAN** function (see page 19).

by calculating a weighted average of each stock's return. In D2 enter the formula: +0.5*B2+0.5*C2. This will calculate the return that your portfolio would have earned in 1993. Copy this formula to each cell in the range D3..D6, and then copy the expected return from C7 to D7.

Notice that the expected portfolio return is 12.35%, exactly halfway between the returns on the individual stocks (remember that we put 50% in each stock). Now, let's see what happens to the standard deviation. Copy the formula from C8 to D8. Notice that the standard deviation of the portfolio is only 1.35% — significantly less than the standard deviation of either stock! Exhibit 11-3 shows these results.

EXHIBIT 11-3
PORTFOLIO OF STOCKS A AND B

	A	B	C	D
1	Year	Stock A Returns	Stock B Returns	Portfolio
2	1993	10.30%	10.71%	10.51%
3	1994	-0.10%	25.00%	12.45%
4	1995	23.30%	0.38%	11.84%
5	1996	2.20%	26.20%	14.20%
6	1997	14.00%	11.52%	12.76%
7	Exp. Ret.	9.94%	14.76%	12.35%
8	Std. Dev.	9.43%	10.83%	1.35%

Because the portfolio, consisting of both A and B, provides a higher return and less risk than Stock A, you would certainly prefer the portfolio to Stock A. We cannot, however, definitively say that you would prefer the portfolio to Stock B. To determine which you would pick, we would need information regarding your risk/ return preferences.[8] In this case, it is likely that most people would prefer the portfolio because the difference in returns is slight, but the difference in risk is great.

---

8. More specifically, we would require knowledge of your utility function.

Determining Portfolio Risk and Return

Expected Portfolio Return

As you have seen in the previous example, combining assets into a portfolio may result in the reduction of risk below that of any individual asset. You have also seen that the expected return for a portfolio will be between that of the lowest return asset and the highest return asset. In general, we can say that the expected return for a portfolio is a weighted average of the expected returns for the individual assets. The weights are given by the proportion of total portfolio value that each asset represents. In mathematical terms:

$$E(R_P) = \sum_{t=1}^{N} w_t E(R_P) \tag{11-6}$$

where w_t is the weight and $E(R_t)$ is the expected return of the tth asset. Equation (11-6) is applicable regardless of the number of assets in the portfolio. From the previous example, the expected return for the portfolio is:

$$E(R_P) = 0.5(0.0994) + 0.5(0.1476) = 0.1235 = 12.35\%$$

Portfolio Standard Deviation

While the expected return of the portfolio is a weighted average of the expected returns for the assets, the portfolio standard deviation is not so simple. If we calculated a weighted average of the standard deviations of Stocks A and B, we would get:

$$\text{Weighted average } \sigma = 0.5(0.0943) + 0.5(0.1083) = 0.1013 = 10.13\%$$

But we know that the portfolio standard deviation is only 1.35%. Obviously, there is something else going on here.

What is going on is that we have ignored the *correlation* between these two stocks. Correlation describes how two assets move together through time. The easiest way to measure correlation is with the correlation coefficient (r). The correlation coefficient can range from -1 to 1. Figure 11-5 illustrates the extremes that the correlation coefficient can have.

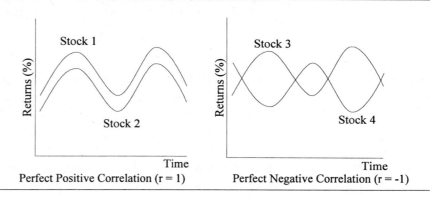

FIGURE 11-5
PERFECT POSITIVE AND PERFECT NEGATIVE CORRELATION

Another way to measure the co-movement of returns is with the *covariance*. The covariance is calculated in the same way as the variance, except that we have two securities rather than one. The covariance is calculated by:

$$\sigma_{X,Y} = \sum_{t=1}^{N} \rho_t (X_t - \bar{X})(Y_t - \bar{Y}) \qquad \text{(11-7)}$$

The covariance is a very useful statistic, but it is difficult to interpret. The correlation coefficient is related to the covariance as the following equation shows:

$$r_{X,Y} = \frac{\sigma_{X,Y}}{\sigma_X \sigma_Y} \qquad \text{(11-8)}$$

So the correlation coefficient is the same as the covariance, but the correlation coefficient has been transformed so that it will always be between -1 and +1.

Assume that you wish to form a portfolio consisting of 50% in Stock 1 and 50% in Stock 2 (from Figure 11-5). Because these stocks are perfectly positively correlated, a plot of the portfolio returns would be exactly halfway between the plots of the returns for Stocks 1 and 2. Your portfolio returns would be as volatile as either stock alone. On the other hand, a similar portfolio of Stocks 3 and 4 would result in a substantial reduction in volatility. Notice that the volatility of returns of Stock 3 are canceled out by the volatility of the returns of Stock 4. This risk reduction is due to diversification.

The correlation is obviously important in the calculation of the portfolio risk. For a portfolio of two securities, the portfolio variance is given by:

$$\sigma_P^2 = w_1^2\sigma_1^2 + w_2^2\sigma_2^2 + 2w_1w_2r_{1,2}\sigma_1\sigma_2 \qquad (11\text{-}9)$$

where the w's are the weights of each security, and $r_{1,2}$ is the correlation coefficient for the two securities. The standard deviation of a two-security portfolio is:

$$\sigma_P = \sqrt{w_1^2\sigma_1^2 + w_2^2\sigma_2^2 + 2w_1w_2r_{1,2}\sigma_1\sigma_2} = \sqrt{\sigma_P^2} \qquad (11\text{-}10)$$

From the above equation, it is clear that the lower the correlation ($r_{1,2}$) between the securities, the lower the risk of the portfolio. In other words, the lower the correlation, the greater the benefits of diversification.

Returning to our example with Stocks A and B, we can calculate the correlation coefficient with 1-2-3's built-in function @CORREL. This function is defined as:

@CORREL(*RANGE1*, *RANGE2*)

where *RANGE1* and *RANGE2* are the two ranges containing the stocks' returns. Before using @CORREL, let's create a graph of the returns to see if you can guess what the correlation coefficient is. Select A2..C6 and then create an XY chart of the returns.

Examining the chart, it is clear that when Stock A's returns are high, Stock B's returns are low and vice versa. The correlation coefficient is obviously negative, and probably near -1. We can confirm this by using the @CORREL function. In B9 enter the formula: @CORREL(B2..B6,C2..C6). The answer is -0.974, so our suspicions are confirmed. This low correlation is the reason that the standard deviation of the portfolio is so low. Your worksheet should now resemble that in Exhibit 11-3.

EXHIBIT 11-4
WORKSHEET DEMONSTRATING LOW CORRELATION BETWEEN A AND B

	A	B	C	D	E	F	G	H	I
1	Year	Stock A Returns	Stock B Returns	Portfolio					
2	1993	10.30%	10.71%	10.51%					
3	1994	-0.10%	25.00%	12.45%					
4	1995	23.30%	0.38%	11.84%					
5	1996	2.20%	26.20%	14.20%					
6	1997	14.00%	11.52%	12.76%					
7	Exp. Ret.	9.94%	14.76%	12.35%					
8	Std. Dev.	9.43%	10.83%	1.35%					
9	Correlation	-0.9741							

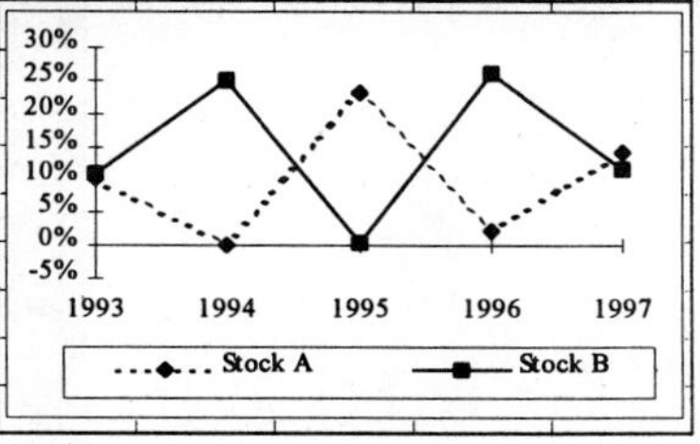

As one final exercise, we can examine the portfolio standard deviation as we change the weights of A and B. Place the following labels in your worksheet. In A11: Stock A. In B11: Stock B, and in C11: Port Std Dev. Enter a series in A12..A22 ranging from 1 down to 0 in increments of 0.1. These will represent the weights allocated to Stock A. In B12 we want the weight of Stock B, which is equal to 1 - weight of Stock A,[9] so enter: +1-A12. The portfolio standard deviation, in cell C12 can be found with the following formula: +SQRT(A12^2*B8^2+B12^2*C8^2+2*A12*B12*B$8*C$8*B$9).

Now simply copy the formulas in B12..C12 down to the rest of the range. If you create a chart of the data (use the range C11..C22 and make A11..A22 the X-Axis labels) your worksheet should resemble that in Exhibit 11-5.

It is instructive to examine the extremes in the chart in Exhibit 11-5. First, note that when 100% of your funds are allocated to Stock A, the portfolio standard deviation is equal to that of Stock A. Similarly, if 100% is allocated to Stock B, the portfolio standard deviation is equal to that of Stock B. Also notice that the minimum standard deviation is achieved with about one-half of your funds allocated to each stock.[10]

---

9. The weights must sum to 100%.

10. The actual weights are 54% in Stock A and 46% in Stock B. We leave it as an exercise for you to find these weights using the Solver.

EXHIBIT 11-5
PORTFOLIO STANDARD DEVIATION AS WEIGHTS CHANGE

	A	B	C	D	E	F	G	H	I
10		Weights							
11	Stock A	Stock B	Port. Std. Dev.						
12	100%	0%	9.43%						
13	90%	10%	7.44%						
14	80%	20%	5.46%						
15	70%	30%	3.51%						
16	60%	40%	1.74%						
17	50%	50%	1.35%						
18	40%	60%	2.95%						
19	30%	70%	4.87%						
20	20%	80%	6.84%						
21	10%	90%	8.83%						
22	0%	100%	10.83%						

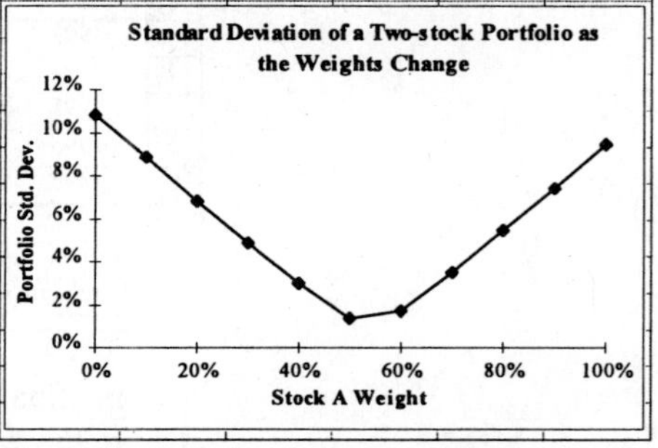

Standard Deviation of a Two-stock Portfolio as the Weights Change

Portfolios with More Than Two Securities

There is no reason that we can't create portfolios of more than two securities. Most individuals that own stocks own more than two. And, many mutual funds own hundreds of stocks and/or other securities.

Regardless of the number of securities in a portfolio, the expected return is always a weighted average of the individual expected returns. The standard deviation is, however, more complicated. Recall that when we were evaluating the standard deviation of the two-stock portfolio, we had to account for the correlation between the two stocks. Similarly, when we have a three-stock portfolio, we must account for the correlation between each pair of stocks. The standard deviation of a three-stock portfolio is thus given by (using the covariance form):

$$\sigma_P = \sqrt{w_1^2\sigma_1^2 + w_2^2\sigma_2^2 + w_3^2\sigma_3^2 + 2w_1w_2\sigma_{1,2} + 2w_1w_3\sigma_{1,3} + 2w_2w_3\sigma_{2,3}} \quad \text{(11-11)}$$

Obviously, the expression for the portfolio standard deviation gets to be cumbersome for more than two securities. Therefore, when more than two securities are included, the expression is usually simplified to:

$$\sigma_P = \sqrt{\sum_{i=1}^{N}\sum_{j=1}^{N} w_i w_j r_{i,j}\sigma_i\sigma_j} \quad \text{(11-12)}$$

or, in the equivalent covariance form:

$$\sigma_P = \sqrt{\sum_{i=1}^{N} \sum_{j=1}^{N} w_i w_j \sigma_{i,j}} \qquad \text{(11-13)}$$

Equations (11-12) and (11-13), while not exactly simple, will calculate the standard deviation of a portfolio of any number of securities.

Summary

We began this chapter with a discussion of risk and determined that risk is roughly equivalent to the probability of a loss. The higher the probability of a loss, the higher the risk. We also found that we could measure risk in any of several ways, but that the standard deviation or coefficient of variation is the generally preferred method.

The primary method of incorporating risk into the analysis of capital investments is the risk-adjusted discount rate technique. This technique involves the addition of a premium to the *WACC* in order to account for the riskiness of the investment. We also discussed the certainty-equivalent method whereby the risky cash flows are deflated according to a decision maker's utility function. Other methods mentioned were the decision (probability) tree method and Monte-Carlo simulation.

Finally, we introduced the concept of diversification. Diversification involves the forming of portfolios of securities so that some of the risk of the individual securities will be canceled by other securities whose returns are less than perfectly correlated.

TABLE 11-9
EQUATIONS USED IN THIS CHAPTER

Purpose	Formula
Expected value	$$E(X) = \sum_{t=1}^{N} \rho_t X_t$$
Variance with known probability distribution	$$\sigma_X^2 = \sum_{t=1}^{N} \rho_t (X_t - \bar{X})^2$$
Standard deviation with known probability distribution	$$\sigma_X = \sqrt{\sum_{t=1}^{N} \rho_t (X_t - \bar{X})^2}$$
Coefficient of Variation	$$\gamma_X = \frac{\sigma_X}{X}$$
Covariance	$$\sigma_{X,Y} = \sum_{t=1}^{N} \rho_t (X_t - \bar{X})(Y_t - \bar{Y})$$
Correlation coefficient	$$r_{X,Y} = \frac{\sigma_{X,Y}}{\sigma_X \sigma_Y}$$
Expected return of a portfolio	$$E(R_P) = \sum_{t=1}^{N} w_t E(R_P)$$
Standard deviation of a two-security portfolio	$$\sigma_P = \sqrt{w_1^2 \sigma_1^2 + w_2^2 \sigma_2^2 + 2w_1 w_2 r_{1,2} \sigma_1 \sigma_2}$$
Standard deviation of an N-security portfolio	$$\sigma_P = \sqrt{\sum_{i=1}^{N} \sum_{j=1}^{N} w_i w_j r_{i,j} \sigma_i \sigma_j}$$

TABLE 11-10
FUNCTIONS INTRODUCED IN THIS CHAPTER

Purpose	Function	Page
Calculate an arithmetic average	@AVG(*LIST*)	248
Calculate a weighted average	@WEIGHTAVG(*DATA-RANGE*, *WEIGHTS-RANGE*, *TYPE*)	249
Calculate a population variance	@VAR(*LIST*)	249
Calculate a sample variance	@VARS(*LIST*)	250
Calculate a population standard deviation	@STD(*LIST*)	250
Calculate a sample standard deviation	@STDS(*LIST*)	250
Lookup a value from a table	@VLOOKUP(*X*, *RANGE*, *COLUMN-OFFSET*)	256
Calculate the correlation coefficient	@CORREL(*RANGE1*, *RANGE2*)	266

Menu Descriptions

The File Menu[1]

```
 New

 Open...        Ctrl+O
 Close

 Save           Ctrl+S
 Save As...
 Doc Info...
 Protect...
 Send Mail...

 Print Preview...
 Page Setup...
 Print...        Ctrl+P
 Printer Setup...

 Exit
```

New — Opens a new (blank) workbook.

Open — Opens an existing workbook. Can also be used to import text files.

Close — Closes an open workbook. If changes have been made, 1-2-3 will prompt you to save the workbook before it is closed.

Save — Saves changes to an open workbook using its current name.

Save **As** — Saves an open document. 1-2-3 will prompt you for a new name, with the current name as the default. You can also use this choice to change the file format (e.g., to .wk3).

Doc Info — Create or display information about the current workbook such as title, subject, keywords, etc.

Protect — Protects the file when working in a network environment.

Send **Mail** — Send the file to another user via your e-mail application.

---

1. The menus described in this appendix are those that appear in Lotus 1-2-3 Release 5 for Windows.

Print Preview — Shows a page by page preview of how the page will look when printed.

Page Setup — Shows the details of the page format (e.g., margin settings, headers and footers, etc.) and allows you to change them.

Print — Sends the file to the printer.

Printer Setup — Specify the printer to use and the options for that printer.

1 .. 5 — Lists the last several files that have been opened. Clicking on one of these choices will open that file.

Exit — Quits 1-2-3.

The *E*dit Menu

Undo	Ctrl+Z
Cut	Ctrl+X
Copy	Ctrl+C
Paste	Ctrl+V
Clear...	Del
Paste Special...	
Paste Link	
Arrange	▶
Copy Down	
Copy Right	
Insert...	Ctrl +
Delete...	Ctrl –
Find & Replace...	
Go To...	F5
Insert Object...	
Links...	

Undo — Undoes the last action if possible, or indicates that the last option cannot be undone.

Cut — Copies the current selection to the clipboard, and deletes it when it is pasted elsewhere.

Copy — Copies the current selection to the clipboard without deleting it.

Paste — Pastes the contents of the clipboard into the worksheet at the current location.

Clear — Deletes the contents of the selected area. Can also be used to delete only the formats, only the data, or notes attached to the cells.

Paste Special — Same as Paste, but allows you to change the format of the data.

Paste Link — Pastes data from the clipboard as a file link, DDE link, or OLE link.

Arrange — Edit drawing objects (lines, arrows, etc.).

Copy Down — Copies the top row of a selection down to the rest of the selection.

Copy Right — Copies the left column of a selection right to the rest of the selection.

Insert — Inserts columns or rows, blank cells, or new worksheets into the current workbook.

Delete — Removes the current selection, rows, or columns from the worksheet.

Find & Replace — Locates the specified text string in the selected worksheet(s) and optionally replace it with another.

Go To — Makes the specified cell active.

Insert **O**bject — Places an OLE object (e.g., a word processor file) into the worksheet.

Lin**k**s — Opens linked workbooks, or allows you to edit OLE and DDE links.

The *V*iew Menu

Zoom In
Zoom Out
Custom - 125%
Freeze Titles...
Split...
Set View Preferences...

Zoom **I**n — Increases the displayed size of the worksheet by 10% each time this choice is selected.

Zoom **O**ut — Decreases the displayed size of the worksheet by 10% each time this choice is selected.

Custom — Increases or decreases the displayed size of the worksheet by a user-defined amount.

Freeze **T**itles — Freezes or unfreezes the top row and/or left column of the worksheet.

Split — Divides the worksheet into independently scrollable regions at the active cell.

Set View **P**references — Set defaults for the appearance of the worksheet.

The **S**tyle Menu

Number Format...
Font & Attributes...
Lines & Color...
Alignment...
Gallery...
Named Style...
Column Width...
Row Height...
Protection...
Hide...
Page Break...
Worksheet Defaults...
Fast Format

Number Format — Sets the number format of the selected cells.

Font & Attributes — Change the typeface and style of the selected cells.

Lines & Color — Sets the borders and colors of the selected cells.

Alignment — Align the data in the selected cells.

Gallery — Sets a predefined display style for the selected cells.

Named **S**tyle — Define styles that can be applied to the selected cells (you must format a cell before the style can be named).

Column Width — Set the width of the selected column.

Row Height — Set the height of the selected row.

Protection — Protects the formatting, but not the contents, of the selected cells.

Hide — Hides, or unhides, the selected rows or columns.

Page **B**reak — Inserts, and removes, a page break at the selected cell.

Worksheet Defaults — Set the default colors, fonts, column widths, etc. for the current worksheet.

Fas**t** Format — Copies the format of the selected cells so that it can be pasted onto other cells (press ESC to return to editing).

The **T**ools Menu

Chart	
Map	▶
Draw	▶
Database	▶
Spell Check...	
Audit...	
SmartIcons...	
User Setup...	
Macro	▶
Add-in...	

Chart — Creates a chart of the selected data.

Ma**p** — Creates and changes maps using data in the worksheet.

Draw — Draw lines, arrows, other shapes, and text boxes.

Data**b**ase — Read and modify database tables created in other programs.

Spell Check — Checks the spelling in the worksheet.

Audit — Helps you locate errors in the worksheet.

Smarticons — Displays or hides Smarticons, and can also create custom sets of Smarticons.

User Setup — Sets various options such as recalculation, auto-save, directories, etc.

Macro — Record, run, or debug macros.

Add-in — Loads add-in functions.

The Range Menu

Version...
Fill...
Fill by Example
Sort...
Parse...
Transpose...
Name...
Analyze ▸

Version — Starts the Version Manager.

Fill — Enters a series of numbers, dates or times into a range of cells.

Fill by Example — Completes a series entered into the selected range (i.e. type: Jan. and Feb. into adjacent cells and 1-2-3 will fill in the rest of the months).

Sort — Sorts the data into ascending or descending order based on one or more key fields.

Parse — Separates data from a text file into more than one cell.

Transpose — Copies and rotates selected cells (i.e., a row of data is copied to a column of data).

Name — Applies a name to a range of data.

Analyze — Activates the data analysis tools such as regression analysis, What-if tables, Solver, etc.

The Window Menu

Tile
Cascade
✓ 1 Untitled

Tile — Displays all open worksheets side by side.

Cascade — Displays open worksheets one over the other.

1 .. 9 — Activates the selected workbook.

| Contents |
| Search... |
| Using Help |
| Keyboard |
| How Do I? |
| For Upgraders |
| Tutorial |
| Movie Guide |
| Online Books |
| About 1-2-3... |
| About SmartHelp... |

The *H*elp Menu

Contents — Displays the help file contents.

Search — Search the help file for keywords.

Using Help — Provides help on how to use the on-line help system.

Keyboard — Describes 1-2-3 keystrokes.

How Do I? — Provides a tutorial on common tasks.

For Upgraders — Describes new features for users of previous versions of 1-2-3.

Tutorial — Starts one of the eight on-line step by step tutorials.

Movie Guide — An index to the tutorial movies on the multimedia CD-ROM.

Online Books — Opens the manuals that are available on the CD-ROM.

About 1-2-3 — Displays the version number and copyright information about the program.

About Smarthelp — Displays copyright information about the help system in the multimedia CD-ROM version of 1-2-3.

Using COMPUSTAT®
Data with 1-2-3

The Standard and Poor's COMPUSTAT database and accompanying PC Plus software on CD-ROM contains a wealth of financial data on over 10,000 publicly-traded U.S. and Canadian companies. The data consists primarily of financial information from the companys' income statements, balance sheets, and statements of cash flow. Further, there are over 300 predefined concepts (formulas) for easy access to financial ratios, stock returns, growth rates, etc. The data is available for up to 20 years. If your university or business is not a subscriber, further information can be obtained by calling (800) 525-8640.

These data are accessible, directly from the CD-ROM, in 1-2-3 with the tools provided by COMPUSTAT. The tools include:

- The *Universal Report Builder* which helps you to design 1-2-3 worksheets which access the database.
- The *Formula Builder* which helps you to easily construct individual formulas.
- The *Chart Builder* which creates and displays charts of the data.
- Pre-built 1-2-3 templates for income statements, balance sheets, statements of cash flow, financial ratios, etc.

Using 1-2-3 and the PC Plus software can help you to more easily gather "real world" financial data so that you can concentrate on analysis, rather than data entry. In this appendix, we will show you how to access these data. However, this appendix is not a substitute for the COMPUSTAT manuals which should be available from your system administrator.

In this appendix we will build two reports as examples of accessing the COMPUSTAT database. Unless you have the LAN version of the product, you will need to use a PC which has both PC Plus and 1-2-3 installed.[1] PC Plus must be installed since 1-2-3 cannot access the data directly from the CD-ROM. Instead, it uses dynamic data exchange (DDE) commands to request data through PC Plus.

Using Pre-defined Reports

When PC Plus is installed on a PC with Lotus 1-2-3, two things happen: (1) a new SPWS menu is added to 1-2-3; and (2) 76 1-2-3 templates are added to the SPWS\LOTUS directory on your hard drive. In this section, we will demonstrate the use of the CIS5 report, which provides five years' income statements for a specified company.

Using the pre-defined reports is mainly a matter of loading the file into 1-2-3 and then specifying the company that you are interested in. To load the CIS5 report, choose File Open from the 1-2-3 menus and then change to the SPWS\LOTUS directory on your hard drive. (The exact location of the 1-2-3 templates may be different on your PC.) Now, select the CIS5.WK4 file and click on the OK button.

The template will initially show the data for the last company that was displayed. To change the company, click on the Company button in the upper left corner of the worksheet. You will be presented with a dialog box into which you enter the ticker symbol for the company of interest.[2] Type MSFT and press Enter to display the last five years' income statements of Microsoft. Exhibit B-1 shows a portion of the CIS5 report for Microsoft.

---

1. This appendix was written for version 5.1 of PC Plus. Other versions may be available when you read this and certain details may vary.

2. Ticker symbols are the abbreviations for company names that are used to conserve space on the ticker tape. If you do not know the ticker symbol for a company, you can click on the Companies button to search by the company name.

You can easily create charts of the data by clicking on the Charts button. Printing the report can be accomplished simply by clicking on the print icon. Before continuing to the next section, you should examine several of the other pre-defined reports. For a description of each report, see the *S&P PC Plus for Windows Report Library*.

EXHIBIT B-1
THE CIS5.WK4 REPORT

| Company | Charts | Print | Exit |

MICROSOFT CORP
msft
SIC: 7372

ANNUAL INCOME STATEMENT
($ MILLIONS, EXCEPT PER SHARE)

	Jun95	Jun94	Jun93	Jun92	Jun91
Sales	5,937.000	4,649.000	3,753.000	2,758.725	1,843.432
Cost of Goods Sold	608.000	526.000	495.000	365.486	295.107
Gross Profit	5,329.000	4,123.000	3,258.000	2,393.239	1,548.325
Selling, General & Admin. Expense	3,022.000	2,160.000	1,794.000	1,296.322	834.001
Operating Income Before Depreciation	2,307.000	1,963.000	1,464.000	1,096.917	714.324
Depreciation, Depl. & Amortization	269.000	237.000	138.000	100.938	67.482
Operating Profit	2,038.000	1,726.000	1,326.000	995.979	646.842
Interest Expense	2.000	2.000	1.000	1.988	4.515
Non-Operating Income/Expense	177.000	88.000	76.000	47.274	28.317
Special Items	(46.000)	(90.000)	0.000	0.000	0.000
Pretax Income	2,167.000	1,722.000	1,401.000	1,041.265	670.644
Total Income Taxes	714.000	576.000	448.000	333.205	207.901
Minority Interest	@CF	0.000	0.000	0.000	0.000
Income Before Extra Items & Disc Ops	1,453.000	1,146.000	953.000	708.060	462.743
Preferred Dividends	0.000	0.000	0.000	0.000	0.000
Available for Common	1,453.000	1,146.000	953.000	708.060	462.743
Savings Due to Stock Equivalents	0.000	0.000	0.000	0.000	0.000
Adjusted Available for Common	1,453.000	1,146.000	953.000	708.060	462.743
Extraordinary Items	0.000	0.000	0.000	0.000	0.000
Discontinued Operations	0.000	0.000	0.000	0.000	0.000
Adjusted Net Income	1,453.000	1,146.000	953.000	708.060	462.743

Using the Universal Report Builder[3]

If the pre-defined reports do not fit your needs, you can define your own reports. The easiest method of creating reports is to use the Universal Report Builder (URB). The URB makes creating reports easy because it takes you step by step through the report building process. Exhibit B-2 shows the first dialog box.

---

3. If you do not have an SPWS menu, you will need to use **T**ools Add-**in** to add the SPWS123.ADW and SPWSMENU.ADW files from the SPWS\LOTUS directory.

281

The URB can create four types of reports:

1. **Standard** reports display data items for several periods for a single company. Each time period occupies a column. The CIS5 report in Exhibit B-1 is an example.

2. **Table** reports display a single periods' data for several companies. Each company's data occupies a single row.

3. **Time series/trend analysis** reports are the same as standard reports, except that they are transposed. That is, each time period occupies a row, and each data item occupies a column.

4. **Comparative** reports are the same as Table reports, but they are transposed so that the data for each company occupies a single column.

EXHIBIT B-2
THE UNIVERSAL REPORT BUILDER FIRST DIALOG BOX

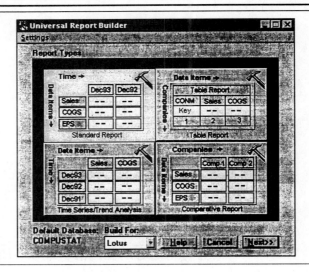

In this section we will use the Universal Report Builder to create a standard report that calculates financial ratios for a specified company for five years. To begin, select Universal Report Builder from the SPWS menu. From the first dialog box (see Exhibit B-2) double-click on the Standard Report button, or click on the Next>> button.

In the second dialog box (see Exhibit B-3) you will specify the data items that your report will contain. Make sure that the All category is selected in the Data Category list. You will select the data items from the Data Item list. If you need an item which is not in the Data Item list, you can always enter the formula in the edit box in the upper-right corner of the dialog box. You can find items in the list more quickly by first clicking in the list and then typing the first few letters of the name of the item

We are creating a report that is similar to that in Exhibit 4-4 on page 80. The first ratio is the current ratio, so select Current Ratio from the Data Items list and then press the Add >> button to enter the ratio. Note that after clicking the Add >> button, the mnemonic will appear in the list to the right of the Data Item list. Since not all of the data items are exactly the same as the ratio names, we have listed the items to select in Table B-1

We have purposely left the return on common equity out of Table B-1 because there is no mnemonic for this ratio. Therefore, you must enter a formula to have it included on the report. To enter the formula, first click in the edit box above the list of mnemonics. Now, from the Data Item list select "Net Income Adj. for CSE." Type a / and then select "Common Equity-Total" from the list. Finally, click on the downward-pointing arrow to the left of the edit box to insert the formula. The dialog box should now look like the one in Exhibit B-3.

TABLE B-1
DATA ITEMS FOR THE RATIO REPORT

Ratio	Select Data Item
Current Ratio	Current Ratio
Quick Ratio	Quick Ratio
Inventory Turnover	Inventory Turnover
Accounts Receivable Turnover	Receivables Turnover
Average Collection Period	Average Collection Period
Fixed Asset Turnover	Fixed Asset Turnover
Total Asset Turnover	Total Asset Turnover
Total Debt Ratio	Total Debt/Total Assets
Long-term Debt Ratio	LT Debt/Tangible Assets
Long-term Debt to Total Capitalization	Long-term Debt to Total Capital
Total Debt to Equity	Total Debt/Total Equity
Long-term Debt to Equity	LT Debt/Sharehldrs Eqty
Gross Profit Margin	Gross Profit Margin
Operating Profit Margin	Op Margin Aft Depr
Net Profit Margin	Net Profit Margin
Return on Assets	Return on Assets
Return on Equity	Return on Equity

EXHIBIT B-3
THE UNIVERSAL REPORT BUILDER SECOND DIALOG BOX

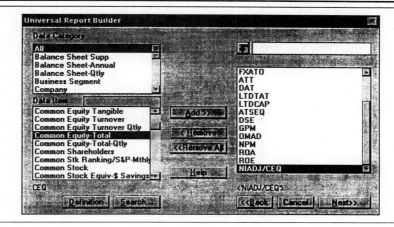

Click the Next >> button to continue to the next step. You should now see the dialog box pictured in Exhibit B-4. Set the Ending Period to – 4 by clicking on the down arrow and then click the Next >> button to continue.

EXHIBIT B-4
THE UNIVERSAL REPORT BUILDER THIRD DIALOG BOX

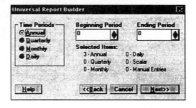

You will now select the company for which you want to display the data. Type MSFT in the Company edit box. Note that if you do not know the ticker symbol, you can click the Companies button to look up the ticker symbol by company name. Before clicking the Build Report button, make sure that the dialog looks like the one in Exhibit B-5.

EXHIBIT B-5
THE UNIVERSAL REPORT BUILDER FOURTH DIALOG BOX

After a few seconds, the finished report will appear in an 1-2-3 worksheet. Note that the report is not formatted. You can apply any type of formatting that you wish to the worksheet without destroying the report. After formatting, your worksheet should resemble that in Exhibit B-6.

Before leaving this report, there are a few points that should be made about reports in general:

1. Once a report is created, there is no reason that you can't or shouldn't edit it. Feel free to change the formatting, edit formulas, etc.

2. All of the formulas in the report in Exhibit B-6 are keyed to the ticker symbol in A2. You can change the ticker symbol to change the company for which data is displayed. For example, to view these ratios for International Business Machines, simply type IBM in A2.

3. Occasionally, instead of a number, you will see a code in the report. For example, several of the leverage ratios for Microsoft are displayed as @IF. This means that the number is an "insignificant figure." @CF indicates a "combined figure," which means that at least one of the components of the formula was combined with another data item. In this case it would probably be misleading to report the ratio. You can get more information about these data codes by searching the PC Plus on-line help for "Data Codes."

EXHIBIT B-6
THE RATIO REPORT

	A	B	C	D	E	F
1	MICROSOFT CORP					
2	msft					
3						
4		Jun-94	Jun-93	Jun-92	Jun-91	Jun-90
5	Liquidity Ratios					
6	Current Ratio	4.723	5.062	3.960	3.506	3.854
7	Quick Ratio	4.479	4.668	3.614	3.169	3.374
8	Efficiency Ratios					
9	Inventory Turnover	4.594	4.651	5.497	5.749	4.422
10	Receivables Turnover	11.437	12.341	10.744	8.689	8.101
11	Average Collection Period	31.478	29.171	33.506	41.431	44.440
12	Fixed Asset Turnover	5.174	4.595	4.255	4.309	4.515
13	Total Asset Turnover	1.014	1.165	1.288	1.341	1.296
14	Leverage Ratios					
15	Total Debt/Total Assets	@IF	@IF	@IF	1.183	0.588
16	L-T Debt/Tangible Assets	@CF	@CF	@IF	0.000	0.000
17	Long-Term Debt/Total Capital	@IF	@IF	@IF	0.000	0.000
18	Total Debt/Total Equity	@IF	@IF	@IF	1.440	0.708
19	L-T Debt/Sharehldrs Eqty	@IF	@IF	@IF	0.000	0.000
20	Profitability Ratios					
21	Gross Profit Margin	88.686%	86.811%	86.752%	83.991%	82.564%
22	Op Margin Aft Depr	37.126%	35.332%	36.103%	35.089%	32.721%
23	Net Profit Margin	24.650%	25.393%	25.666%	25.102%	23.591%
24	Return on Assets	21.369%	25.046%	26.821%	28.144%	25.258%
25	Return on Equity	25.753%	29.395%	32.288%	34.256%	30.394%
26	<NIADJ/CEQ'>	25.753%	29.395%	32.288%	34.256%	30.394%

Building Reports Manually

There are times when the pre-defined reports don't suit your needs, or the Universal Report Builder can't build the type of report that you want. In these cases you will need to manually build a report using the DDE functions that are supplied with PC Plus. In this section we will manually build a report to display monthly closing prices for a set of companies and for the S&P 500 index.

The SPWS Add-in Functions

When PC Plus is installed, it modifies the 1-2-3R5.INI file so that 1-2-3 automatically loads the SPWS123.ADW file. This add-in file contains three functions that access the COMPUSTAT data through Dynamic Data Exchange (DDE).

The SPWS function returns a single data item for a specific company. It is defined as:

$$@SPWS(KEY, EXPRESSION)$$

where **KEY** is the ticker symbol for the company, and **EXPRESSION** is the data item or formula that you want displayed. For example, to display the current ratio for Microsoft for the most recent period, you could use:

```
@SPWS("MSFT","CR").
```

The **@SPWS.SET** function displays a single data item for each company in a defined set. (A *set* is a group of companies. It could be the result of screening in PC Plus, or it can be defined in 1-2-3.) This function is defined as:

$$@SPWS.SET (SET, EXPRESSION, ARRAY\_DIRECTION)$$

where **SET** is the either a set file (saved by PC Plus) or a set definition, **EXPRESSION** is as defined above, and **ARRAY_DIRECTION** is either 0 (down) or 1 (across). **ARRAY_DIRECTION** tells 1-2-3 which direction to insert the data. As an example, let's display the net income for Microsoft, IBM, and Novell. First, in A1 enter: {"MSFT","IBM","NOVL"} which defines the set to use. Now, to display the net income for each company enter: @SPWS.SET(A1, "NI",1) in A2.

There are two important things to know about the **@SPWS.SET** function:

1. This function returns a value for each member of the set. However, the formula is entered only in the first cell, the other cells are filled automatically. Make sure that there is no other important data in the cells that will be filled because it will get overwritten.

2. The function returns the data in alphabetical order, sorted by the ticker symbol. In the above example. the order would be: IBM, MSFT, NOVL which is different than the order in which we defined the set.

Finally, the **@SPWS.TIME.SERIES** function displays several periods' data for a single company. This function is defined as:

@SPWS.TIME.SERIES(*KEY, EXPRESSION, BEGIN_PERIOD, END_PERIOD, ARRAY_DIRECTION*).

In this function, *BEGIN_PERIOD* and *END_PERIOD* specify the starting and ending time periods to display. Note that the current year is year 0 ("0Y") and all previous years are relative to the current year and are specified with negative numbers. Data for 5 years ago would be specified by "-4Y". To specify monthly data, instead of annual, substitute an M for the Y. For example, to display the last six months' closing prices for Microsoft:

```
@SPWS.TIME.SERIES("MSFT","PRCCM","0M","-5M",0)
```

Creating a Monthly Stock Price Report

In this section we will create a report that lists the last 60 months' closing prices for three stocks: Microsoft, IBM and Novell. In addition, the report will contain closing prices for the Standard & Poor's 500 index. This type of report is useful for a number of reasons. For example, it might be used to calculate the beta for the stocks (see "Regression Analysis" on page 101), or to calculate the monthly value of a portfolio. Note that this type of report cannot be created with the Universal Report Builder because it combines a comparative report and time series/ trend analysis report.

To begin, open a new worksheet. So that the report can be used for any set of companies, we will define the set in B1. In A1 enter the label: Set, and in B1 type: {"MSFT","IBM","NOVL"}. Our set definition is simply an array of company ticker symbols.

In B2 we will calculate the number of companies in the set. In A2 enter the label: Companies, and in B2 enter the formula: @SPWS("IBM","@CSIZE("&$B$1&")"). Note that we are using "IBM" as the key, but the value isn't important (i.e., any ticker symbol would work even if it isn't in the set). For this set the result should be 3. Of course this is obvious for this set, but remember that you can change the set definition to the file name of a saved set. So, in other cases, it may be useful to know the number of companies in the set.

In C4:E4 we want to display the ticker symbols for the companies in the set. We could enter the symbols directly, but that would destroy the generality of the report. Instead, we will use a formula. In A4 enter the label: Tickers. Now, select C4 and enter the formula: @SPWS.SET($B$1,"TIC",1). This will display the ticker symbols in alphabetical order in C4:E4.

Next, we would like to enter the dates for the past 60 months in A5:A64. Again, we must use a formula to get the dates from PC Plus because we want the report to display properly even after an update of the COMPUSTAT CD. In A5 enter @SPWS.TIME.SERIES(C4,"@MNT(OM)","OM","-59M",0). Note that we have specified C4 as the key. However, we could have specified any of the ticker symbols because this formula doesn't return data that is specific to any company. Also, note that the @**MNT** function is a PC Plus function that returns the month of the requested time period.

Entering the formula for the monthly closing prices is almost identical to entering the formula for the dates. We will start with Lotus Development, since that is the first ticker. Select C5 and enter the formula: @SPWS.TIME.SERIES(C4, "PRCCM","OM","-59M","DOWN"). PRCCM is the mnemonic for the monthly closing price. To display the prices for Microsoft and Novell, simply select C5 and copy to D5 and E5.

Finally, we want to display the monthly closing prices for the S&P 500 index (the symbol is I0003) in B5:B64. This is accomplished in exactly the same way as for the three companies. However, we always want the S&P 500 data to display, regardless of the set of companies. Further, we would like for this data to always be in column B. Therefore, we will enter the symbol directly. In B4 type: I0003. Note that this symbol can be found in the Universal Look Up List. Now, copy C5 and paste to B5.

Your report should resemble the worksheet fragment in Exhibit B-7.

EXHIBIT B-7
A PORTION OF THE MONTHLY STOCK PRICE REPORT

	A	B	C	D	E
1	Set:	{"MSFT","IBM","NOVL"}			
2	Companies:	3			
3					
4	Tickers	I0003	IBM	MSFT	NOVL
5	Feb96	640.430	122.625	98.687	12.187
6	Jan96	636.020	108.500	92.500	13.500
7	Dec95	615.930	91.375	87.750	14.250
8	Nov95	605.370	96.625	87.125	16.875
9	Oct95	581.500	97.250	100.000	16.500
10	Sep95	584.410	94.500	90.500	18.250
11	Aug95	561.880	103.375	92.500	18.000
12	Jul95	562.060	108.875	90.500	18.125
13	Jun95	544.750	96.000	90.375	19.937
14	May95	533.400	93.000	84.687	19.312

Summary

COMPUSTAT contains a wealth of "real world" data. In this appendix we have shown you how to access some of this data. However, you should spend some time exploring the pre-built reports and building your own. No textbook can provide the educational experience that a few days spent with real data will give you.

TABLE B-2
FUNCTIONS INTRODUCED IN THIS APPENDIX

Purpose	Function	Page
Return a variable	SPWS(*KEY, EXPRESSION*)	288
Return a variable for every company in a set	SPWS.SET(*SET, EXPRESSION, ARRAY_DIRECTION*)	288
Return a time series	SPWS.TIME.SERIES(*KEY, EXPRESSION, BEGIN_PERIOD, END_PERIOD, ARRAY_DIRECTION*)	289